Managing evaluation in education

This book provides a practical, well-structured, yet rigorous introduction to the management of evaluation in education. Managing evaluation is now an area of priority concern in both schools and colleges, but despite a growing number of books on education management few have dealt with the subject of managing evaluation in any depth. The granting of substantial devolved powers to schools and colleges under the Education Reform Act also has fundamental implications for evaluation.

Managing Evaluation in Education is designed to meet this need. It begins by considering the meaning of evaluation and of management and the relation between them. It considers the context in which evaluation must be managed in schools and colleges, and addresses the question of the need for ongoing monitoring and review, before proceeding through the stages of the evaluation process, giving particular consideration to the management issues which arise at each stage. Finally, it considers the importance of developing a culture across the whole organisation which is conducive to evaluation.

The book has a developmental approach which combines accessible text with a series of exercises and photocopiable worksheets which can be used by individuals and teams in their own work contexts.

Kath Aspinwall is Senior Lecturer at the Centre for Education Management and Administration, Sheffield City Polytechnic, and has experience of teaching in the areas of early childhood, further and higher education, and working as an advisory teacher and LEA evaluator. **Tim Simkins** is Head of the Centre for Education Management and Administration, Sheffield City Polytechnic. He has a particular interest in strategic management and has worked in management development in a wide variety of educational contexts both in Britain and overseas. **John F. Wilkinson** is Deputy Headteacher at Shirebrook Community School, Mansfield, with responsibility for students and the community, and has worked in secondary schools since the mid-1970s. **M. John McAuley** is Principal Lecturer in Organisation Behaviour at Sheffield Business School, where, in addition to teaching duties, consultancy and research, he is subject leader in organisation behaviour and human resource management.

EDUCATIONAL MANAGEMENT SERIES
Edited by Cyril Poster

Managing the Primary School
Joan Dean

Teaching and Managing: Inseparable Activities in Schools
Cyril Wilkinson and Ernie Cave

Schools, Parents and Governors: A New Approach to Accountability
Joan Sallis

Partnership in Education Management
Edited by Cyril Poster and Christopher Day

Management Skills in Primary Schools
Les Bell

Special Needs in the Secondary School: The Whole School Approach
Joan Dean

The Management of Special Needs in Ordinary Schools
Edited by Neville Jones and Tim Southgate

Creating An Excellent School: Some New Management Techniques
Hedley Beare, Brian Caldwell and Ross Millikan

Teacher Appraisal: A Guide to Training
Cyril and Doreen Poster

Time-constrained Evaluation
Brian Wilcox

Performance-related Pay in Education
Edited by Harry Tomlinson

Evaluation in Schools: Getting Started on Training and Implementation
Glyn Rogers and Linda Badham

Managing Change in Schools
Colin Newton and Tony Tarrant

Managing Teams in Secondary Schools
Les Bell

Inspecting and Advising
Joan Dean

Opting for Self-Management
Brent Davies and Lesley Anderson

Managing External Relations in Schools
Nick Foskett

Managing evaluation in education

A developmental approach

Kath Aspinwall, Tim Simkins,
John F. Wilkinson and M. John McAuley

London and New York

First published in 1992
by Routledge
11 New Fetter Lane, London EC4P 4EE

Simultaneously published in the USA and Canada
by Routledge
a division of Routledge, Chapman and Hall Inc.
29 West 35th Street, New York, NY 10001

© Crown Copyright 1992. Published by permission of the Controller of the HMSO.
Additional material © Kath Aspinwall, Tim Simkins, John F. Wilkinson and M.
John McAuley

Typeset by LaserScript, Mitcham, Surrey
Printed and bound in Great Britain by
Mackays of Chatham PLC, Chatham, Kent

British Library Cataloguing in Publication Data
A catalogue record for this book is available from the British Library.

Library of Congress Cataloging in Publication Data

Managing evaluation in education : a developmental approach / Kath Aspinwall
[et al.]
    p.   cm. — (Educational management series)
  Includes bibliographical references and index.
  ISBN 0–415–08043–6
  1. Educational evaluation–Great Britain–Management.
I. Aspinwall, Kath. II. Series.
LB2822.75.M36   1992
379.1′54—dc20
92–9347
CIP

Contents

List of figures   vi
List of exercises   vii
List of worksheets   ix
Foreword   x
Introduction   xi
Acknowledgements   xv
List of abbreviations   xvi

1 Management and evaluation   1

2 Understanding the context   17

3 The processes of monitoring and review   48

4 Choosing a focus   77

5 Planning and managing the process   99

6 Resourcing the process   125

7 Using success criteria   139

8 Collecting the data   169

9 Changing practice   189

10 Evaluation and organisational learning   212

   Bibliography   234
   Index   238

Figures

1.1 Dimensions of evaluation   5
1.2 The planning cycle   13
2.1 The role set of a curriculum co-ordinator in a primary school   28
3.1 SWOT analysis   56
3.2 An example of a curriculum audit   64
3.3 GRIDS   68
4.1 Overview of evaluation activity   82
4.2 Stakeholder map of a secondary school   86
5.1 The problem-solving process   116
6.1 Costing a questionnaire for parents   130
6.2 Gathering and processing data: key activities   133
6.3 Diagram of activities   135
7.1 Sheffield University school success criteria   143
7.2 The Joint Efficiency Study's success criteria for further education   144
7.3 Quality of Learning and Teaching (QLT) Profile   145
7.4 Success indicators for a Careers Education and Guidance programme   147
7.5 The quality statements addressed by each evaluation instrument   153
7.6 Developing and using success criteria   155
9.1 Increasing parental involvement: a Force Field Analysis   200
10.1 Questions for reviewing (evaluating) evaluations   216
10.2 The learning organisation   230
10.3 Managing evaluation: three levels of concern   232

Exercises

2.1 Why? What? How?   18
Worksheet: Why? What? How? Who? When? So what?   20
2.2 'I', 'We', 'They'   22
2.3 What do the rules say?   25
2.4 Role set analysis   29
Role set analysis briefing sheet   31
Role expectations worksheet   32
2.5 What kind of place is this?   35
2.6 The cultural implications of evaluation   40
2.7 Diamond ranking   43
Some statements about evaluation   45
3.1 SWOT analysis   57
SWOT briefing sheet   60
SWOT worksheet   61
3.2 Reviewing progress in curriculum development   69
3.3 A wall conversion   72
3.4 Sentence completions   74
4.1 Stakeholder analysis (I)   87
Stakeholder briefing sheet   89
Stakeholder worksheet 1   90
4.2 What do we need to know?   92
4.3 Nominal group technique   94
5.1 Aspects of accountability   105
5.2 Diagnosing group problems   110
Group problem worksheet   112
5.3 Considering group roles   119
Group roles worksheet   120
7.1 Generating success indicators   148
7.2 Stakeholder analysis (II)   163
Stakeholder worksheet 2   165
Stakeholder worksheet 3   166

9.1 Micro-political mapping   196
    Micro-political mapping: worksheet 1   198
    Micro-political mapping: worksheet 2   199
9.2 Force Field Analysis   201
9.3 Reflecting on learning   207
    Factors which help and hinder learning   208
10.1 Diagnosing cultures of evaluation   218
    Diagnosing cultures of evaluation: instruction sheet   220
    Diagnosing cultures of evaluation: questionnaire   221
    Diagnosing cultures of evaluation: scoresheet   224

Worksheets

Note: Some worksheets are located under the relevant exercise.

3.1 Expenditure monitoring sheet	52
4.1 Overview of evaluation activity	83
4.2 Clarifying the purposes of evaluation	96
5.1 Designing an evaluation process (1)	107
5.2 Designing an evaluation process (2)	108
6.1 Preparing an opportunity costing	127
6.2 Activity schedule	134
6.3 Action plan	137
7.1 A framework for generating success indicators	150
7.2 Analysing performance	156
7.3 The quality of performance information	158

Foreword

This is the third book on evaluation to appear in this series and two of them, this being one, have originated in major investigative projects. That fact alone gives some indication of the attention that is currently being paid to this aspect of accountability.

In a national climate in which teachers are frequently being held responsible for 'low standards' – an accusation which is easily made by politicians and the media, and difficult to rebut by practitioners – evaluation may all too readily be seen as yet another stick with which to beat the poor donkey. Yet, like teacher appraisal, provided that the approach is developmental and not judgmental, evaluation is a powerful instrument for school improvement while at the same time providing accurate and impartial evidence about standards. This book, like others in the series, is designed to help teachers to manage more effectively for the good of their institutions, their students and themselves.

In an early chapter the authors quote Drucker's dictum in which he defines *efficiency* as 'the art of doing things right' and *effectiveness* as 'the art of doing the right things'. This book is, to a high degree, by these standards both effective and efficient. A wealth of experience makes it effective; and an exemplary attention to presentation makes it efficient. It is, to employ a term which is perhaps becoming debased through overuse, essentially user-friendly. This does not mean that it talks down to its readers. On the contrary, in its use of *reflections* it constantly challenges readers to consider where they stand, and what they need to do, how they might best go about doing it. Its case study approach through *cameos* demonstrates clearly that the book is dealing with real issues, not abstractions. Yet nowhere does it lose sight of the fact that teachers are busy people with little time or inclination to be led down academic byways.

I am confident that this book will be of great help to managers at all levels of education, not only in the UK but also in other countries confronted by the same challenges, and will become a classic in its field.

Cyril Poster

Introduction

The issue of educational quality is now central to much policy discussion in education. This means that ways need to be found to define and assess quality and to use the results to improve educational processes and outcomes. The aim of this book is to provide an introduction to the management of evaluation processes which is practical, accessible to the busy practitioner, and yet challenging in its approach to what is an area of considerable debate and controversy.

The Department of Education and Science's School Management Task Force (DES, 1990) identified monitoring and evaluation as one of the six management areas which are currently causing greatest concern to those in schools. The evaluation of the pilot phase of TVEI (Lines and Stoney, 1989) also identified the area as one in which considerable development needed to take place. In general, the Education Reform Act with its emphasis on enhanced delegation and accountability in the education system will place a premium over the next few years on the effective management of evaluation processes. Yet our work in schools, colleges and LEAs has shown that this is an area where managers at all levels in the education system feel insufficiently skilled.

The book is about managing evaluation: it is not about management in the purely hierarchical sense or evaluation in the purely technical sense, although both issues will be addressed. It is written for those who manage different aspects of the education service. All teachers and lecturers manage classrooms. Our particular concern here, however, is with those – the vast majority these days – who work *with and through other adults* to improve the quality of the curriculum and of classroom practice. This means, in effect, all teachers and lecturers who are members of year, departmental, pastoral, project, perhaps cluster/consortia or LEA teams or working groups, or who lead such teams. It means, in addition, all those such as senior staff of schools and colleges and LEA officers and advisers who are responsible for creating the organisational structures and climate within which such teams work. At both team and organisational levels the demands of management in education are becoming increasingly complex, not least because of increasing pressure to evaluate the quality of the areas of work for which they are responsible. We believe this book will be of interest and value to all these groups and also to those who are involved in management training and development.

The book arises from work that we have undertaken in a variety of contexts in all sectors of education and elsewhere. The examples in the text reflect this experience. The immediate impetus, however, has arisen from a project which we undertook on behalf of the Employment Department (formerly the Training Agency) on the management of Monitoring, Review and Evaluation (MRE) in TVEI. During that project we worked with teachers, lecturers, officers and advisers in three local education authorities to explore with them their own perceptions of their problems and needs in relation to the management of MRE and to develop responses which were appropriate to their own situations. During that work it became clear that the problems of managing MRE in TVEI are generic ones. They are generic in the sense that they need to be tackled with approaches which address *general* management development issues rather than ones which are specific to MRE alone. Furthermore, these approaches are applicable to the management of MRE in a wide variety of educational contexts, not just those – mainly within the 14–18 age-range – which are the focus of TVEI. We decided, therefore, to combine the lessons from the TVEI project with those from our other experiences of management development to produce this book.

HOW TO USE THIS BOOK

This book is designed to be *used* by all those who want to manage evaluation more effectively. Each chapter has a number of elements:

- discussion of particular aspects of the management of evaluation, exploring ideas and concepts, developing possible approaches and giving brief examples;
- a variety of exercises and activities designed to help individuals, groups and teams to manage the process of evaluation;
- cameos or case studies in which a variety of authors describe their actual experiences of managing evaluation;
- guidance on where to seek further ideas or information.

The chapters are in a sequence based on our experience of the particular steps that need to be taken if the time and effort put into evaluation are to prove really worthwhile. The steps or stages are:

- developing an understanding of, and approach to, evaluation, management and the management of evaluation;
- understanding the context in which evaluation must be managed;
- establishing systematic, on-going monitoring and review;

- determining the focus of more specific investigations;
- preparing plans for this evaluation and ensuring that it is appropriately managed and resourced;
- clarifying its purpose and deciding the criteria on which success is to be judged;
- managing the gathering of data;
- producing and reporting results and using the evaluation to implement action plans.

All of these stages are interrelated. For example, the kinds of data to be gathered must reflect the purpose of the activity to be evaluated, and the planning process must ensure the necessary resources will be available at an appropriate time to maximise the chances of influencing action. Such requirements of effectively managed evaluation may seem obvious but are often forgotten. It is important, therefore, that the book is read as a whole. In particular, it is hoped that readers will not jump to the later chapters, especially that on data collection, without first examining the issues explored in the earlier chapters.

The chapters of the book work through these stages. Chapter 1 outlines the approaches to evaluation and management that underpin the philosophy of the book. Chapter 2 considers the significance of the roles and relationships, culture and values which provide the differing contexts in which any evaluation will be carried out. Chapter 3 suggests processes and methods that will enable regular, on-going monitoring and review of what is taking place. Chapters 4 to 8 then consider the necessary stages of more specific, focused enquiry. Chapter 4 considers methods of choosing an appropriate focus for such evaluation. Chapter 5 considers aspects of the planning and management processes. Chapter 6 considers how evaluation should be costed and how the appropriate allocation of resources, including time, can be made. Chapter 7 explores the development and use of success criteria in relation to a development's purposes. Chapter 8 discusses methods of collecting and processing data. Chapter 9 considers how best to ensure that the results of the evaluation are to be used to maximum effect in influencing future practice. Finally, Chapter 10 provides an overview of the ideas presented in the book by considering more generally the place of evaluation within educational organisations.

Despite this emphasis on key stages, the book is not designed to be prescriptive. The ideas presented in each chapter are intended to stimulate thinking, discussion and debate. The cameos are presented to illuminate the complexity and messiness of 'real life', where best-laid plans meet unexpected obstacles and have unanticipated as well as intended outcomes. Further reading is, of course, optional. The exercises are examples of management development activities which will help you and your colleagues to clarify your ideas and purposes. Most of these activities can be used by individuals as well as groups. However, they are primarily designed for the latter, as this book is based on a belief that the management of evaluation is, at best, a collaborative and shared process. Therefore:

- some exercises (called 'Reflections') simply ask the reader to pause and consider the personal implications of what he or she is reading;
- some exercises are designed to help individuals and groups to develop their understanding and thinking about the management of evaluation processes;
- some can be used by groups and teams to explore in a systematic way how to manage themselves and to evaluate more effectively developments for which they are responsible or in which they are involved;
- some are presented in the form of 'Worksheets' which enable particular aspects of evaluation to be considered more systematically;
- a number of the exercises can be used in other contexts as more traditional training materials, for example, during a whole school or college INSET event or training day;
- some can be used for more than one of these purposes.

Each exercise makes clear how it can best be used. They are copyright free and can be photocopied and enlarged for your use. Do not be constrained to use only these exercises or feel that you *must* work your way through each one. It is sensible to choose and adapt them to match the needs of your particular situation and also to develop ideas of your own.

Managing evaluation involves thinking and planning, checking on progress, rethinking and replanning in a continual cycle. We hope this book will help you with this process.

Acknowledgements

Many people have contributed to the ideas in this book. Officers, advisers and teachers too numerous to mention in the many LEAs in which we have worked have frequently caused us to review our thinking about how evaluation is managed in education; but we must mention the particular contribution of those in the three LEAs – Derbyshire, Rotherham and Sheffield – in which the field work for our project for the Department of Employment was undertaken. In addition to officers and advisors in all three authorities, particular contributions were made by teachers from: Glossopdale Community College and St Philip Howard School in Derbyshire; Aston, Dinnington, Rawmarsh, Spurley Hey, Thrybergh and Wickersley Schools in Rotherham; and City and other schools in Cluster D/E, Myers Grove School and Parson Cross and Stradbroke Colleges in Sheffield. The support and enthusiasm of all these professional colleagues provided the basis for some fascinating work and many of the ideas which appear here have been filtered through their experience. A number of them contributed cameos to the book.

Colleagues in the Centre for Education Management and Administration at Sheffield City Polytechnic – Brian French, Viv Garrett, Roger Mercer and Len Watson – have given us continual support and encouragement as well as improving the draft of the manuscript with their helpful suggestions. Our thanks also go to Beryl Titterton who has been project secretary.

The project from which this book derives was funded by the Employment Department and we have appreciated in particular the supportive management style adopted by Roy Saxby and Don Carter of its TVEI Section. We have also enjoyed and valued our discussions with colleagues from our partner management development projects at Bristol Polytechnic, the Polytechnic of Wales and the Open University in Wales, and the National Development Centre for School Development and Planning at the University of Bristol.

We are grateful to Roger Harrison for permission to adapt his questionnaire on organisational ideologies for use in Chapter 10.

Needless to say, the final responsibility for what follows is ours alone.

Abbreviations

CEG	Careers Education and Guidance
CSt	Computer Studies
DION	Diagnosing Individual and Organisational Needs
EI	Evaluation Instrument
FE	Further Education
GRIDS	Guidelines for Review and Internal Development in Schools
INSET	In-Service Education and Training
LEA	Local Education Authority
LMS	Local Management of Schools
LMSC	Local Management of Schools and Colleges
MRE	Monitoring, Review and Evaluation
QLT	Quality of Learning and Teaching Profile
QS	Quality Statement
ROA	Records of Achievement
SAT	Standard Attainment Target
SDP	School Development Plan
SMT	Senior Management Team
SSR	Staff: Student Ratio
SWOT	Strengths, Weaknesses, Opportunities, Threats
TVEI(E)	Technical and Vocational Education Initiative (Extension)

Chapter 1

Management and evaluation

We frequently evaluate what we do, although most of the time this is not done in any structured way. Sometimes such evaluation is done privately. This can be satisfying, perhaps a momentary warm glow after a well-run meeting or a successful lesson. During a long and sleepless night it can be agonising. Sometimes the evaluation is shared, informally in the staff room or more formally during a meeting. These 'evaluations' vary greatly in depth and rigour but it is unlikely that you will get through a day without some reflection and without drawing some conclusions about your effectiveness or otherwise. How often did you talk over aspects of your work with a colleague or perhaps your partner or a friend? Were there any moments when you changed your behaviour in reaction to feedback from others? However busy you were, it is likely that some events like these occurred at some time. If, however, if you were asked to list all the evaluation activities in which you engaged yesterday, your response would most probably have been different. It may well have been, 'None at all'.

We have frequently found that people tell us that they are not involved in any evaluation process. However, further conversation reveals a considerable number of review activities and that they are taking a generally reflective approach to their work. However, such activities are often fragmented, not clearly linked to planning except in the most immediate sense, not recorded in any way and not regarded as evaluation. We are not suggesting that any momentary reflection can be counted as sufficient basis for saying that evaluation is taking place. However, we *are* suggesting that recognising, valuing, building on and developing the already existing processes of reflection and evaluation is the best way to start.

Reflection 1.1

When am I evaluating?

Think about your last week at work.

- How often did you talk over an issue with a colleague or colleagues or think through systematically what you had done or what happened?
- Did you reach any conclusions that resulted in your changing anything?
- Did you write anything down?

Talking things over is not in itself enough to be described as evaluating. However, doing so systematically and reaching conclusions that lead to action can be described as informal evaluation. You can build on this.

In this chapter we will first explore the issue of 'evaluation' in some detail. After considering the difference between research and evaluation, we identify what, to us, are the key characteristics of the latter and the implications of each of these. We then offer our thinking on 'management', once again providing key definitions and exploring implications.

WHAT IS EVALUATION?

At the most straightforward level it can be said that *evaluation means placing a value on things*. However, we would like to propose a more exhaustive definition:

Evaluation is part of the decision-making process. It involves making judgements about the worth of an activity through systematically and openly collecting and analysing information about it and relating this to explicit objectives, criteria and values.

Before expanding on this definition we will explore the differences, as we see them, between *evaluation* and *research*. These terms are, of course, open to a variety of definitions. It is not uncommon for people to undervalue the evaluative work that they are doing because they are measuring themselves against a largely mythological spectre, that of 'real research'. This is seen to necessitate rigorous, in-depth study, involving large, representative samples, using specific and often difficult techniques, and resulting in some kind of formal report.

In most schools and colleges, time for teaching, preparation and marking are all at a premium. New initiatives and demands such as those of the National Curriculum, appraisal and new requirements in relation to testing and examinations, arrive at an increasing rate. Research seems an unimaginable luxury that needs to be carried out by outsiders or, with some difficulty, by insiders struggling for a higher degree. There can also be some suspicion that this kind of activity, perhaps like 'management', is not real work.

We have found it helpful to think of a continuum from

Research ←——————————————— to——————————————→ Action

It may not be possible for busy practitioners to spend much, if any, time engaged in pure research. However, it is essential from time to time to take deliberate steps back from 'hands on' activity in order to make some assessment or evaluation of progress. Sometimes the step will be a small one, at other times it may be necessary to move a considerable way towards the 'research' end of the continuum. For example, in the context of introducing SATs for seven-year-olds, some schools held review meetings at an early stage in the process. This enabled staff to identify problems facing Year 2 teachers and to take some steps to minimise these. These were relatively informal processes. Meanwhile, however, their LEA was carrying out a more formal evaluation of the situation by circulating questionnaires and carrying out classroom observations and interviews with samples of teachers. These activities resulted in a report containing more general findings.

Evaluation shares some characteristics with research, but there are also differences. For example, while it is necessary to establish that findings have some validity, validity in evaluation relates more to the careful match of the quality of information to the claims that are being made rather than to the quantity of information collected. Evaluation generally requires a greater degree of pragmatism than research: information is often required quickly and the activity must be possible within the time and the resources that are available. The greatest need of those engaged in action is for *formative* evaluation: reliable information about the strengths, weaknesses, advantages and disadvantages of a particular initiative or development which enables the most effective next steps to be identified. Less often do we need *summative* evaluation which assesses the worth of an activity or programme after it has been established or its funding is finished. Many evaluation activities will need to be small scale and carefully focused. This does not mean, however, that they can be slipshod or overly biased.

The crucial first step in managing evaluation is to recognise and value what is already taking place. This enables us to to make existing processes more systematic, more accessible, more appropriate and therefore better able to contribute more effectively to planning and decision-making processes.

The characteristics of evaluation

The evaluation landscape may be a broad and varied terrain, but it has particular characteristics. Nuttall lists the necessary components of what he terms accountability schemes, suggesting that such a scheme needs to:

(a) be fair and perceived as fair by all the parties involved;
(b) be capable of suggesting appropriate remedies;
(c) yield an account that is intelligible to its intended audience(s);
(d) be methodologically sound;
(e) be economical in its use of resources;
(f) be an acceptable blend of centralised and delegated control.

(Open University, 1982: 30)

This a helpful summary of what might be expected of an evaluation process, but there are three key attributes which define more clearly what in our view evaluation should be. These are:

- Evaluation involves making judgements.
- Evaluation is, at best, open and explicit.
- Evaluation contributes to decision-making.

First, *evaluation should involve making judgements* about the worth or value of an activity. This includes setting clear criteria, standards, values against which to measure success. Sometimes values or criteria are assumed to be shared. The process of identifying criteria explicitly may involve considerable debate and disagreement about what is appropriate. Sometimes criteria are set without sufficient thought or without realising what the unintended consequences might be. It may be tempting, for example, to set easily attainable objectives in order to guarantee success. Conversely, over-ambitious criteria may result in unnecessary disappointment and a failure to recognise the successes that are achieved. It is very important to be sure that success is recognised along with areas for improvement, and to set criteria that are achievable but sufficiently demanding.

It is essential to recognise that evaluation is in itself value-laden. The current attempts to identify means, or performance indicators, by which schools and colleges can be identified as more or less effective are leading to controversy and debate about the values that are implicit in different indices. In general, who decides what is evaluated, who evaluates whom and for what purpose are far from neutral matters. In subsequent chapters we endeavour to offer means by which bias and the distortions of particular agendas can be minimised; but the first step is to acknowledge that our values influence our perspective to a considerable degree.

Our perspective on evaluation will almost certainly be influenced by what we see to be its central purpose. Educational evaluation has tended to emphasise its developmental potential through such activities as action research and school self-evaluation mechanisms such as GRIDS (McMahon *et al.*, 1984). More recently there has been an increasing demand for accountability, for example for evidence that grant-related funding is being spent in the ways stipulated or is producing 'value for money'. These two dimensions, of development and accountability, are sometimes held to be contradictory. Whilst recognising the tension between them, we would argue that an evaluation activity could be high in both aspects or perhaps sadly lacking in either.

For example, in the context of an annual review which is part of an external project's requirements, responses could fall into any of the quadrants in Figure 1.1.

We suggest that there is a legitimate need for both developmental and accountability dimensions of evaluation and that the important consideration concerns which is appropriate in what situations. It is, however, important not to confuse the two, nor to allow one's own orientation towards one aspect to cloud one's judgement to the point of excluding consideration of the other.

Reflection 1.2

Think for a moment about your previous experiences of evaluation. Can these be placed in relation to Figure 1.1? If so, do they all fit neatly into one box or can you think, for example, of an incidence of accountability such as an HMI inspection which was subsequently used for developmental purposes?

Figure 1.1 Dimensions of evaluation

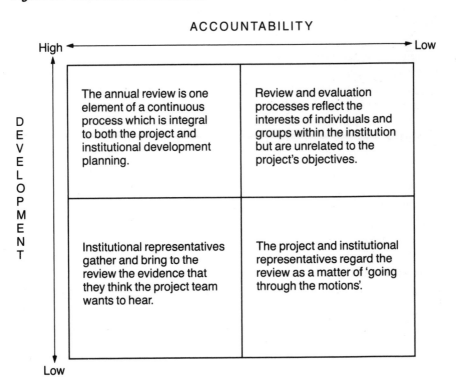

Second, *evaluation should be open and explicit.* It is not possible to improve practice without checking and analysing the strengths and weaknesses of what we are doing. However, questions such as 'How well am I doing?' or 'How well are you doing?' are not always comfortable ones. The link between evaluation and future funding is even more threatening with a temptation to put on a good face or conceal or deny problems. Any element of secrecy or of evaluation being done to the weak by the more powerful will compound these problems. What is shared ought to be more than conclusions and recommendations. Who has been involved, what has taken place, the success criteria used, all need to be clear. Managing evaluation includes managing the inclusion of others in different ways. In addition, the limitations as well as the strengths of our evidence or data need to be recognised and the connection between the data and the conclusions clearly made. The need to be open does not mean that all evaluation activities must result in written reports, although some written record, preferably brief and to the point, is a necessary part of a continuing process. For example, brief notes recording the content and conclusions of a review meeting are an important part of the evaluation record. However, the sharing of experience, the drawing of conclusions, the setting of future actions during the meeting are a vital part of the public process. The fact that evaluation should be open does not mean that every piece of information generated should be available to absolutely everybody. It is unlikely that teachers would ever undertake any evaluation of their own practice if this meant they must expose all their weaknesses to other staff, parents and pupils.

We recognise that evaluation is multi-level. Different actions are appropriate in different circumstances. For example, you will not wish to call a staff meeting or circulate a report to make public your insights on a particular meeting or lesson. However, some forum where reflections on a new project or on continuing practice may be shared and shaped at intervals is appropriate, perhaps as part of the process of identifying staff development and INSET needs.

Finally, evaluation should produce a result that *contributes to decision making*. It is possible to argue that 'researchers' are not responsible for ensuring that action is taken as a result of their findings, but this is not so for those engaged in evaluations. Evaluation is a crucial and integral part of both formal and informal planning cycles. Unfortunately, it is not uncommon for evaluation findings, or reports, to be shelved or archived.

Reflection 1.3

Think for a moment about any evaluation reports you have ever received. How closely did you read them? Where are they now? Did they influence your own behaviour or your institution in any way?

Readers and hearers often reject evidence or data that they find uncomfortable or which suggests they should make changes they do not wish to make. Again, much of this book is concerned with establishing ways of managing the process to minimise the chance of the rejection of findings. It is, however, possible that even when a development appears to have 'proof' that it is successful, funds may prove too short to continue its promotion. However, even in those circumstances, what is learned about one issue or development may prove transferable to other situations. Managing the transfer of insight gained in one situation to another is as important as the more direct application.

In this context it is also essential to recognise that evaluation is not primarily a technical issue. Viewing it as a 'puzzle' involving identifying and carrying out the 'right' technique usually creates problems. If the activity is not carefully managed and set into context its effects can be minimal or even harmful. For example, in one school it was decided that a small group of teachers would evaluate a major change in curriculum delivery at the end of the first term after its introduction. Staff and pupils were interviewed and questionnaires circulated. The feedback was devastating. The staff were feeling de-skilled by the many changes. Much of the feedback from pupils was not encouraging. Some staff were clearly exposed, although not named, as less successful than others. Perhaps the school was attempting to do too much too quickly, but the evaluation was intensely depressing in its effect. It also tended to fix a perception of failure in an unhelpful way. An attempt to identify staff development support needs at this stage of the project might have enabled the same difficulties to be recognised but in a more positive and purposeful way. There is always a danger that evaluation which focuses on technique rather than context may have negative consequences, rather like the proverbial technically successful operation during which the patient died.

In evaluation, as in so many circumstances, the process is as important as the product. *How* things are done is often at least as important as *what* is done. Often the factors that distinguish 'successful' evaluations from those that prove less effective in influencing developments relate to the way in which each evaluation has been managed. It is possible to identify a considerable number of helpful strategies and behaviours but not to delineate any aspects of management that are exclusive to evaluation. Once again the best way forward appears to be to build on what is already known and apply general principles to the particular context. We will, therefore, in the next part of this chapter, outline the general principles that we have found to underpin the most effective management approaches.

WHAT IS MANAGEMENT?

We define management as *getting things done with and through others*. Implicit in this definition are two key points: the fact that management is a purposeful activity, and the wide range of activities which can be considered to be managerial. We will now explore each of these in turn.

Management is purposeful

First, management is *purposeful*. It is not an end in itself – although too often this may seem to be the case! This sense of purpose does not necessarily mean that management involves the pursuit of 'objectives' in any narrowly defined sense, although many management writers would argue that it does. Rather, it involves *'getting things done'* in ways which make sense to those involved and which enhance the capacity of the group or the organisation to perform better in the future. What it means to perform better or how this might best be achieved may be the subject of debate or even conflict, and dealing with these is as much a part of management as is finding and implementing the best way to achieve relatively uncontroversial goals. We will explore the implications of this point for the management of evaluation later. Here, however, it is important to note that, if management is concerned with purposes, evaluation in its broadest sense should be a central element in *all* management processes.

The idea that management is purposeful can be explored in a number of ways. One is to use the concepts of efficiency and effectiveness which are currently much in vogue. Drucker (1974) defines *efficiency* as 'the art of doing things right', and *effectiveness* as 'the art of doing the right things'. It is possible to conceive of management – and hence evaluation – as being concerned with either or both of these things. There are many pressures in the current climate for the emphasis to be placed on efficiency. Such an emphasis tends to focus on specific areas of activity within the school or college and how they might be improved: in particular how present results might be achieved with fewer resources or how the current level of resources might be managed to achieve more. This is important, especially when resources are tight. However, such an approach has a tendency to be inward-looking and to be more concerned with the short term than the long term. In contrast, an effectiveness perspective is constantly concerned with whether the things we are doing continue to be appropriate, particularly in the context of a rapidly changing and increasingly demanding external environment. Of course, the two perspectives are not alternatives – they are complementary. All management activities must be concerned both with the 'why?' and the 'what?' (an effectiveness perspective) as well as the 'how?' (the efficiency dimension). Evaluation should help us to address all of these.

It should not be assumed, however, that the definitions of efficiency and effectiveness in any particular situation are unproblematic: 'Let us get our objectives clear and everything else will fall into place.' Such an approach – which is still common in much management literature – begs a lot of questions about relationships within an organisation. Management occurs in a *micro-political* context. It cannot be assumed that all the members of an educational organisation, let alone its diverse external constituencies, share a common view about purposes, priorities or practice. We all view particular issues in terms of our own values and interests. These will deeply colour our views about what is desirable and what is undesirable in our organisations. For example, there may be fundamental disagreement about the priority which should be given to the teaching of basic skills or to examination success as against broader aspects of education in primary or secondary schools. Or there may be conflict in a college about the degree to which special needs provision should be generously resourced at the expense of other areas of work. There can be disagreement about methods as well as purposes. For example, teachers with different subject backgrounds may view very differently the appropriateness of mixed ability teaching methods to their subject. Such differences are not easily resolved. They render the idea of purpose problematic and subject to constant renegotiation. This means that management can never be viewed as a purely 'rational' activity.

Finally, management involves *choices*. As has already been seen, it clearly involves choices in the micro-political sense that values may be in conflict. But even if there is broad agreement, the economic concept of *opportunity cost* tells us that a decision to allocate resources to one particular activity implies foregoing something else. This arises at all levels from the use of people's own time to major questions relating to balance and choice in the curriculum. The choices which individuals and groups actually make in allocating time and other resources demonstrate powerfully what their *real* priorities are, whatever their rhetoric may say. A good example here is evaluation itself: statements about its importance are frequent, but this does not prevent it from being constantly marginalised.

The activity of management

It is not unusual in schools and colleges for people to talk about management tasks as if they are the sole prerogative of those who hold defined positions of responsibility, such as headteacher, principal or head of department, and who are paid higher salaries to manage other people. There are two problems with this approach. First, it is often experienced as deprofessionalising, reducing the amount of control that individuals have over their work. Some teachers may be happy with this – it often makes life a lot simpler! It does not, however, reflect the reality in many cases nor does it reflect our conception of management. Second, this view of management leads people – especially those who do not think of themselves as 'managers' – to underestimate their power to influence the world in which they work. Too often individuals and groups claim to have very little power to influence the organisational environment within which they work; they feel unable to take decisions or implement actions without referring to, or waiting for, approval from their 'superiors'. Yet very often it can be shown that they have a good deal of power – provided only that they think more clearly about the managerial dimension of their professional activities.

Our view is that, while some posts in schools and colleges are clearly managerial in a formal sense, it is more helpful to think of management as an activity than as a job. From this perspective, all teachers in schools and colleges are managers for part of their time, as, often, are other adults such as caretakers, secretaries and technical staff, and pupils and students too. While much managerial activity is carried out through the formal structures of the organisation (the 'organisation chart'), it also involves the complex network of informal relationships through which much of the real work of the school or college actually gets done. Management roles, too, can be formal or informal: the main-grade teacher who develops a method of evaluation and then shares it with others is fulfilling a managerial role just as much as, and possibly more effectively than, the head of department who gathers some of the data required for a TVEI annual review. Indeed, one can find many examples in TVEI, as in other initiatives, of main-grade teachers and lecturers who are either representing their school or college at cluster or pyramid meetings, or are taking responsibility for cluster or pyramid working groups.

However, few of these people would view themselves as involved in *management*, even though they are performing, in many cases, complex management activities. One reason for this is a tendency to see management primarily in hierarchical terms. Thus, those teachers who hold a relatively lowly place within the hierarchy often feel disempowered and see themselves as having little influence over what happens in the wider context. This often leads to the feeling that 'I' or 'we' have carried this out as far as we can, but 'they' have not given their blessing or, sometimes, have blocked what 'we' want to do. Yet often those in senior management positions do have a genuine desire to share responsibility, create autonomy and promote imaginative ideas, wherever they are generated in the hierarchical structure.

This apparent contradiction between the perceptions of senior managers and those of their more junior colleagues may be less alarming than it first appears. The former often have a philosophical view of management which supports the notion of greater collegiality in schools and colleges, but find themselves working within a multi-layered management structure which they may allow to negate their best intentions. The latter, being in the middle or at the bottom of the hierarchy, are all too aware of the structure and frequently their perception of the structure's potential for control is enough. They internalise their initial perception of lack of power and do not see opportunities for action when they arise. In effect, they control themselves, either out of a belief that if they do not others will, or out of a reluctance to accept responsibility which they believe to be above and beyond their formal status.

The way around this dilemma is to develop a shared conception of management that is richer than the simple hierarchical model. Thus, while it may be accepted that top-down approaches are appropriate in some circumstances, this must not blind us to the very real possibilities of managing upwards and horizontally with colleagues. Indeed, in our view, steep hierarchies are not the most helpful structures for promoting creativity, autonomy and effectiveness within schools or colleges. It is far more useful to think of management as a multi-dimensional process which, in addition to 'top-down' elements, involves:

- working in departmental or cross-institution teams with colleagues of equal or varied status – sometimes as 'leader', sometimes as 'follower' and sometimes as co-equal;
- influencing upwards – 'managing the boss';
- managing across the institution's boundaries – working with parents, employers, members of other institutions, and so on.

Increasingly we find ourselves in a variety of management roles virtually simultaneously. At one time we may be leading a team; at another exercising functions delegated to us by a formal superior; at another working in a team which is perhaps being led by a colleague who is formally junior to us. Each of these roles requires us to choose an appropriate approach for the situation and to exercise certain management skills.

The challenge is not to choose one approach whatever the situation, but to adopt that which seems most appropriate in the circumstances. In doing this we need to be constantly aware that all management activities comprise both *task* and *process* elements. As has already been seen, the effective manager needs to pay attention both to *what* is to be done and *how* it is to be achieved. Here, however, the 'how' dimension is not so much concerned with seeking the best technical solution to a problem – this is part of the 'task' dimension – but rather with ensuring that adequate attention is given to the needs and expectations of the people involved. Often individuals in management roles have a preference for one or other of these dimensions. When managing evaluation in particular, people can become so fascinated by the technical requirements, say of designing a questionnaire, that the need to ensure the interest and commitment of those who will be expected to fill it in is forgotten. Conversely, in running a review meeting, so much attention may be given to ensuring the experience is an enjoyable one that the meeting's original purpose may be forgotten.

Some readers may feel that this emphasis on how people feel about an evaluation to be inappropriate or overprotective. However, such feelings will inevitably influence how willing individuals and groups will be to change their behaviour and approaches in the light of any findings. Furthermore, it is important to be aware that effective management should comprise a long- as well as a short-term perspective. If a particular evaluation activity lasts a few weeks or months, with a report being prepared and presented and that being the end of it, it will be of limited usefulness. If, however, the evaluation process has been managed in such a way that it has not only influenced decisions about the way forward but also enhanced the capacity of the school or college to carry out future evaluations and has widened understanding in a more general sense, much more will have been achieved. Therefore, in addition to achieving the task at hand and maintaining the team while we do so, we often need to consider two further factors:

- developing the team to enhance its capacity to perform in the future; and
- developing the individual.

You may wish to consider your abilities in relation to these various aspects of management by undertaking the following reflection:

Reflection 1.4

Task, group and individual

Think about some recent situations where you have been engaged in management roles. Can you identify your natural bias in terms of the following alternatives?

- You tend to put the *task* first and are low on concern for group and individual.

                    Yes   No

- For you the *group* seems the most important; you value happy relationships more than productivity or individual job satisfaction.

                    Yes   No

- Individuals are supremely important to you; you always put the *individual* before the task or the group for that matter. You tend to over-identify with the individual.

                    Yes   No

- You can honestly say you maintain a balance, and have feedback from colleagues to prove it.

                    Yes   No

Give some illustrations from experience.

It is likely that you found that you prefer or are stronger in some of these areas than in others. Such an awareness is the first stage towards personal development. An understanding of, and sensitivity to, the situations in which we operate is vital if we are to manage effectively the fine balance between achieving the task, maintaining the team, and developing the individual and process. The demands placed on educational institutions by recent legislation, and a whole range of initiatives, makes it imperative that all those who work *with and through others* think critically about their management roles. This needs to be done at an organisational, team and personal level. In the following chapter we will try to enable you to think more effectively about these issues.

MANAGING EVALUATION

Having discussed our understanding of the meaning of evaluation and of management, it is now necessary to consider the interrelationship between the two. How do evaluation processes fit into the broader framework of school or college management? Evaluation is most commonly viewed as part of the planning cycle. In their work on school development planning, Hargreaves *et al.* (1989: 5) identify four key stages in this cycle:

- *Audit*: a school reviews its strengths and weaknesses;
- *Plan construction*: priorities for development are selected and then turned into specific targets;
- *Implementation*: of the planned priorities and targets; and
- *Evaluation*: the success of implementation is checked.

These stages are shown in Figure 1.2. In more user-friendly terms, they can be encapsulated by four questions:

Figure 1.2 The planning cycle

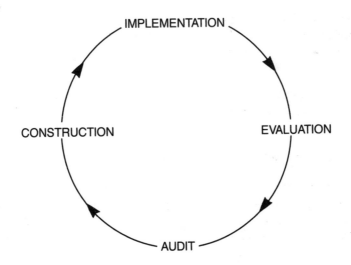

IMPLEMENTATION

CONSTRUCTION

EVALUATION

AUDIT

- Where are we now?
- Where do we want to go?
- How do we get there?
- How shall we know whether we have got there?

Although audit and evaluation are distinguished in this model, they share many characteristics. Not least, both are concerned to find out how we are doing, first as a basis for preparing plans, then in order to assess their achievement. In Hargreaves' work, audit is identified as the point at which the planning process gets started, but once that process is under way, audit and evaluation blend into each other as the evaluation of the results of one planning cycle feed into the auditing process which prepares for the next one.

This formulation of the place of evaluative activities in schools and colleges is helpful, but it is important that this model is not used, as unfortunately it sometimes is, as a reason for thinking about evaluation only at particular times. Such an emphasis may occur at the beginning of the planning cycle with quite elaborate exercises undertaken to take stock of where the school or college is, but then with little attention being given to ensuring that the implementation of plans is effectively monitored and outcomes assessed against objectives. Conversely, the emphasis may be on the end of the cycle: little attention is given to questions of evaluation until implementation is well under way with the common result that meaningful evaluation cannot be undertaken because the appropriate foundations have not been laid in terms, for example, of making arrangements for collecting information or gaining the necessary commitment of individuals who are key to the evaluation process.

The underlying assumption of this book is that evaluative activities will only be effective if they embody principles both of good evaluation practice *and* of good management practice. We began to explore these principles in the earlier sections of this chapter. Here we will make three points which link them.

First, as indicated earlier, evaluation needs to be seen as an integral part of the management process. It is not enough to think of it simply as something which is a stage in the planning process, let alone something which is 'bolted on' as an afterthought. It must be a continuous subject of attention and must be soundly embedded in the structure and culture of the organisation. If it is a stage in the process it can be put off; if it is integral to the process it cannot. Attention needs to be given to how evaluation relates to individuals' roles and to the values and ways of working in the organisation. If this is not the case, the problem of the marginalisation of evaluation activities, which is so common in educational organisations, will never be overcome. This fundamental issue is addressed throughout the chapters that follow. However, because it is so central, it is the focus of the next chapter and is revisited in the concluding chapter.

Second, and building on the distinction between audit and evaluation, it is helpful to think of evaluative activities as being of three kinds. Hargreaves *et al.* (1989) distinguish between 'checking progress', 'taking stock' and 'checking success'. We term these activities *monitoring, review* and *further enquiry* respectively. We define these as follows:

- *Monitoring*: The process of gathering information about an activity, on a continuing and systematic basis over a period of time, normally in relation to the implementation of a plan.
- *Review*: The periodic systematic assessment of an activity's, or programme's, progress and achievements in relation to its objectives or targets, with a view to determining a course of action.
- *Further enquiry*: The design and implementation of procedures to gather and process information to address in some depth an area of specific concern.

Regular monitoring and review are clearly essential elements in the well-managed planning cycle. Further enquiry, in contrast, can be seen as something with a slightly different, but complementary emphasis. It is typically a discrete, 'one-off' activity rather than a continuous or cyclic one, but it informs these others.

The final point to be made here concerns the management of evaluation as a process. As has already been noted, evaluation is too often seen as an essentially technical task, with the main problem for managers being the design and application of appropriate data-gathering mechanisms. Nothing could be further from the truth. The best-designed data-gathering tool will be ineffective if it is used within an evaluation process that has not been thought through or managed *as a whole*. This means carefully thinking through all the key stages of the evaluation process at the outset, and ensuring throughout that they are managed in an integrated way. Before we consider these stages in more detail, however, we need to explore the organisational context within which evaluation needs to be managed.

FURTHER READING

There are a considerable and ever-growing number of books on evaluation in education. Many of these are theoretical rather than practical. If you want a comprehensive overview of the evaluation literature, start with Murphy and Torrance, *Evaluating Education: issues and methods* (1987). This contains over a dozen articles and papers by writers, such as Cronbach, McDonald, Parlett and Hamilton, and Stenhouse, who have influenced thinking about, and approaches to, evaluation over many years. A more practical book, specifically written for teachers, is Hopkins, *Evaluation for School Development* (1989). This gives guidance on evaluation methods, on evaluating classroom practice and curriculum developments, on whole-school, INSET and project evaluation, and includes plenty of examples of evaluation in practice. McCormick and James, *Curriculum Evaluation in Schools* (1988), is another comprehensive and helpful book which focuses on the professional, political, ethical and theoretical issues involved in curriculum evaluation. Adelman and Alexander, *The Self-Evaluating Institution* (1982), deals with post-compulsory institutions.

The literature on management in education is also fast growing, and there are, of course, many books on management in general. A good way to start thinking about your approach to management is by using a self-development handbook such as Pedler, Burgoyne and Boydell, *A Manager's Guide to Self Development* (1986). This provides a list of qualities of effective managers against which to assess yourself and diagnose your needs; it then offers a wealth of practical activities and reflective processes through which to work. If you want to read more about the management of educational organisations, you may enjoy Handy and Aitken, *Understanding Schools as Organisations* (1986), in which the authors address such matters as what is particular about schools as organisations, effective methods of managing and the resolution of power struggles within them. A more extended view of Handy's thinking on organisations can be found in his book *Understanding Organisations* (1986b). Two useful books specifically on management in secondary schools are Torrington and Weightman, *Management and Organisation in Secondary Schools: a training handbook* (1989b) and Kemp and Nathan, *Middle Management in Secondary Schools: a survival guide* (1989), which are full of practical activities. Southworth, *Readings in Primary Management* (1987) stresses the importance of relationships and considers such matters as the different roles in primary schools and how teachers learn to perform them; staff development; team work; curriculum management and evaluation; and effectiveness.

For a discussion of development planning see Bryson, *Strategic Planning for Public and Nonprofit Organizations* (1988), and Hargreaves and Hopkins, *The Empowered School* (1991).

Chapter 2

Understanding the context

Having outlined in the last chapter the principles and thinking that underpin our approach to managing evaluation we now move on to consider the organisational context within which evaluation has to be managed. This is done through the examination of two key concepts: *role* and *organisational culture*. Understanding these – and the interrelationship between them – is an essential precondition for deciding how to carry out any management task. For example, whether one is a head or principal or a standard-scale lecturer or teacher will affect the kinds of evaluation that one can initiate; and the possible strategies and styles of operation which can be considered depend very much on the accepted patterns of behaviour and relationships embodied in the culture of the school or college. To give a further example, on taking up a new appointment, a lecturer was advised not to step on anyone's toes with the additional warning 'People around here tend to have very big feet!' In this college, sensitivity about role had become a feature of the organisational culture.

As the chapter develops, it will become clear that the issue of *values* is central to these concerns, as it is to other aspects of evaluation. The implications of this will be considered further in the final section. At this point, however, it would be useful to begin to think through the implications of these issues by working through Exercise 2.1.

EXERCISE 2.1

WHY? WHAT? HOW?

Purpose

To enable participants to reflect on a past experience of evaluation. It will help to separate out the various elements that are involved in an evaluation activity, to understand the connections between these, and to identify the factors that influence the successful management and implementation of evaluation activities.

Context

The exercise can be undertaken individually or, preferably, as a group. It is a useful method for enabling a group with a range of different experiences of evaluation to share these.

Materials required

Flipchart sheets and pens are needed when used as a group exercise.

The exercise

Individual activity

Divide a sheet of paper into six columns as on the attached worksheet. Now think about one specific piece of evaluation that actually took place and involved you in some way and:

- In column 1 (Why?) write the reasons for the evaluation being carried out;
- In column 2 (What?) describe the activity, project, curriculum development, etc. that was evaluated;
- In column 3 (How?) describe the evaluation methods used;
- In column 4 (Who?) list all the people who were involved in any way in the evaluation activity;
- In column 5 (When?) say at what stage in the lifetime of the project, development, etc. the evaluation was carried out;
- In column 6 (So What?) describe what happened as a result of the evaluation.

When you have done this, reflect on the insights that are emerging.

© Routledge 1992

Group activity

1 Participants are each asked to carry out the individual activity for 15–20 minutes.
2 They are then asked to share their analyses in groups of about four people. Each member talks through his or her sheet with colleagues and answers questions.
3 The group chooses one example from those it has discussed and transfers it on to six flipcharts, one for each of the six questions, which have been previously prepared. This can be done one group at a time. If there are more than four or five groups it is probably not wise to take an example from each as the process can become too repetitive.
4 When this stage of the activity is completed, the whole group discusses the insights that are emerging.

Points to note

• The insights that emerge from this exercise can be considerable. For example, how do the intentions under 'Why', for example, connect with the outcomes of the 'So what' column? How were these outcomes affected by what people expected from past experience? How was the evaluation influenced by the stage of the developments being evaluated? Spend some time thinking about the 'Who' column. Who was involved? How were they involved? Did anyone feel that their particular role was being overlooked or threatened? How committed did this make them to the process? How did this influence outcomes?
• From this process it should be possible to draw out the matters that help or hinder evaluation. Almost certainly, whatever the outcomes of this particular exercise, you will have noted that what needs to be managed is far more than the actual method of evaluation.
• Once you are familiar with this method of analysing past experience, you can use the same process as a means for planning future enquiry or as a checklist against which to check your plans.

WORKSHEET

WHY? WHAT? HOW? WHO? WHEN? SO WHAT?

Why?	What?	How?	Who?	When?	So what?

ROLES AND RELATIONSHIPS

Exercise 2.1 provides a simple yet very rich framework for beginning to organise our thinking about the ways in which monitoring, review and evaluation are managed. It is useful in that it is likely to raise all kinds of issues and we will be referring back to this exercise at several points in the future.

In considering how evaluation can be managed most effectively, it is helpful to think of management activities operating at three interconnected levels in an organisation: that of the *individual*, that of the *group or team*, and that of the *organisation* as a whole. It also involves the management of relationships with individuals, groups and organisations *beyond the boundaries* of the organisation in question, particularly those who, although outside the school or college, feel they have a legitimate interest in what is going on. Therefore, we need to be clear about how individuals and groups relate to one another and what roles they perform within a given context. The head of a primary school embarking on whole school evalu- ation will be able to work in different ways from a TVEI co-ordinator on Scale B who is attempting to achieve the co-operation of colleagues, many of whom will be senior to him- or herself, in conducting an annual review. A common mistake in managing evaluation is to take insufficient account of the roles and expectations of those whose commitment is essential if the evaluation is to be effective. Exercise 2.2 provides a simple framework for beginning to do this.

EXERCISE 2.2

'I', 'WE', 'THEY'

Purpose

To help to identify the action that needs to be taken by those involved in managing a process of evaluation, and the power they have to influence others.

Context

A group activity to be undertaken by a group that is involved in managing an evaluation process.

Materials required

Flipchart paper and pens.

The exercise

As a group, identify an evaluation task that needs to be undertaken. Make sure that you all agree on the nature of the task. Then ask the following questions about what needs to be done to enable this work to be undertaken as effectively as possible:

- What do *I* – each individual in the group – have to do?
- What do *we* – the group as a whole – have to do?
- What do *they* – other groups who can affect the work – have to do?

1 *What do I have to do?* Group members should spend about 15 minutes thinking about what they, as individuals, need to do in their individual roles. They should jot down their ideas on a piece of paper, noting at least five action points. Each individual then spends a few minutes sharing his/her ideas with the rest of the group.

2 *What do we have to do?* The group now considers the second question. There may be a need, for example, to gather additional information, to consult more widely, to meet more regularly or to develop better networks of communication. One of the group should note down the salient points on a flipchart. The group should try to come up with at least five points of action for the coming months.

© Routledge 1992

3   *What do they have to do?* This third question can appear to be the most difficult. It is an opportunity to think about what members of the group would like to happen and then to consider how best they can help to bring it about. Another question emerges: 'What do we have to do to help them to do it?' For example, have we provided the relevant information? Are our recommendations clear and well argued? It may be necessary to consider how effective members are at managing upwards. As before, the group should try to devise five action points for the coming months.

The focus on 'I', 'We' and 'They' in this exercise quickly indicates the complex web of tasks and relationships which evaluation activities commonly embody. It helps us to think critically about the role we play in a given context and how we relate in this role to others with whom we are directly, or indirectly, involved. Our role may be one of leadership, supervision, administration or co-ordination; but it may also simply be that of 'team member' or 'classroom teacher'. Whatever the particular role we are called upon to take, the recognition that 'I' or 'We' may be able to contribute to the decisions which 'They' make or the action that 'They' take can be liberating and help to counter feelings of dependency or powerlessness which are so inhibiting. The exercise also helps us to avoid confusing role with position or office: a headteacher, principal or head of department will, invariably, have to occupy a number of roles within his or her school or college, and these roles will change from time to time depending on the particular demands of the situation.

At first sight, role may not seem a difficult idea for us to conceptualise, as most of us readily see the actor's role as analogous. It is the actor's ability to change role from character to character, and play to play, that we so admire. Indeed, a play is judged, for the most part, by how well the individual actors perform their roles together. Similarly, the success of a particular initiative, programme or evaluation will depend on how well the individuals involved perform their roles in relation to one another. However, even though the concept of role may seem relatively unproblematic, the practicalities can be far from straightforward. It is difficult, if not impossible, to separate our professional roles from our personal roles, for example. Our role as parent may well conflict with aspects of our role as a headteacher. And within the work situation, too, we may have to play a number of roles simultaneously which can cause considerable stress. We shall return to some of these role problems a little later. Before we do, however, we need to consider the concept of role rather more systematically.

Formal role

If people are asked to explain their roles within the organisation they may well, in the first instance, give a summary of their job descriptions. In other words, they will answer the question in terms of 'this is what I am supposed to do'. The key question here, therefore, is *What do the "rules" say?'* Exercise 2.3 tries to help you think about your *formal* role. After engaging in it, you should be in a position to consider the potential of your formal role for managing evaluation effectively.

EXERCISE 2.3

WHAT DO THE RULES SAY?

Purpose

To enable individuals to explore the formal aspect of their roles, particularly as these relate to evaluation, to consider the consequences of these, and to share their findings with others.

Context

An individual exercise, although it can also be used in other ways (see 'Points to note').

Materials required

None.

The exercise

1 Consider your formal role by asking the questions below:

- Is there a job description for it? If not, should there be?
- If there *is* a job description, consider its contents:
  - ◆ how clear is it?
  - ◆ is it realistic?
  - ◆ place the elements in a rank order of priority. On what basis have you done this? Do you think the order would be shared by those with whom you have to work – for example, your boss, your subordinates or your peers?

2 Write your own job description, identifying in particular your understanding of:

- those areas where *demands* are placed on you: what things must you do, or must you do in a particular manner?
- those areas of *constraint:* what are the areas in which you are not allowed to act, you cannot act, or in which particular ways of acting are prescribed?
- those areas of *choice* in what to do or how to do it: in which areas do you have flexibility and how much?

3 After carrying out these tasks consider where responsibilities relating to *evaluation* fit in. Are your responsibilities in this area explicit? Where does evaluation come in *your* order of priorities, and those of others who may have expectations of your role? How far are your evaluation responsibilities the subject of *demands*, of *constraints* or of *choice*? Is the balance appropriate? If not, what might be done to change things?

Points to note

- This exercise can usefully be undertaken by an individual when he or she is reflecting on how a role is to be undertaken. It might also be done with an assessor as part of an appraisal process.
- A useful approach is to enable holders of similar roles, such as heads of department or curriculum co-ordinators, to share their understandings. This can be organised by assigning people to groups or allowing more informal group activity. This approach is particularly fruitful in the context of cluster, consortium or similar contexts, where those holding apparently similar roles in different institutions can compare their perceptions of their jobs.
- If undertaken seriously, this exercise will take some time. However, the effort will prove worthwhile.

Your analysis may or may not have shown the management of evaluation to be clearly part of your formal role. If it is, this will usually be helpful; but it will rarely be sufficient to guarantee effective action. First, formal role descriptions do not in themselves necessarily guarantee the formal power or authority to carry out the evaluation task effectively. Others may co-operate on the basis of your formal authority alone, but they may not do so, especially if their conception of their own role causes them to give lower priority to evaluation than you do. Perhaps more importantly, formal statements of what we are expected to do usually tell us little about *how* our role should be played. To understand this we need to adopt a much more dynamic conception of role.

Expectations and role

Role is much more complex than job descriptions or other formal statements imply: it involves us continually interacting with others to perform as head-teacher or principal, head of department, curriculum co-ordinator, or class-room teacher. In performing this role, we will interact with a wide variety of other people, all of whom will have expectations about how we should play our role. These are the members of our 'role set'. How we choose to behave in our role will reflect to a significant degree our perceptions of how these 'others' *expect* us to behave.

This second view of role, therefore, is one where role involves behaviour which arises from patterns of expectations and communication in our role set. The key questions are as follows

- Who are the key members of my role set?
- How much influence do they have over me?
- What are their expectations of me? (and how do I know?)

These questions can be explored by using 'Role Set Analysis'. The members of the role set comprise all those individuals with whom we interact and who are in a position to influence our concept of our role (called the 'focal role') by having expectations, or even stereotypes, of it. A simple example of a role set for a mathematics curriculum co-ordinator in a primary school charged with a particular piece of evaluation is shown in Figure 2.1. The lengths of the lines indicate perceptions of relative influence: those members of the role set who are closer to the focal role are judged to have the more influence. The set includes other curriculum co-ordinators in the school, the teachers who contribute to the area of work being reviewed, the headteacher, the deputy head who has overall responsibility for curriculum review, the subject adviser, the head of Year 1 in the neighbouring secondary school, and pupils and parents. Exercise 2.4 outlines a process for analysing role in some depth.

Figure 2.1 The role set of a curriculum co-ordinator in a primary school

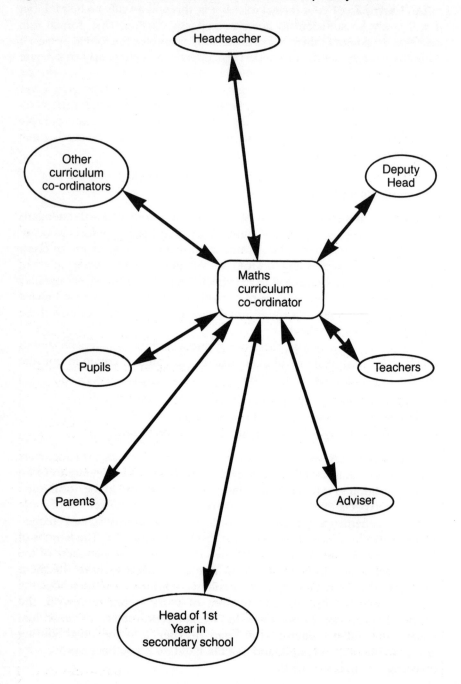

EXERCISE 2.4

ROLE SET ANALYSIS

Purpose

To enable individuals and members of a role set to consider in some depth their mutual expectations of each other.

Context

Preferably a group activity involving members of one or more role sets.

Materials needed

Plenty of copies of the Role Set Analysis Briefing Sheet and the Role Expectations Worksheet.

The exercise

1 A brief introduction is given to the concept of role set.
2 Individuals spend about 10 minutes reflecting on their current role using the Role Set Analysis Briefing Sheet.
3 Individuals are then placed in groups which, as far as possible, relate to their roles with regard to managing evaluation. Ideally these groups should comprise role sets. These groups should then:

   - spend approximately 10 minutes sharing their experiences and comparing the patterns of expectations which have emerged from their sheets;
   - then spend anything up to an hour producing their own role set diagram and an analysis of role expectations for key members of the role set.

4 This is followed up by:

   - *either* an art gallery display of the products of all the groups, with time for people to look at them, followed by the facilitator commenting on the main points of similarity and difference between the groups and plenary discussion (30–45 minutes)
   - *or* pairing groups so that they can talk through the key points of similarity and difference in their expectations of each other and consider the implications (45 minutes).

© Routledge 1992

Points to note

- Role set discussions can be very rich. The idea of talking through mutual expectations rather than simply defining job descriptions provides a much more dynamic context for discussions about the perceived freedoms and constraints within which individuals work. This can lead to the identification of areas of role ambiguity, role conflict and role overload, and to discussion of ways of reducing these.
- Role Set Analysis can be done individually using stage 1 only. However, it is of limited value without the possibility of structured feedback by members of the role set.

ROLE SET ANALYSIS BRIEFING SHEET

Reflect on your current role with particular reference to its components which relate to evaluation. Consider in particular:

1 Who are the members of your role set? Draw a diagram.
2 What is their relative influence on your role? Represent this by the length of the lines in the diagram with more influential members being placed closer.
3 What do you think are their expectations of your role performance? What do they want you to do (their 'hopes')? What do they not want you to do but think you might do (their 'fears')?
4 What are your expectations of their role performance ('hopes' and 'fears' as above). Use the Role Expectations Worksheet to record these.

ROLE EXPECTATIONS WORKSHEET

Your role:
The other role:

Your expectations of them:	Your perceptions of their expectations of you:
Hopes	*Hopes*
Fears	*Fears*

Possible role problems

The use of role analysis will lead us to examine the implications for ourselves, our colleagues and the wider organisation. They produce a useful framework for thinking about the kinds of problems which might arise for those who perform management roles. Potential areas of difficulty include:

- *Unclear expectations about role performance:* the requirements of the role are not made clear and the individual, therefore, has no way of telling the sorts of criteria on which his or her performance is likely to be judged – for example, how important *really* is the management of evaluation in the role?
- *Conflicting demands by different members of role set:* for example, the headteacher expects a team leader to take a whole-school view in his or her approach to evaluation, while team members expect him or her to defend the team's interests in the competition for resources.
- *Conflicting elements within the role:* for example, to act as both appraiser and adviser/supporter of colleagues.
- *Conflict with other roles held by the same person:* for example, teacher and parent of a child at the school.
- *Role overload:* too many roles, for example those of head of department, head of year and class teacher with a heavy teaching load in a small secondary school.

Such difficulties can arise at a number of levels. Organisational frameworks may be inappropriate: for example, job descriptions have not been thought through or the structure of posts in the school or college is no longer appropriate to current needs. Or they may occur at an interpersonal level: poor communication or negotiation resulting in unrealistic or misunderstood expectations about what particular roles involve. Effective role analysis in itself can often help to resolve role issues or problems, because so many of these are a product of unrealistic or taken-for-granted assumptions. The three keys to managing roles effectively are:

- communication about expectations of oneself and others;
- negotiation to achieve mutually acceptable definitions of role where expectations appear incompatible;
- empathy with the problems others face in carrying out their roles effectively.

Sometimes these are not enough, however, and consideration has to be given to fundamental restructuring or the redesign of roles; alternatively individuals may need to be retrained or shifted to roles that are more compatible with their personal qualities. The way we play our role is not just a product of the expectations and influence of others but also of our own values, preferences, personality and skills. Many individuals find themselves in roles with which they are uncomfortable, because they are unable to carry them out effectively in ways compatible with their personality or personal values. The key questions are: How can I best reflect my preferences for particular forms of behaviour in this role, and how much freedom do I have to do this?

Reflections of this kind should lead to the realisation that effective role performance is not merely the product of an individual's skill, experience, preferences of style and confidence, but depends on the expectations, and behaviour, of all the other people with whom he or she interacts in carrying out the role. Role performance is easier, therefore, in situations where there is a considerable degree of commonality of expectations about behaviour, preferably based on shared values. Where this is the case, it is likely to reflect a strong organisational culture.

ORGANISATIONAL CULTURE

Whenever teachers from different schools and colleges come together to discuss their work, it emerges that the fact that a particular approach is working well in one situation does not lead everyone else to adopt it. 'You couldn't do that in my situation', 'We tried that but it didn't work', or 'That might work for us but we'd have to adapt it to take note of . . . ', will all be familiar responses. What the teachers are recognising is the fact that different schools and colleges have different 'cultures', although this may not be the word that they use. Culture is sometimes defined as '*the way things are done around here*'. Shared, and often undiscussed, notions of what is done – or is not done – can act as powerful control mechanisms. New staff find they have to start behaving the same way as everyone else if they are not to remain outsiders. Some things will never be attempted because everyone *knows*, rather than assumes, that they cannot work here. An initial insight into an organisation's culture can be gained by undertaking Exercise 2.5.

EXERCISE 2.5

WHAT KIND OF PLACE IS THIS?

Purpose

To help members of an organisation to begin to think about the culture of their organisation and their feelings about this.

Context

This is a group activity. It can be undertaken in a small group which is planning an evaluation in its organisation, or it can be undertaken by a very large group during a whole-school or whole-college event.

Materials needed

Flipchart and pens.

The exercise

1 Each person in the group writes a list of ten words or phrases that he or she feels most aptly describe the organisation.
2 The whole group combines their lists on to a flipchart. If several people have used the same word or phrase this should be recorded with the appropriate number of ticks. However, nothing should be paraphrased or re-phrased at this stage.
3 The group then discusses whether any words or phrases have clearly positive or negative connotations and a + or − is placed next to these. The proportion of pluses or minuses will immediately tell something about the culture in which the group is working. At this point it is helpful to look for words or phrases that have the same or similar meaning. It will almost certainly be found that similar characteristics may be viewed in very different ways. For example,

+	−
hardworking	demanding
busy	hyperactive
stable	resistant to change

Whether individuals view a particular characteristic as positive or negative may be an indicator of how much they feel in tune with the organisation. If it is felt to be appropriate, the list can be prioritised in relation to how widely particular perceptions are shared, but this is not essential.

4 Finally, the group should discuss why things are done like this around here. It may be that certain characteristics can be attributed to leadership style or powerful staffroom groups or cabals. But do not be surprised if it is not easy to do this: culture is a complex interaction of values, attitudes, language and symbols.

Points to note

- This activity can be done individually, but this will not generate a very rich list of ideas and will not permit perceptions to be shared. The ideal group size is eight or less.
- This exercise is designed to raise awareness of the significance of the culture of an organisation, not to establish 'the' definition and not to decide who is to blame.

In trying to answer the question 'What kind of place is this?', we are striving to fathom the intricate weaving of values, attitudes and beliefs that come together and cause people to behave in ways identifiable as a particular culture. The term 'organisational culture' is not really in common usage in staff rooms. However, many comments made by individuals about the context in which they work are concerned with issues of culture. For teachers in the classroom, this is certainly true. Often, when they talk of their enjoyment of teaching one particular group but their dislike of teaching another, they are referring to the group's culture and the way in which they interact with it. The nature of this interaction creates an atmosphere, or climate, which reflects a variety of values and assumptions which are, to a greater or lesser degree, shared by the members of the group and are embodied in their behaviour. Those things that the teacher prefers to be going on in the class are, as far as he or she is concerned, the components of a good cultural environment; but beyond this, every teacher feels that, if he or she could have sufficient time with a class in a leadership role, then the culture of the class could be profoundly affected. This is well illustrated in cases where particularly experienced and accomplished teachers are given pastoral responsibility for tutor groups which are thought of as 'difficult to handle'. In the best cases this is done not as a crude control mechanism, but as a way of changing the group's culture. The teacher works on gradual change, particularly in attitudes and values.

Just as classes and groups have their own culture, so too do schools and colleges. In any LEA one can visit schools which are similarly resourced, with populations of similar socio-economic backgrounds, with staff of broadly similar philosophies, and yet the places feel very different. One school, for example, might have a 'tight ship' feel about it, while another has a feeling of relaxed purposiveness, and yet another feels anonymous.

So far we have referred to these matters as things that are felt – we sense the culture of a school or college. However, culture is far more deep-seated than an atmosphere. A poor atmosphere, for example, can be changed quite quickly by a highly unpopular but influential person leaving the organisation. However, the working culture of that organisation will take much longer to change, as such change will probably involve shifts in values, attitudes and beliefs. These may be transmitted consciously or unconsciously. One of the enduring problems with culture is that it is difficult to define: it has the quality of 'now you see it, now you don't'. There are a number of reasons for this. One arises from the fundamental nature of cultural assumptions and values which tend to be so deep-seated that those who share them are unaware that they are there: they can conceive of no other way of seeing their world. Another difficulty is that schools and colleges often do not have a single and unified culture, unless they are very powerfully controlled from the centre. They are usually pluralities of cultures with one of them more dominant at a given time while others compete for dominance.

One way of looking for the culture of an organisation is to consider the *symbols* and *language* which are often its outward representations. Symbols may be found in all spheres of school or college life. For example, in one school there may be plaques which celebrate those students who have successfully attained places in higher education; considerable attention may be given to the publication of examination results in newspapers; and students may be openly encouraged to compete for success. In another, attention may be given to the recognition of a wide range of student achievements of all kinds; examination results may be de-emphasised despite the legal requirement to publish them; and efforts may be made to ensure that all students can be seen to succeed. Another potent symbol is dress codes: a school where considerable attention is given to regulating the dress of both students and staff will almost certainly have a very different culture from one where dress codes are much less formal. In some colleges, the key symbols may embody ideas of businesslike efficiency: there may an emphasis on corporate style in letterheads and logos, the drawing up of a 'mission statement' and business plan, the production of performance indicators of various kinds and of a glossy annual report. Such symbols are likely to be potent expressions of what is valued in the institution, although we need to be sure that they do not represent simply a veneer which covers a very different set of 'real' beliefs and assumptions in the school or college, and which are more faithfully reflected in the ways in which people treat, and interact with, one another on a day-to-day basis.

Culture is also reflected in the language which is used to describe and understand the world of the school or college. For example, the way in which the people who come to institutions for educational purposes are referred to is interesting. Are they referred to as 'girls and boys', 'students', 'pupils', 'course members', 'learners' (a term used in schools of nursing), or even 'customers'? Or, as Handy and Aitken (1986: 43) ask:

> Are the children workers, clients or products?
> The words may shock but they distinguish between three different ways of relating to an organisation:
>
> - A *worker* is a member of the organisation, who co-operates in a joint endeavour.
> - A *client* is a beneficiary of the organisation, who is served by the endeavour.
> - A *product* is the output, which is shaped and developed by the organisation.

These various ways of thinking about and describing those involved in the educational process reflect quite different sets of cultural assumptions. They will influence many aspects of the behaviour of those who work in the school or college, including the ways in which processes of monitoring, review and evaluation are addressed. The processes used – both formal and informal – will embody assumptions about *how* things should be done; the items chosen for consideration will give important clues about *what* is felt to be important. It is interesting – because it is revealing – to ask first what it is that these processes value, and then, how are their outcomes celebrated? Exercise 2.6 provides a way of doing this.

EXERCISE 2.6

THE CULTURAL IMPLICATIONS OF EVALUATION

Purpose

To enable individuals and groups to explore the cultural assumptions which underlie approaches to evaluation in their school or college.

Context

This exercise can be undertaken individually or in a small group.

Materials needed

None.

The exercise

1 List the main ways in which evaluative statements about the work of the school or college have been derived or used in the past year. Examples might include:

   - formal review processes;
   - discussions at meetings such as head of department meetings or governors' meetings;
   - statements about the performance of individual pupils or students through reports, records of achievement, announcements in assembly, etc.;
   - notices or stories in the press.

2 Consider what these tell you about:

   - what members of the organisation think is important about its performance;
   - how success can best be assessed;
   - how information about performance should be disseminated.

Points to note

- This exercise is best carried out in a group in order that a wide variety of ideas can be generated.

The outcomes of this exercise will tell you something about the school or college and its values. But they will also reflect the external pressures on institutions to do things in particular ways. There is currently concern among many in education about the pressures to express values in a very public, quasi-business way, with all that this implies for processes of monitoring, review and evaluation. The world of education has only comparatively recently become used to terms such as performance indicators, success criteria, and curriculum audit; and many will view the terms as synonymous with unacceptable forms of accountability and quantitative approaches to evaluation. They may perceive them to be in contradiction to the values which underpin such terms as peer review, action research, classroom observation and student perception questionnaires. This language, and its associated symbols, may well suggest a more developmental approach, with an emphasis on qualitative rather than quantitative data. There is un-doubtedly tension between these two approaches. However, as we argued in the previous chapter, the management task is to develop strategies which marry the two cultures to provide an overall framework for evaluation.

EVALUATION AND VALUES

A dominant theme throughout this chapter has been the centrality of values to the processes of management and evaluation. The management of evaluation, therefore, cannot be separated from values. Personal experience and attitudes, different roles, different demands and different cultures all influence understanding and expectations of evaluation.

Different attitudes and opinions can prove very difficult to handle. For example, an LEA project team, which had been working for two years on a school-based project, was developing a framework for asking heads and teachers about the effects of the team's work. As they discussed the questions – how to pose them, how to check that the information they were given reflected what was actually happening in the classroom – they were taken aback when an adviser who was new to the group questioned the whole process. She suggested that only a questionnaire, circulated to schools by someone not involved with the group, could provide an accurate picture. Such differences of understanding about what counts as evaluation are most problematic when perceived of as either 'right' or 'wrong'. This is particularly difficult when differences of status are also involved, especially if higher status is held to confer superiority of opinion.

Difficulties do not just arise, however, when differences in perspective are associated with status differences. Teaching is a very personal occupation. We invest a lot, if not all, of what we are in what we do. This tends to magnify the natural human response that to criticise or question an idea or viewpoint is to criticise the person who holds it. Values are even more difficult. The value positions we take on evaluation and management, for example, are likely to be rooted in more deep-seated beliefs. Darling-Hammond *et al.* (1983) suggest that the approach we take to evaluation will be influenced by our view of teaching. They propose four possible views of teaching – as a labour, a craft, a profession or an art – and argue that each of these views influences how we regard the role of the head or principal and senior management, and how we believe that 'good practice' may best be promoted. They suggest that the first leads to an expectation that evaluation will require inspection and monitoring; the second to attempts to ensure that teachers have the requisite skills; the third to a preference for review by peers; and the fourth to an emphasis on staff development with some help from colleagues. It is not surprising that an attempt by a group of colleagues to establish some success criteria against which to evaluate progress can turn into a lengthy and difficult process.

We outlined in the last chapter the principles and thinking that underpin our approach to managing evaluation; we now ask you to reflect upon your own. Of course, you will already have begun to do so, not least through a process of identifying with, or rejecting, all or some of what we have already said. As a writing team, we have set some specific structured time aside and have had a considerable number of informal conversations sharing and clarifying our value position. We had no choice but to do this. It is not possible to write a book together, or work with groups of fellow professionals, if you are all struggling to promote different views. This may seem a luxury that those in schools and colleges simply cannot afford. However, we have come across (and on occasions lived through!) several instances when a reluctance to acknowledge, discuss, resolve, accommodate or assimilate differences of opinion has caused problems. Delaying tactics, subversion, failure to take any action, ineffective action or developments that grind to a frustrating halt have been some of the consequences. A serious attempt to address and use differences of opinion positively can be developmental, resulting in a mutual expansion of understanding. Such processes can be more useful and productive than uncritical agreement.

It is encumbent, therefore, upon anyone charged with managing an aspect of evaluation, to be as clear as possible about the values which they will bring to the task. It can be helpful to consider the question of values as an issue in itself. You may wish to do so as a separate activity or at a very early stage in an evaluation process rather than let an argument based on different viewpoints become so entrenched that it is hard for anyone to back down. One way to initiate discussion is to use a diamond ranking exercise (Exercise 2.7).

EXERCISE 2.7

DIAMOND RANKING

Purpose

To examine how different value positions influence approaches towards evaluation and to open up some ways of coping with these differences.

Context

This is a group exercise.

Materials needed

Sets of cards with relevant statements on them (see below).

The exercise

1   A set of nine statements is prepared about the issue being con-sidered. These statements should cover a wide range of possible perspectives and values. A list of possible statements about evaluation is appended, but you may wish to develop others. Each of the statements is written on a separate piece of paper or card, providing enough sets for the people taking part. Each individual could have his or her own set to begin with, or a small group can be given a set between them.
2   Individually, or in pairs or small groups, the statements are placed in an order of priority: from that which people consider most important or agree with most strongly to that which they consider least important or disagree with most. Priorities are expressed by placing the cards in the following pattern:

1

2   3

4   5   6

7   8

9

Points to note

- The process of prioritising should lead to some interesting discussions. The following strategies help in dealing with disagreements. It is important to recognise this possibility and have such strategies ready to use.

  - Carry out the activity twice. The first time base your prioritising on how evaluation is viewed in your institution at the moment. The second time rank the statements on how you would like evaluation to be seen. Discussion can then focus around any steps that might help to move the situation towards the ideal.
  - If fundamental differences emerge, focus the discussion on how evaluation activities can be devised that will acknowledge these different perspectives and provide the kinds of activities and evidence that will meet different expectations.
  - It is equally important to review the situation if there is a very large measure of agreement. What are the consequences, for example, if you as a group are heavily biased towards accountability or development? What might you be missing?

- Carrying out this activity helps people to clarify their own perceptions and feelings and, in so doing, reveals what can sometimes be fundamental differences between different individuals.

SOME STATEMENTS ABOUT EVALUATION

The statements we suggest using about evaluation are:

- Evaluation is about being accountable to other people.
- Evaluation takes up so much time that its advantages are out-weighed by its disadvantages.
- Evaluation is about making judgements.
- Evaluation is a necessary component of self-development.
- Evaluation by outsiders ensures objectivity.
- Evaluation by insiders ensures commitment to necessary changes.
- Evaluation requires considerable skill and expertise.
- Evaluation enables professionals to provide clear evidence of their effectiveness or otherwise.
- Evaluation is concerned with gathering information in order to make judgements about future action.

As with role and culture, values are seldom discussed in schools or colleges. Shared values are often assumed, and differences and potential conflict denied or avoided. It is then particularly difficult if such differences are exposed only at the point when targets are being set or evaluation methods decided.

At the outset of this chapter we recommended the use of the 'Why? What? How?' exercise (Exercise 2.1) as a way of starting to think about the issues around the management of a piece of evaluation. The exercise, though apparently simple, helps to focus upon issues relating to role and culture, which have been the theme of this chapter. However, more important, it allows us to think critically about real situations, to place theories of role and culture into real management contexts. We do not perform our management roles in a vacuum, but within a variety of situations which are created by a complex interaction of relationships, attitudes and values, made manifest in the language and symbols we use and display within our organisation.

The first two chapters have examined generic management issues such as role and culture in an effort to focus the reader's attention on vital matters of process. It is important to raise awareness and deepen understanding of these matters. Otherwise the chapters that follow will be of reduced value – for sensitivity to the context in which we manage is vital.

FURTHER READING

There are a number of accessible introductions into the issue of role analysis. Recommended are Handy, *Understanding Organisations* (1986b, Chapter 3), and Plant, *Managing Change and Making It Stick*, (1987: 44–55), which provides a Role Effectiveness Profile against which to measure yourself.

You can read more about culture in some of the chapters in Westoby, *Culture and Power in Educational Organisations* (1988). In Handy, *Gods of Management* (1986a), the author proposes four management cultures and their gods: Club – Zeus; Role – Apollo; Task – Athena; and Existential – Dionysus, and describes their characteristics and the consequences for organisations. An interesting and important book by Morgan, *Images of Organisation* (1986), considers various metaphors that can be applied to organisations – machines, organisms, brains, cultures, political systems, psychic prisons, flux and transformation, and instruments of domination – and explores what these images can contribute to our reading and understanding of organisations. It contains a useful chapter entitled 'Organisations as cultures'.

The issue of values is addressed in *Secular and Spiritual Values: grounds for hope in education* (1990) by Plunkett and *Understanding Educational Aims* (1988) by Winge. Some relevant and interesting ideas and activities can be found in *Global Teacher, Global Learner* (1988) by Pike and Selby: for example, how to manage the processes of creating a learning climate, engaging in enquiry, arriving at general principles and taking action (see especially pp. 91–3). This book is designed for junior teachers but many of the activities are transferable to other age groups and to adults.

Chapter 3

The processes of monitoring and review

The processes of monitoring and review form the basis of any evaluation programme. They were defined in Chapter 1 as follows:

- *Monitoring*: The process of gathering information about an activity, or programme, on a continuing and systematic basis over a period of time, normally in relation to the implementation of a plan.
- *Review*: The periodic systematic assessment of an activity's or programme's progress and achievements in relation to its objectives or targets, with a view to determining a course of action.

This chapter focuses on these essential processes, offering practical guidelines and examples of specific monitoring and review activities. Well-planned, systematic yet economical processes for monitoring ('checking progress') and review ('taking stock') may in themselves provide sufficient information to enable a development to be evaluated. Through establishing strengths and weaknesses and demonstrating 'value', they will indicate what should happen next.

Such activities are regularly carried out in schools and colleges. For example:

- on-going monitoring of what is happening, for example by minuting meetings or recording the number of boys and girls choosing particular options;
- reviewing progress regularly through staff, departmental or group meetings designed for this purpose;
- keeping brief diaries of events, developments and issues, the contents of which are themselves reflected upon and reviewed at intervals;
- feedback meetings when individuals or groups of staff report back to others on particular developments;
- establishing the status quo or starting points through audits of various kinds.

Reflection 3.1

An initial audit of evaluation activities

As a starting point to thinking about these issues, jot down two lists of the methods that are being used in your institution at the moment.

Monitoring   *Review*

Now put these lists to one side ready to come back to them later in the chapter.

It is useful to think of evaluation processes in terms of information management, because this highlights a number of key questions which all of these processes need to address. In this context, 'information' has a particular meaning. Unlike 'data', which comprise all the mass of stimuli that impinge upon us daily, 'information' comprises only data that have been selected and processed to help us carry out a particular task. This means making choices about what is important and how relevant information can best be gathered and used. Of course, choices embody values, and information can therefore never be value-free.

Information can also be put to different purposes. Sproull and Zubrow (1981) suggest four ways of using information:

- *Symbolically*, to demonstrate that a development or programme is being managed in a rational, responsible way. The mere fact that information is being collected is enough. For example, a project would be seen to be accountable whether the information collected was used to inform practice or not. It is not at all unusual for information to be gathered apparently for its own sake in all kinds of organisations. Sometimes the original reason for the collection may have been forgotten. A key question that needs to be asked is 'Would it make any difference if this collection ceased?'
- As a *scorecard* to let interested parties know that things are on course. A good example of this approach is the traditional school report which provides regular feedback at a relatively low level of sophistication to parents on a regular basis. Such reports indicate that attention is regularly

being given to each child's performance, but their design often means that parents may not actually be aware whether they should be concerned about the levels of performance being achieved.

- In an *attention-directing* way: the information is used to indicate where problems may be arising and to highlight the need to find out why. Attention-directing systems normally embody clear indications of acceptable levels of performance and concern is aroused when these levels are breached. Many schools and colleges use examination results for this purpose, for example.
- Towards *problem-solving*: this is the most sophisticated type of information system. The way in which the information is collected and presented not only indicates that difficulties are occurring but also provides the basis for seeking a solution. Some of the review processes described later in this chapter are designed for this purpose.

This book is written in the anticipation that its readers will not be satisfied with the first two uses of information described above. Even when information is collected for symbolic purposes it can often be put to more significant use. Nevertheless, it is important to be sure at all times that the information which is needed to make management more effective is actually being collected.

MONITORING

As part of the process of information management, it is important to establish early on what aspects of a development need to be monitored. Retrospective monitoring is difficult, if not impossible: if arrangements have not been made in advance to collect the necessary information, it is unlikely that it will be retrievable later. However, once a straightforward system for monitoring is in place, it is usually not difficult to manage.

What distinguishes monitoring information from that used for review or further enquiry is that it is collected on a systematic, regular basis and is normally produced in a standardised, and often quantified, form. In establishing a monitoring system, a number of basic questions need to be answered:

- *Why* is this monitoring information needed?
- *What* information will best meet these needs?
- *How* should the information be collected and disseminated?
- *When* should the information be collected?
- *From and to whom* should the information be passed?

Effective monitoring processes provide the right information to the right people at the right time in the right way to achieve specified purposes. In deciding what it is necessary to monitor, consider what information you are required to collect by external agencies what you need to collect in order to support your school or college, TVEI or other development plans, and what other groups might reasonably expect.

Reflection 3.2

A further audit

Refer back to the list you drew up earlier of what you monitor – the information which is routinely collected – and ask yourself the following questions:

- What use do we make of this information in evaluating our practice?
- Is there any other on-going information that we need?
- Are we using resources to collect information that we don't need?

Again put your answers on one side.

In terms of Sproull and Zubrow's categorisation, monitoring information is most likely to be collected for symbolic, scorecard or attention-directing purposes. Most commonly, three kinds of things need to be monitored: expenditure, actions and outcomes.

Expenditure

Anyone managing a programme of any kind will be concerned to ensure that money, time and other resources have been expended according to budget. This may be required by an external party – for example, under a directly funded programme such as TVEI – but it should be considered a matter of good practice in any case. Monitoring here typically involves the regular reporting and analysis of expenditure against budget. This can be done using a form of the type illustrated as Worksheet 3.1.

Actions

In addition to monitoring expenditure, it will normally be necessary to check regularly whether the things that were planned have been done as planned and on time. Here regular updates are required of progress against plans, probably linked to previous agreements about the distribution of responsibilities for ensuring that particular actions are carried out. This might be done by using for monitoring purposes the kind of planning schedule outlined in Chapter 6 (see Worksheet 6.3). Other kinds of information might be used too. Minutes of meetings are usually filed. These provide a record of

WORKSHEET 3.1

EXPENDITURE MONITORING SHEET

Month	Planned monthly expenditure	Planned cumulative expenditure	Actual cumulative expenditure	Balance
April				
May				
June				
July				
August				
September				
October				
November				
December				
January				
February				
March				

matters discussed, action decided and action taken. Working groups are often asked by senior management to provide reports on their activities at regular intervals. It is important to note that many of these activities happen as a matter of routine, but the most effective use is not always made of the resources which they generate. For example, a review of minutes can provide a useful insight into the progress a group is making, and groups can use such a review as an impetus for more effective work in the future.

Outcomes

Information about outcomes puts on record what has been achieved by the actions and expenditure in the period in question. There will be a limit to the amount of information about outcomes which can usefully be collected through routine monitoring as opposed to more rigorous investigations. However, it is important that monitoring does address the issue of outcomes, first because we need to be sure that we are 'on course' in the periods between more substantial evaluations, and second because information about key aspects of implementation which has been regularly and system-atically collected will be an important source for the evaluation process itself.

This is the area where performance indicators of various kinds may be collected. Sometimes what needs to be monitored is decided for us:

The proportion of male and female students in year 10 receiving a minimum of five days experience of work:

- on school and college premises
- on employers' premises

(Training Agency, 1990)

Or we may choose to monitor particular matters for ourselves. For example, information may be gathered regularly on the number of pupils or students selecting 'non-traditional' work experience as an indicator of the success, or otherwise, of a school's or college's equal opportunities or open-access strategy. A close look at statistical information can be very informative. One secondary school, with a large number of pupils for whom English was not their first language, attributed disappointing examination results to 'lang-uage problems'. However, a closer study of the pattern of results revealed that many of these pupils had achieved their highest marks in the English exam. This provided the impetus for a considerable reappraisal.

Although collecting this kind of information is not difficult, the use to which it is put is more problematic. For example, schools are now required to publish examination results in their brochures. One of the most contro-versial aspects of the Standard Attainment Targets (SATs) is the requirement that these too must be published. Such publication must inevitably lead to comparisons being made that the data alone cannot substantiate.

Examination and test results are influenced by a variety of factors, of which home background and the process of schooling are but two. Yet many assume that higher test or examination results equate straightforwardly with 'better' schooling. What we measure, what we report, and how we report it are indicative of the values espoused by an institution and the wider society. This issue will be addressed further in Chapter 7.

REVIEW

As we have said, good monitoring processes should be established as a matter of routine. They provide the information to enable us to check whether we are still on course. It will also be necessary, however, to supplement these with more specific activities which enable us to take stock regularly. Time for review needs to be set aside on a systematic yet manageable basis. Where possible this time should be found within the existing pattern of meetings. Such time may already be set aside. If so, check the quality of the discussion. Is it relatively unstructured, dominated by particular individuals and not recorded? Do the most interesting discussions only occur when the business agenda finishes earlier than expected? If time is clearly set aside on the agenda for on-going review, is the process deferred because an 'urgent' matter has arisen which must be dealt with immediately? It is important to recognise that on-going review can be a way of ensuring that emergencies are less likely to arise.

There are many ways to set up review meetings. However, we suggest that in essence the processes of review outlined here are those that provide structured group events designed to explore different perceptions or to gather together available evidence in a fairly quick but systematic and balanced way. The results of review sessions should always be recorded in some way in order to add to the evaluation evidence about a particular activity. The purpose of a review session is to reflect on what has happened, to clarify the present situation and to identify what might happen next.

Review meetings can make a significant contribution to the process of evaluation and have many advantages:

- Existing meetings can be set aside for a process of review so that other time is not intruded upon.
- Issues are openly shared and discussed and participants are able to be active in the process of establishing conclusions.
- A lot of ground can be covered quickly, enabling more in-depth study to focus on issues identified as requiring this.
- The process of clarifying issues and ideas can be satisfying and give everyone the sense of moving forward.
- If problems are revealed and shared, there is the possibility of shared commitment to take appropriate action.

- It is possible to establish some picture of what a whole staff is feeling about development in a short period of time.
- There is opportunity for definitions and conclusions to be fully discussed.

However, there are some areas of difficulty. These need to be recognised, and in being recognised their effects can be minimised. Examples here are:

- Status or difficulties in relationships may make some people unwilling to be open about their ideas or opinions.
- Individuals may dominate a group discussion and push it in certain directions.
- Only the perceptions of the moment can be captured, and other outside events may affect the mood of a meeting in a way that influences outcomes.
- These events need to be carefully structured and managed and not everyone has the necessary skill or confidence.
- Some people may be reluctant to recognise such activities as a legitimate method of evaluation.
- Some people may hesitate to express criticism that may hurt others.
- Conversely, the isolation of individuals who do not share the consensus may be painfully revealed.

Review sessions can play a key part in managing the inclusion of all of those who may have a direct interest in an area of development. Staff who have been involved in the process of identifying any necessary next steps will have a commitment to carrying these out. More will be said about the use of groups in evaluation activities generally in Chapter 5. The rest of this chapter will be devoted to the consideration of a number of specific contexts in which review might take place, and ways in which it might be carried out.

Whole-institution review

When systematic evaluation strategies have not been developed in a school or college, it is often helpful to begin with an activity that can include everyone and take a 'broad brush' view of the current state of the organisation. One way of doing this is to engage in a 'SWOT Analysis'. Such an analysis is based on the assumption that any overall view of the organisation's 'health' must explore the fit between what goes on within it and the demands and pressures arising from its environment. Only by considering both internal and external circumstances can a strategy be developed which achieves an appropriate balance between a *proactive* stance, which seeks developments which reflect internal values and preferences, and a more *reactive* stance, which is primarily concerned with responding to perceived external demands. SWOT Analysis addresses these issues. It is most commonly used within individual institutions but should also be considered in other contexts. It may be a helpful instrument for clarifying understanding about, and within, a cluster or consortium, for example.

Essentially, SWOT Analysis consists simply of an analysis of the strengths and weaknesses of the organisation, and the opportunities and threats with which it is faced (see Figure 3.1). A method for carrying it out is described in Exercise 3.1. SWOT typically raises many issues about the challenges the school or college faces and how 'healthy' it is as an organisation. Some of the points to which it might give rise include:

- How much consensus is there about the main areas of concern? For example, did most groups identify similar issues?
- What is the balance of concerns? Relatively how long are the lists of strengths and weaknesses? And the opportunities and threats lists? What does this tell us about the school and the attitudes of people in it?
- With respect to particular areas:

  ♦ Are we doing enough to build on our strengths and to communicate them to others?
  ♦ Have we fully identified areas of opportunity, or are we mainly concerned with threats? Could threats be used positively as opportunities if viewed differently? (It may be possible here to focus on groups which put similar items under different headings.) Schools and colleges which manage their threats will survive; but those which can capitalise on their opportunities are more likely to thrive.
  ♦ How specific are the statements of our weaknesses? Are they very specific (e.g. 'no teaching schemes in English') or are they quite general and difficult to pin down (e.g. 'poor communications')?
  ♦ Would other individuals and groups not represented here (e.g. parents, pupils, LEA officers or inspectors) share our perceptions? How do we know?

Figure 3.1 SWOT Analysis

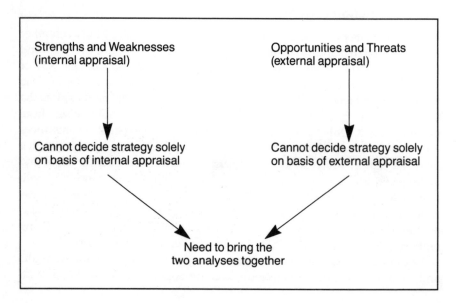

EXERCISE 3.1

SWOT ANALYSIS

Purpose

To enable members of a school, college or programme team to carry out an internal assessment (strengths and weaknesses) and an external assessment (opportunities and threats) of their organisation.

Context

This activity is an excellent one for carrying out at a whole-school or whole-college event, especially one which includes groups such as support staff, parents, governors or employers as well as teaching staff. It can also be carried out by a smaller team which is concerned with a particular area of work. In larger-scale contexts it will require a facilitator.

Materials needed

- Enough SWOT Briefing Sheets for all participants, and enough SWOT Worksheets to give one to everybody and to give one extra to each group.
- Flipchart and pens.
- Overhead projector transparencies and pens.

The exercise

1 The idea of SWOT is briefly introduced (10 minutes).
2 Individuals are given the SWOT Briefing Sheet and Worksheet. This asks them to spend about 10 minutes individually identifying the major strengths, weaknesses, opportunities and threats in relation to their organisation or team.
3 Individuals then share and discuss their individual lists as a group or groups, producing a consolidated list with the three most important items under each heading marked with an asterisk. They can be given extra worksheets to do this.
4 If there are a number of groups, activity 3 is completed using flipchart paper, and the products are placed on the walls in art gallery form, with individuals given time to browse among them.

© Routledge 1992

5 The facilitator prepares a final consolidated statement which lists all the items which groups have asterisked under each of the four headings. This can best be done on an overhead transparency, perhaps during a coffee or lunch break.

6 The facilitator presents the final collation, and plenary discussion then takes place. This may lead to an agreement that particular issues need further consideration and to the development of strategies for doing this.

Points to note

- In discussions of SWOT, the following may be helpful:

  ♦ Particular items may appear under more than one heading – for example, a mature staff may be seen as a strength (because of their accumulated experience) or as a weakness (because they find it hard to change and there is no room for 'young blood'), while LMS or the National Curriculum may be felt to contain elements of both opportunity and threat. It is important, therefore, that people are as specific as possible about their analysis: they must be clear *why* an item is a strength, a weakness, an opportunity or a threat.

  ♦ It can be helpful to consider which items are within the control of the school or college, and can therefore be managed, and which are not. Policies and plans will clearly need to treat the controllable and the uncontrollable differently. It is important, however, to think this issue through carefully: often things are more controllable than than they appear to be at first sight.

  ♦ The prioritising element is very important in this exercise. Very long lists of strengths, weaknesses, opportunities or threats need to be refined to provide a feasible basis for action.

- SWOT Analysis is a very flexible diagnostic tool which can be used in a variety of contexts:

  ♦ During a whole-school or whole-college event, especially one which includes teaching and support staff, governors, etc. This is perhaps the most appropriate as it embodies the organisation-wide perspective which is at the heart of SWOT. It can capitalise on the complementary experience of 'insiders' and 'outsiders', generate understanding among different groups, and provide a shared basis for action. To ensure this, it is important that groups are mixed to represent all the stakeholders (teachers, support staff, governors, etc.) present.

- ◆ As part of a general review process in a governing body or a senior management team. A SWOT framework, perhaps used quite informally, can help to structure thinking about where the school or college is.
- ◆ In a departmental team. Although the focus here may be relatively narrow, any organisational unit can benefit from a SWOT Analysis of its work.

- The SWOT process will help to focus attention on the potential for opportunity or threat in carrying out evaluation activities. It may raise questions and provide insight relevant to the issue of how best to handle feedback. In general, analysis of the results of this process can help with decisions about *how* priorities for evaluation are to be set.

SWOT BRIEFING SHEET

You are asked to carry out a SWOT Analysis of your organisation. Spend about 10 minutes individually identifying the major strengths, weaknesses, opportunities and threats using the accompanying SWOT Worksheet to record your lists.

It is important to be *as specific as possible* in your analysis: you must be clear *why* an item is a strength, a weakness, an opportunity or a threat (it may be more than one of these for different reasons).

Opportunities and *threats* should be addressed first as they often receive less attention in policy discussions. It may be helpful to consider these in terms of:

- forces and trends (e.g. educational, political, economic, social, technological);
- clients, customers and funders;
- competitors, collaborators.

Strengths and *weaknesses* may be considered in a variety of ways. One simple classification is:

- resources: human, physical, financial, organisation (e.g. reputation, location, relations with community);
- strategies;
- performance.

SWOT WORKSHEET

Opportunities	Threats	Strengths	Weaknesses

© Routledge 1992

Such questions can provide a very helpful starting point for considering areas for further action or for more detailed strategies for evaluation.

Carrying out an audit

Another way of asking the question 'Where are we now?' is to engage in an audit of such matters as staffing, resources or curriculum content or processes. The use of the word 'audit' (which is borrowed from accountancy) in the context of curriculum review in particular is perhaps a reflection of the new, more competitive, finance-driven world or culture into which the education service is being propelled. Local Management of Schools and Colleges (LMSC), is increasing the need for the careful auditing of staffing and other resources, with other innovations, most particularly the National Curriculum and TVEI Extension, creating an urgent need for auditing the curriculum. Once schools and colleges are legally or contractually obliged to teach certain things, it is essential to devise means that can both check and ensure that these are being taught.

Here the first step is to identify the question that is being asked. This will inevitably be different in different situations. It may be a matter of thinking about the current situation in a different way. For example, for many primary and special schools, one problem in coming to terms with the National Curriculum has been separating what is being taught through project and topic work into its subject components. For secondary schools and colleges, the problem has almost been the reverse: that of identifying the National Curriculum and TVEI cross-curricular themes, issues and dimensions within the existing more subject-centred and vocationally-centred curriculum.

In offering some guidance on auditing, we will take as an example the auditing of the National Curriculum cross-curricular themes. In this context the National Curriculum Council (1990) states:

> The most important consideration in planning is to make sure that each topic appears at least somewhere in the curriculum and that overlaps, where they occur, are deliberate and complementary.

This reflects audit at a fairly basic level, dealing with quantity rather than quality, but is an essential first step. It is clear that the quality and depth of the information gathered can vary enormously, but it is as important in this area as any other not to be over-ambitious and therefore overwhelmed by the amount of information or data that you collect.

Before the audit begins a number of things need to be established:

- *Exactly what is being audited?* The objectives for each of the National Curriculum cross-curricular themes are given within the relevant documentation, but those who are to be involved in the audit will need to be familiar with these and to develop some common understanding of what each involves. The size of the task also needs to be identified. For example, it is possible to decide on a relatively superficial overview of all five themes across the whole curriculum, to focus on one theme within one year group, or any other combination in between.

- *Exactly who will be involved in the audit?* In this context, all staff may necessarily be involved in providing information about what is being taught. They may all wish to be involved in deciding what will be audited and how, or they may prefer to delegate decisions to a small group with the majority of staff undertaking to provide the information that is requested. The task may be delegated to departments, curriculum areas or faculties, with representatives from each forming a group that brings the information together.
- *Exactly how will the audit be carried out?* The processes most commonly used are those of answering specific or general questions or completing a checklist. These tasks are usually given to staff to carry out, but it is possible to ask pupils which of the objectives *they* perceive as being met. This may seem too difficult or even too alarming at the beginning of an audit, but might well be introduced once the auditing process has become established. It is unlikely that any school will find that all aspects of all themes are being covered, and the auditing process will necessarily be repeated at intervals. Providing new ways of finding out what you need to know may provide additional impulse and insight.

There are a number of ways of approaching an audit. You may decide to opt for a checklist. For example, one school asked all staff to complete a list in which they recorded whether each objective for each of the five National Curriculum cross-curricular themes made:

1 a major contribution;
2 a significant contribution;
3 a minor contribution or no contribution

to their curriculum content. Figure 3.2 shows two stages of this process for one theme: that of education for economic and industrial understanding. Twenty key objectives for key stages 3 and 4 were identified and staff were asked to use the three categories to record the extent to which these objectives were being met in their own subject areas. By collecting and collating these responses, it was possible to provide a graphic representation to staff of what was, and was not, being provided for pupils at key stages 3 and 4 in this area.

Gathering information in these ways is, of course, only the beginning. The audit will have implications for your future planning. The task will need to be managed carefully. It will not be possible to take all the action that may be necessary at once.

- Check whether you have gathered enough information for some necessary decisions to be made.

Figure 3.2 **An example of a curriculum audit**

CROSS-CURRICULAR THEMES SUMMARY GRID

NCC 4: EDUCATION FOR ECONOMIC & INDUSTRIAL UNDERSTANDING

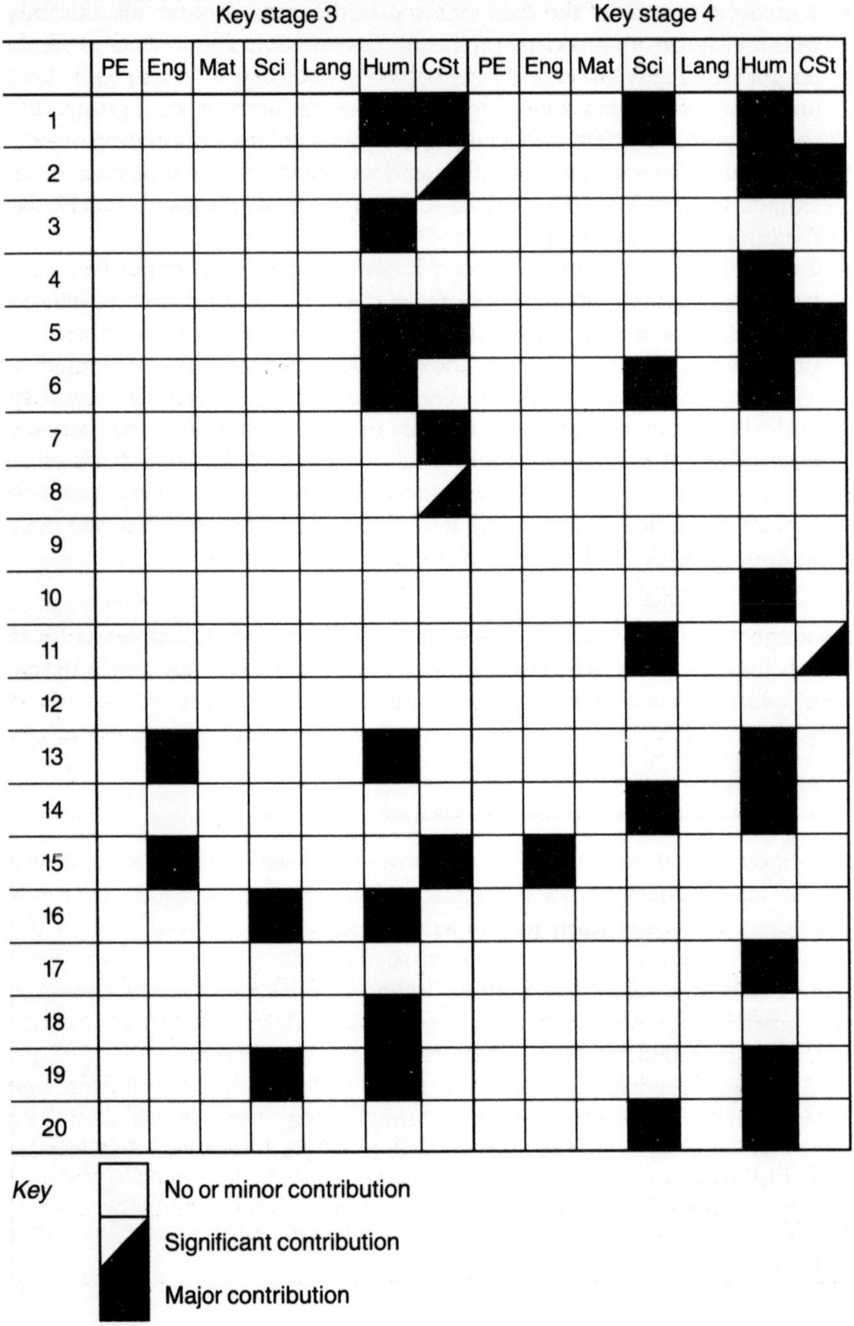

	Key stage 3							Key stage 4						
	PE	Eng	Mat	Sci	Lang	Hum	CSt	PE	Eng	Mat	Sci	Lang	Hum	CSt
1						■					■		■	
2							◣						■	
3						■								
4													■	
5						■							■	
6						■					■		■	
7						■								
8						◣								
9														
10													■	
11											■			◣
12														
13		■				■							■	
14											■		■	
15		■					■		■					
16				■		■								
17													■	
18						■								
19				■		■							■	
20											■		■	

Key

☐ No or minor contribution

◪ Significant contribution

■ Major contribution

- Decide where and how to focus attention on possible next steps. For example, the whole school or college may decide to focus on one cross-curricular theme. Alternatively, different groups of staff may wish to work on different themes and then exchange insight and information.
- Within the context of the decisions above, the audit may (almost certainly will) reveal that some themes are being covered several times and others do not appear at all. How can a better balance be achieved? Who needs to give up what? Are certain areas not being covered because no one has the requisite expertise? If so, what help can be obtained from outside the school?
- Check if you have ignored any significant matters. For example, work experience or residentials may be covering key aspects of cross-curricular themes but may have been ignored in the audit.
- Consider what the implications of the audit are for the School Development Plan and for staff development. New tasks need new skills and information, and time and resources will need to be found for these.
- Clarify what else you need to know or do and decide the time-scale in which the necessary work will be completed. For example, you may decide the time has come to gather some pupil perceptions; or you may wish to set a date to repeat the existing audit in order to check what progress has been made. You may wish to draw up a checklist on which new cross-curricular developments can be added as they are developed. You may decide the key issue is one of resources and the task to find the money or means to improve these.

Although this issue of audit has been discussed in the context of the National Curriculum, the process is transferable to other situations. The cameo below describes the way that a cross-curricular audit in a tertiary college led to consideration of the way in which the organisation's structure influenced the delivery of cross-curricular themes.

Cameo

Cross-curricular audit in a tertiary college

TVEI-E is finally becoming part of the vocabulary in this college as its resources permeate the depths of the academic/vocational divide. What is also becoming apparent is that it represents an opportunity to embed practices of monitoring, review and evaluation as an integral part of college life. As college co-ordinator I realised that I didn't have much of an idea of what was happening across college in a whole range of TVEI-E entitlement areas ranging from Records of Achievement to Equal Opportunities. What I have realised after undertaking a comprehensive curriculum audit is that no one else in college did either.

Before the audit I found myself putting together an institutional plan which made all the right noises in terms of post-16 speak – open-access workshops, modularisation, etc. but did not involve staff or management. I felt powerful in my TVEI-E role armed with resources but powerless to operate in a real cross-college dimension. The breakthrough was getting out to talk to a few course teams in an internal audit. This simply involved asking 'What are you doing?' in relation to a number of specific areas such as information technology, records of achievement and so on. I found that course teams were keen to talk and that some surprising areas of good practice already existed. Another bonus was that I gained support of one member of the senior management team who was committed to curriculum-led staff development.

At about the time I was carrying out the TVEI audit, the college development plan 'fell out of the sky', inviting comments but looking rather finished. Against this background I undertook to plan a college curriculum audit with the sympathetic senior manager. We looked at a document from the Further Education Unit (FEU, 1989) which gave us some useful guidelines. We tried to establish a broad audit team and identify a process that ultimately would inform both the allocation of TVEI-E resources and, hopefully, the college development plan. The audit imposed a set of external agendas from TVEI-E and asked staff to review existing provision. It also created space for course teams to put forward their own agendas.

A number of strategic points contributed to the success of the exercise:

- A day out of college for thirty-five middle managers offered them the chance to comment on the documentation and process.
- The senior management team allowed classes to close so that this event could take place.
- The day focused on a key issue for staff: the confusion over what constitutes a course team and therefore how these units of curriculum delivery could be supported by the existing college structure.

A document was drawn up as a result of our discussions. Subsequently all staff were given a copy of the document and invited to complete it with colleagues with whom they identified. The outcome was a course team map and the identification of one of the units through which cross-college activities would operate. The result was that twenty-four course teams and 70 per cent of the staff responded.

The analysis was painstaking but interesting. Sometimes I worked with people interested in particular areas, but more often I worked by myself or with my senior manager. Knees were worn out poring over flipcharts.

What of the outcomes? The first section was on course team processes. In the monitoring and evaluation section it became clear that some people collect data, some don't. Some feed it upwards and few receive any sort of feedback. It is not surprising that course teams haven't rushed to be involved in cross-college developments. Staff need a framework within which to review their curriculum and a mechanism to influence the direction of college and to receive feedback – the audit has started this process.

Reviewing a specific area

As a result of a SWOT Analysis or similar exercise it may be decided that a specific area of work needs to be reviewed It may be possible to adapt procedures from within available materials on school review for this specific purpose. For example, GRIDS (Guidelines for Review and Internal Development in Schools) outlines the following useful procedures for specific review (see Figure 3.3) or you may wish to devise your own questions. Alternatively, you may wish to use the procedure outlined in Exercise 3.2.

Figure 3.3 GRIDS

Step 2   **Find out what is the school's present policy/practice on the specific review topic.**

Tasks   (i)   Search school handbooks, information sheets, schemes of work, etc., extract any relevant policy statements and write a brief description of the school's formal policy on this topic (if there is no formal policy, ignore this task).

(ii)   Try to establish what actually happens and what people do.

(iii)   Write a short report which summarises existing practice.

Step 3   **Decide how effective present policy/practice actually is.**

Tasks   (i)   If there is a formal policy on this topic, decide how closely it represents actual practice.

(ii)   Agree upon some criteria and procedures for assessing the effectiveness of existing policy/practice.

(iii)   Carry out these procedures and apply the criteria.

(iv)   Decide how effective the existing policy/practice is.

Source: McMahon *et al.* (1984: 21–2)

EXERCISE 3.2

REVIEWING PROGRESS IN CURRICULUM DEVELOPMENT

Purpose

To enable a group to review rigorously and systematically, but relatively quickly, progress in a particular curriculum area and to identify specifically:

- Changes, developments or materials that have been produced during the lifetime of a particular project, programme or group.
- Which factors have helped or hindered these processes.
- What the existence of the working group has contributed to these processes.
- Next steps and implications for the future.

Context

An activity for a group or groups which have been involved in a particular activity or development.

Materials

- Post-its;
- Flipchart paper and pens.

The exercise

1 Bring together the group or groups which have been actively involved in the process.
2 Give each participant some post-its, or equivalent, and ask each of them to write down actual changes or products that they can confidently state have taken place or been produced during the lifetime of the working group.
3 In groups of five or six sort, group and classify these outcomes on a large sheet of paper. Each person then reads one in turn and everyone else says if they have similar outcomes recorded. If more than one group is involved in this process, it will be necessary to reach agreement on the way issues are to be classified and to gather together all items under each agreed category.

4 As a whole group, discuss and record on a flipchart what factors
   have helped or hindered developments. Give particular attention
   to what the working group has contributed specifically to the
   process.
5 Draw conclusions about priorities for moving forward.
6 Produce a written report that records the outcomes of stage 2 in
   full and summarises those of stages 4 and 5.

Points to note

• It takes at least twice as long to carry out stage 3 – recording and
  sorting the changes – as it does the other stages, so divide the
  available time proportionately.
• This process of recording and sorting is, of course, transferable to
  many other situations. It is therefore extremely useful.

Quick reviews of specific events

As part of managing the process, it is helpful to provide time during review sessions for participants to write down their perceptions or to ask them to bring to a meeting written evidence of what they know to be happening. The process of sharing, sorting and collating written statements helps to prevent dominant individuals from forcing conclusions on others. In general, it is useful to open up possibilities, share perceptions and report on actions during the first part of the meeting. Processes which help to sort and classify should follow. The meeting should end with setting priorities for the next steps that need to be taken in the light of what has been revealed. Exercises 3.3 and 3.4 are examples of procedures which can be used in such contexts.

EXERCISE 3.3

A WALL CONVERSION

Purpose

To review quickly and immediately a particular event or activity.

Context

A review activity for all who have participated in a programme or event.

Materials needed

Flipchart paper and pens.

The exercise

1 Put on the wall sheets of flipchart paper, each headed with a question or statement about the matter under review. For example, after an INSET day:

   • What were your expectations of the day?
   • Have these expectations been met?
   • What have you learned about — today?
   • What have you learned about yourself?
   • What kind of follow-up would you like?

   These questions can be decided in advance or at the beginning of this activity, although the latter would be difficult with a large group. Space the flipcharts well and provide enough sheets for each question to give space for all the group to write comments. Give participants a felt tip pen and ask them to write up their responses. It is important to stress the need to write not talk. Participants move about freely. Encourage them to agree or disagree with other statements perhaps with ticks or 'me too'. When participants have written all they wish, ask them to wait until others have finished. This process usually takes about 15 to 20 minutes.

2 When everyone has finished, the flipcharts are read, also without talking, before discussion and summary of what has been said on each sheet.

Points to note

- This activity is quite short, is usually enjoyable and provides a fairly accurate picture of feelings about a particular event. It can also be used at the end of a period of development as a shared review of what has taken place. The activity can be undertaken by small or large groups, although a group of fifty or more will need considerable space to work in.
- The summary of sheets is more difficult the more people there are. Practice helps with this, as does sharing the task out so that individuals sum up responses to one question only. The flipcharts can be taken away, analysed more carefully and written up as part of the evaluation record.
- Some people may be put off by the public nature of this exercise and may refuse to take part, but when everyone is moving about and writing it can feel surprisingly anonymous. It is clearly more public than an unsigned questionnaire but is more private than group discussion. No one can dominate a wall conversation and those who find group discussion difficult, or who are worried by their status, often find this process liberating. Major advantages are that everyone sees the span of opinion expressed and the process is not subject to the delay caused by the analysis of data gathered by more standard means when reports often arrive long after the event.

EXERCISE 3.4

SENTENCE COMPLETIONS

Purpose

To review an event quickly and to share perceptions and experiences.

Context

A review activity for all who have participated in a programme or event.

Materials needed

Previously prepared sheets (see below).

The exercise

1 At the end of an event, hand out sheets with several unfinished sentences to complete.

> One thing I learned today was . . .
> One thing I found difficult was . . .
> I wished that . . .

2 After completing the sentences, participants take turns to read out their responses, one question at a time.
3 Sentence completion and statements participants want to make can be restricted to two or three and written on different coloured cards. These are then collected in and redistributed to be read by others so that individual contributions can remain anonymous.

Points to note

- As with the Exercise 3.2, this requires a public expression of opinion, although redistributing the cards can help with this if it is a problem. However, hearing others' views can be illuminative for everyone. Regularly ending meetings in this way, for example, can help a group work more effectively together. It may also be important for people to feel responsible for expressing their own opinions in a way that others can hear.

- Similar activities can be used at the beginning of an innovation, perhaps recording participants' hopes, fears and expectations. These can be collated and recorded and used at later stages in the project to remind participants of their starting points and the progress made.

These exercises are examples of methods for monitoring on-going developments and carrying out whole-institution, specific-area or specific-event review. You may already use or be able to create other ways of achieving the same ends.

Reflection 3.3

Yet a further audit

At this point, go back to the two lists you drew up at the start of the chapter. Do you want to add to either of these lists? Now ask yourself the following questions about both lists:

- Why are these activities being carried out?
- Are any findings and conclusions recorded succinctly and systematically?
- What use is made of these?
- Are there any areas that need to be investigated in more detail? What else do you need to know?

Chapters 4 to 8 are designed to take you from this point through the process of carrying out more detailed enquiry. Such enquiry will not be a matter of routine and may involve quite a commitment of resources, including time. Developing effective processes of monitoring and review will help to estab- lish what is already known. It then becomes possible to establish what else needs to be found out and to direct energies most effectively into new and necessary forms of enquiry. Chapter 4 will take this focusing process a stage further.

FURTHER READING

A number of approaches to review are described in some detail in David Hopkins, *Doing School Based Review* (1988). They include GRIDS (Guidelines for Internal Review and Development in Schools) and DION (Diagnosing Individual and Organisational Needs), which are dealt with in more detail in books by McMahon et al. (1984) and Elliott-Kemp and Williams (1980) respectively. You will find more interesting and relevant ideas in Plant, *Managing Change and Making It Stick* (1987), particularly in Section 5, 'Where are we now?' For a discussion of management information, see Davies *et al.*, *Education Management for the 1990s* (1990, Chapter 2), and Fidler and Bowles, *Effective Local Management of Schools* (1989, Chapter 7), which both discuss the use of management information in schools.

Chapter 4

Choosing a focus

It is at this point that we begin to focus on evaluation activities that require more in-depth enquiry. As with monitoring and review, these may already be taking place in your school or college. Each activity may be part of a well-planned sequence, closely and clearly tied into your overall development plan. On the other hand, it may not. How many of the following situations do you recognise?

- Fragmented evaluation or pockets of enquiry about which little or nothing is known in the wider institution.
- Inappropriate evaluation, often set up in a hurry in response to a request from senior management for evidence of some kind.
- Mistimed evaluation, which occurs too early in a process for there to be any chance of positive findings or too late to fulfil a formative function.
- Unanticipated outcomes of evaluation where, for example, findings indicate that changes are required in the wider system and not just the area under review. It is comparatively rare for such findings to be acted upon.
- Evaluation which seems to grow exponentially, where the task gets out of hand through the collection of unmanageable amounts of data or the pursuit of an issue in more and more depth.
- Evaluation overload, where staff feel bombarded with questionnaires or other intrusions which may be unco-ordinated to the point of different people asking the same or similar questions.
- Irrelevant evaluation, imposed by insensitive outsiders (or insiders) where this is seen to be over-demanding and pursuing interests that are perceived as contrary to those of the school or college (or other groups within them).
- Threatening evaluation, where the activity is imposed and suspected to be part of an internal or external need for control.
- Unfocused evaluation, where, in the rush to know something about a particular area, we neglect to establish more precisely the nature of the information we require.

The careful identification of both focus and purpose is an essential part of the process of minimising the chance of these unhelpful consequences. This chapter is designed to build on the on-going processes of monitoring and review, to select the focus or foci for more in-depth investigation, and to ensure that you are clear about the purpose(s) for which the evaluation is intended.

THE NEED TO FOCUS

This book is written in the light of experience that such evaluation must be carefully managed. In some cases, it is a matter of managing the individual evaluation activities more effectively, in others it is a matter of more strategic, whole-institution management planning. The following cameo illustrates how some of the kinds of problems we have been describing were managed in one secondary school

---

Cameo

Co-ordinating evaluation across a cluster

As the co-ordinator of a TVEI-E cluster of a number of schools and a college, I was aware from an early stage that the management of evaluation would be one of my responsibilities. Although I had been given some limited training in the techniques of evaluation, I had received no help in how to manage evaluation. This was probably because there were very few people who knew how!

On reflection, I was hampered by three major problems. First, very few teachers or lecturers were used to carrying out or managing evaluation. Second, those who *did* invariably believed that an evaluation should involve never-ending questionnaires and the need to ask nearly everyone everything! Third, very few schools in the cluster had an existing policy for evaluation and review.

In the cluster there were seven members of staff, each of whom was given one half-day per week to co-ordinate the work across the cluster of a particular area of development such as Technology, Records of Achievement, Economic and Industrial Understanding, and Balanced Science. All of them worked with colleagues from other institutions in order to promote their particular development. Each area had specific targets which they set themselves and which fitted in with the major cluster targets. Therefore it seemed sensible to me that each co-ordinator should be responsible for managing the evaluation of their particular area of development and the criteria for success should be whether or not their targets had been met. My view was that delegation had now taken place, and that from now on it was the responsibility of those co-ordinators to evaluate the progress of their developments, measured against their targets. This they did – with a vengeance!

The teaching staff of the cluster institutions were suddenly inundated with five-page questionnaires about such things as their attitudes to gender issues, their teaching and learning styles, and how much they used technology in their lessons. The complaints started to pour in across the cluster. The area co-ordinators argued, quite rightly, that they were merely doing as they had been told. They too, by this stage, were encountering real problems in handling all the data they had collected. They simply did not have the time to process all the information or carry out any useful analysis. It became obvious that the whole review and evaluation process needed managing at a strategic level, and that schools do not have the time to carry out lots of large-scale evaluations. In addition, more thought needed to be given to the best ways of gathering information.

In common with most other management problems, this one could not be solved by any one individual. I needed to bring the seven key individuals together and see how we could solve the problems as a team. We began by reviewing what had already been done in each area and sharing any conclusions we had drawn. What emerged was how many areas of overlap there were and how interesting many of the findings were to the members of the group. It became obvious that it was not feasible to carry out more than one major evaluation across the cluster in any one year, and that we needed an evaluation plan which covered a longer period than a year. All the group felt they had taken too much responsibility for actually carrying out the evaluation, as opposed to managing the process. It was also mentioned that there were a considerable number of small-scale evaluations already being carried out within institutions (e.g. in departments or faculties), of which few people were aware. It was felt that many of these could be extremely useful in involving staff in TVEI and avoiding duplication of data.

It was decided to adopt the following two principal strategies for the future:

- For each area co-ordinator to go away with a month-by-month, three-year time plan proforma, on which they could map their evaluation strategy. This could be completed after consultations with the members of their various groups. On its completion, this would be returned to me and I would produce an overall, three-year review and evaluation plan for the cluster. This would be discussed, at a later date, by this evaluation group and a plan submitted to the cluster's Management Group for their consideration.

- To ask each cluster institution to carry out a survey of any recent or forthcoming evaluation, and consider how it might inform, or fit in with, the cluster's evaluation plan.

This approach will, hopefully, help us to construct a framework for managing evaluation in the cluster and to focus more acutely on what really needs evaluating.

In this situation, the three levels of involvement that we described in Chapter 2 emerge quite clearly. Matters needed to be managed at the *organisational* level. What had been thought of as separate activities needed to be brought together as part of institutional and cluster planning. This would ensure that staff were less overburdened and would give all those involved time to make sense of what they were finding. The situation included a *team* dimension. The act of bringing the co-ordinators together to find a solution enabled the group both to identify what they were learning from their experiences and to plan ahead more effectively. Finally there was an important *individual* element in that each evaluation had to be managed in itself as well as within the wider context. In general, the evaluation activities needed to be more carefully and coherently managed.

It is helpful to keep these three levels in mind when considering how to choose a focus for any more detailed evaluation. At an organisational level evaluation must form a central part of development planning. Development plans may include a clear recognition from the beginning that evaluation requiring in-depth enquiry will sometimes be needed. The resources necessary to carry out such tasks can then be identified and planned for. On-going monitoring and review may reveal gaps in understanding and knowledge that need to be informed by further evaluation. This, too, must be planned at an institutional level. It must also be possible for departments, faculties, groups or individuals to meet their own evaluation needs, but these activities must be logged in some way at an institutional level with thought being given to how learning from such situations can best be shared.

As part of institutional planning it is extremely helpful to set aside some time for those most centrally involved in evaluation to come together to review progress and engage in joint planning as a group or team. In the context of choosing a focus, this could influence planning in several ways. For example, it might be decided to identify a general focus on pupil/student experiences and perceptions. These could be explored in diverse areas such as new courses, work and other out-of-school experience, starting school, transfer from one stage of schooling to another, Records of Achievement, destinations post-16 or vocational training. Conversely, it might be considered more profitable to consider pupils in only one or two areas and to explore parent or teacher perceptions in others. Any combination is possible. The choice of method is also important (see Chapter 8). These also need to be balanced, to prevent the overuse of particular methods, or particular groups. Time set aside for review of evaluation plans and processes in themselves will prevent a feeling of consultation overload in which no one feels able to do anything without consulting everyone individually first.

At an individual level, there will be a wide variety of reasons for choosing to evaluate a particular area of development. It may be that evaluation is a requirement of the funding body. It may be that things are not running quite smoothly and there is a need to find out why. For example, in one secondary school, on-going review of a new curriculum development indicated that there was a mismatch between teacher and pupil perceptions of which parts of the course were most difficult. This needed further investigation. In a primary school it was realised that the school was feeling under pressure from a small group of parents without knowing what the majority of parents thought about the apparently contentious issue. In a tertiary college, staff recognised that their efforts to ensure continuity and progression required them to know more about pupil expectations pre-16. It may simply be a desire to know more. For example, in the context of both TVEI Extension and the National Curriculum, introduction of cross-curricular themes has given rise to the need to carry out an initial curriculum audit to establish if and where each theme is being taught (see Chapter 3).

In essence, each activity needs to be carefully focused within itself and to be set into the wider context of the institution. In each case it is helpful to consider the following:

- The *area* of focus – specific curriculum area, issue, year group, staff activity, etc.
- The *location* of focus – the whole institution, department/faculty or individual classroom;
- The *nature* of focus – monitoring, review or in-depth study.

If each of these is recorded for each evaluation activity, it is possible to see almost at a glance whether a balance is being kept across the whole institution (see Figure 4.1). Worksheet 4.1 provides a framework for you to do your own audit of evaluations currently being undertaken. Such an audit is an essential and continuous record of what is happening and what is already known. Few things irritate more than being asked for information that has already been given albeit in a different context.

Figure 4.1 Overview of evaluation activity

Area of focus	Location of focus	Nature of focus
1 National Curriculum – cross-curricular themes	4th and 5th Year curriculum	Curriculum audit – checklists and questionnaires
2 Records of Achievement	2nd Year pupils	In-depth study of pupil perceptions – interviews, questionnaires
3 Staff INSET activities; use of in-service budget	All staff	Monitoring which staff attend which INSET activities

WORKSHEET 4.1

OVERVIEW OF EVALUATION ACTIVITY

Area of focus	Location of focus	Nature of focus
1		
2		
3		
4		

WHO SHOULD BE INVOLVED IN THE FOCUSING?

Before going further into how teachers might choose a focus for evaluation within a particular context, it is helpful to step back and ask the question 'Whose interests and perceptions are we taking into account?' If we see the world too much from our own point of view, we may find ourselves feeling satisfied with practice that others question, or conversely dissatisfied with something that others find valuable. The 'Why? What? How?' exercise (Exercise 2.1) enabled us to think critically about the purposes and outcomes of an evaluation and the people who are, or should be, involved. It is all too easy when examining the 'Who?' dimension to focus too narrowly upon the teacher and the pupil or student. This tends to neglect other groups, or individuals, who can be seen to have a legitimate interest in a particular development or the institution in general. It also fosters an insularity which stops us taking account of other legitimate values and opinions. Within the context of evaluation, it assumes that the only valid measures of success are ones determined by the professionals.

All teachers, but senior managers in particular, should be aware of the key role they perform on the boundary of the institution and wider community. Indeed, recent trends in education, such as community education, TVEI and local management of schools and colleges, have served to emphasise the need for schools to be more responsive to those who are perceived to have a legitimate stake or interest in the school or college. A useful concept here is that of stakeholder:

> A *stakeholder* is any group or individual who is affected by or can affect the future of the organisation, programme or activity.

In the early stages of planning any evaluation process, it is important to identify those who have a stake in the activity or programme which is to be evaluated and to consider their expectations and potential influence. Stakeholders will broadly be of four kinds:

- *Clients or customers*: all the individuals and groups who are served by the programme in question. This clearly includes pupils or students, but it also may include, for example, parents and local employers who depend on the skills and attitudes of school and college leavers.
- *Suppliers*: all those who provide resources of energy, finance and materials to enable the programme to take place. The major suppliers are, of course, the staff, but there will be a range of other important providers of key resources, including possibly outside funding agencies.
- *Competitors and collaborators*: all those who provide an alternative to the service provided by the programme, or whose collaboration is necessary if it is to operate effectively. This obviously includes other educational institutions, but it might also include, for example, firms who attract

school-leavers at 16 (who might otherwise enter the sixth form) or who collaborate with the school to provide work experience.
- *Regulators*: all those, such as Government agencies and examination boards, who establish policies and rules which those running the programme must abide by.

A number of points can be made about stakeholders:

- Stakeholders can be both internal (e.g. staff) and external (e.g. parents) to the school.
- Stakes can relate to present or future relationships (e.g. parents of children not yet enrolled as well as those already in the school).
- Some groups may have more than one kind of stake in the school (e.g. parent governors, who are both clients and regulators; other schools, who act both as competitors under open competition but also as collaborators in relation to TVEI schemes).
- The relative importance of stakeholders may increase or decrease over time (for example, local education authorities are generally becoming less important and the DES and governors more so).

The stakeholders of a school or college can be 'mapped' as in Figure 4.2. The institution is placed at the centre and the perceived importance of each group is indicated by the length of the arrows, with the more important stakeholders placed nearer the centre.

It is essential for those with responsibility for planning and evaluation to be well aware of *who* the stakeholders are and, following on from this, *what* they might think and require. Not all stakeholders will play a part in *managing* the evaluation process. However, being aware of who the stakeholders are, and of the expectations they hold, should allow the process to be managed in a more meaningful and effective manner. Stakeholder Analysis is one method of thinking critically about one's situation as it focuses upon the people who are, or might be, involved. The degree of importance we attribute to a particular stakeholder will reflect current local and national priorities and developments, as well as the relative influence of individuals and groups inside and outside a particular institution.

Exercise 4.1 incorporates this notion of the stakeholder and requires us to focus upon our own institution, a curriculum development or a programme, and carry out an analysis of the stakeholders and their expectations.

Figure 4.2 Stakeholder map of a secondary school

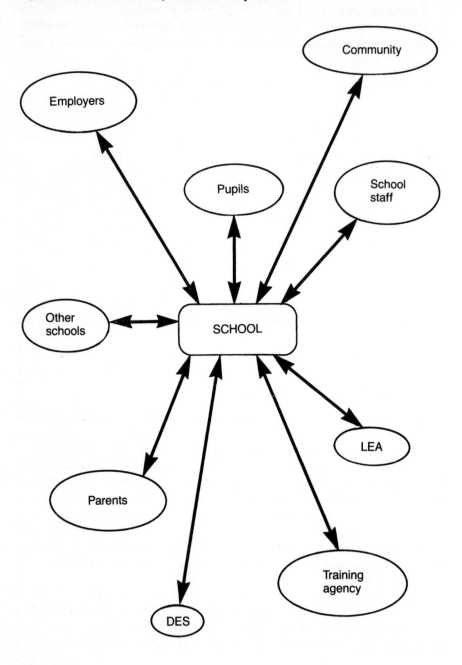

Note: The length of the arrows indicates the perceived importance of each stakeholder group: the shorter the arrow, the greater the perceived importance

EXERCISE 4.1

STAKEHOLDER ANALYSIS (I)

Purpose

To identify those individuals and groups who have a stake in an evaluation and to explore what their expectations of the evaluation are.

Context

This activity is an excellent one for carrying out at a whole-school or whole-college event, especially one which includes groups such as support staff, parents, governors or employers as well as teaching staff. It can also be carried out by a smaller team which is concerned with a particular area of work. In larger-scale contexts a facilitator is necessary.

Materials needed

- enough Stakeholder Briefing Sheets for each member of the group;
- flipchart paper and pens.

The exercise

1 The concept of stakeholder is introduced to the group (10 minutes).
2 Hand out the Stakeholder Briefing Sheet. Individuals are asked to spend 10 minutes identifying the individuals and groups who they consider to be the key stakeholders in the evaluation activity being considered. They are then asked to rank the stakeholders in an order of importance and draw a stakeholder map (see Figure 4.2)
3 Individuals then go into pairs and compare their lists and orders of importance, exploring the reasons for the similarities and differences.
4 On the Stakeholder Worksheet 1, each pair categorises all the stakeholders which they have identified into 'Internal' and 'External'. Then, next to each stakeholder, they list very briefly what they consider the stakeholders' expectations might be.

5 Finally, a number of larger groups are formed, consisting of four or six people, and each chooses four of the stakeholders – perhaps two internal and two external – who are common to most of their lists. Then, using a flipchart, each group agrees, in rather more detail than before, what each of the stakeholder's expectations might be. The contents of the flipcharts can be either shared verbally or, in the case of a large group, placed on the walls for others to view.

Points to note

- Where a number of stakeholders are represented at an event, it is important to give careful consideration to the composition of groups. It is probably preferable to use mixed groups which represent a number of stakeholder interests, although consideration might be given also to using homogeneous groups, each of which contains one kind of stakeholder only.
- It is important not to give too much guidance about who we might mean by internal and external stakeholders. The ambiguity can bring out interesting comparisons and promote discussion. For example, is a parent an internal or external stakeholder? The answer to this question may be a revealing comment upon an individual's personal philosophy or of the culture of the institution within which he or she works.
- At the end of this exercise there is often a desire to involve stakeholders who are not represented at the session much more closely in the planning and evaluation process. It may well be useful, as a follow-up, for the group to identify ways in which this might be done.

STAKEHOLDER BRIEFING SHEET

At an early stage in planning an evaluation, it is helpful to spend time considering the perspectives of those who have some kind of stake in the development. This activity will help you to clarify the context in which you are working and the expectations you may have to meet. It may influence the criteria you choose for success and which aspects of the development you choose to evaluate.

Remember that a stakeholder is *any group or individual who is affected by, or can affect, the future of a development.* In order to be effective it is necessary to understand and respond to the expectations of the key stakeholders. In identifying these, the following questions may be helpful:

- Who has an interest in the development?
- Who can affect its adoption or implementation?
- Who has expressed an opinion?
- Who ought to or might care about it?

Relevant groups might include the following:

- students
- teachers
- parents
- employers
- LEA
- governors
- Training and Enterprise Councils (or Local Enterprise Companies in Scotland)

It is important to consider both internal and external stakeholders, and to differentiate between subgroups if these have differing expectations. You should also consider future as well as present stakeholders. Now:

1 Identify the individuals and groups who you consider to be the key stakeholders.
2 Rank the stakeholders into what you consider to be an order of importance. Draw a stakeholder map.

STAKEHOLDER WORKSHEET 1

Internal		External	
Stakeholder	Expectations	Stakeholder	Expectations

© Routledge 1992

The Stakeholder Analysis presented here enables us to think critically about the 'who' dimension and asks us to go a step further to examine what the stakeholder's expectations might be with regard to the institution, development or programme. The intention is for us to be aware of the context in which we work and to be sympathetic to the range of values and perspectives that exist in an increasingly pluralistic society. In a later chapter, when we deal with the issue of success criteria, we shall return to the idea of stakeholder.

SOME OTHER APPROACHES

So far in this and previous chapters we have proposed the building-up of a stock of evaluative evidence through on-going processes of monitoring and review. We have suggested one method of ensuring that we take the perspectives and expectations of people other than teachers into account. These processes enable us to establish what we know about a development and its consequences. At the same time, we must be asking ourselves the further question 'Is there anything else we need to know?' Sometimes the answer to this question will lead to an expansion of the monitoring process. However, at other times it will be clear that the necessary further knowledge and understanding can only be gained through systematic and in-depth investigation.

As we saw earlier in Chapter 3, the discovery that many second language learners were achieving their best result in English meant that the school had to reappraise its assumptions about their examination results in general. They needed to know more about the problems their pupils faced. A stakeholder analysis in one school led to the teachers realising that they had very little evidence about parents' expectations of a Record of Achievement. They too needed to know more. Sometimes what else we need to know may appear painfully obvious but at other times this may be less so. When choosing a specific focus, and bearing in mind what you learned from the Stakeholder Analysis, you may find it useful to undertake Exercise 4.2.

It is, of course, possible that there will be no clear agreement about priorities. In such circumstances, to avoid positions becoming entrenched with different individuals and groups arguing for different priorities, it may be necessary to use a systematic prioritising process such as Nominal Group Technique (Exercise 4.3).

EXERCISE 4.2

WHAT DO WE NEED TO KNOW?

Purpose

To identify what further enquiry is really necessary and to ensure time used for this is well spent. The task is first to clarify what you need to know about a particular development, project, curriculum area or other issue and then to consider what is already known.

Context

An individual or group activity to be undertaken by those preparing for an evaluation.

Materials needed

Flipchart paper and pens, if being undertaken as a group.

The exercise

1 Draw up a list of what you need to know about a development, remembering to include what is required of you as well as what you would like to know.
2 Consider each item and decide whether or not you already have enough information available about it. Check this carefully. Do you have evidence or information or are you relying on assumption? Gut feelings about how well or badly things are going are a kind of evidence, but it is worth exploring this further. Does everyone share the same feeling? Feelings are almost always based on more solid evidence of some kind, and it is worth identifying just what this evidence is.
3 This process almost always reduces your original list considerably – or even completely. Rewrite the list of issues that are left.
4 Work through this list again, this time deciding the nature of each task. For example, is more monitoring what is needed? Have you found that the necessary information is available but fragmented in a way that could be resolved through a structured review? Which issues will require in-depth exploration?

5 If several items occur in all or any of these categories, priorities
   will need to be set. It may be possible to monitor or review more
   than one issue but it is not advisable to undertake more than one
   in-depth study at a time. Ask everyone to indicate their first
   priority. If there is agreement, this will indicate your focus.

EXERCISE 4.3

NOMINAL GROUP TECHNIQUE

Purpose

To develop, through a process of structured review, priorities for further action.

Context

This exercise can be used by groups in a wide variety of contexts where there is a need to clarify priorities.

Materials

Flipchart paper and pens.

The exercise

1 A relevant question is posed to a small group (twelve or less) without discussion, for example: 'Which areas of further evaluation enquiry might we consider?'
2 Individuals are asked to write down their answers to this question without discussion.
3 Each person gives his or her answers to the question in turn and all of these are recorded on a flipchart or board, again without discussion or comment.
4 At this point the items are clarified though discussion and questions until similar points have been combined where possible and a list is available that everyone understands.
5 Everyone is then asked to consider their own priorities and award points from 5 to 1 to the five items that are considered to be most important. The points are then tallied to provide the group's priorities.
6 The group then discusses the implications of the priority list and decides on the future action to be taken.

Points to note

• This is another process that can be helpful in many contexts. For example, it can be used as another review process to supplement those described in Chapter 3. In this case, the initial questions identified might include, 'What have been the strengths of — so far?' or 'What have been the limitations?'

Although these processes may sound complicated and take time to work through, they can reduce what seems to be a very difficult task to manageable proportions. It can be very cheering. For example, a group of secondary teachers who were worried that they had very little evaluation evidence about pupil experience produced the following list of existing knowledge in a very short period of time.

- examination results;
- attendance levels (staff/pupils);
- destinations;
- the content of the curriculum pupils are offered;
- the work they produce;
- the experiences and opportunities they are offered;
- the value put on these experiences, e.g. work experience may be followed up in several curriculum areas and valuable feedback can be given by pupils in these situations;
- lesson review;
- comments, slips, feedback at the end of sessions/modules;
- pupil self-assessment and other aspects of Records of Achievement;
- units of Accreditation;
- what is said in tutorials and counselling and guidance sessions (not breaking confidentiality);
- interviews by the Youth Service;
- aspects of COMPACT – target setting – action planning;
- feedback from parents' evenings (and attendance at these meetings);
- visitors' reports;
- HMI reports.

What they were not doing was managing this knowledge and drawing it together in any coherent way that could inform decision-making. They needed to do this before checking again if there was anything else they still needed to know.

As a final step in this process, it may be helpful at this point to go back to the Accountability/Development diagram in Chapter 1, duplicated here as Worksheet 4.2.

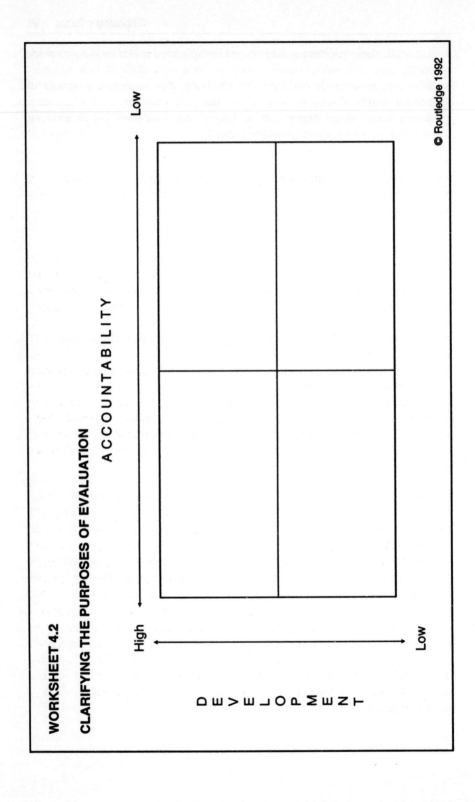

WORKSHEET 4.2

CLARIFYING THE PURPOSES OF EVALUATION

ACCOUNTABILITY

High — Low

DEVELOPMENT

Low

- Can you place your organisation's current or recent evaluation activities on to this?
- Which of these purposes is being met? Is there a bunching of activity in one quadrant?
- Whose interests are being met? Is there a balance or are the interests of one group – perhaps the senior management team, the LEA or an external funding body – predominating?

The Overview of Evaluation Activity (Worksheet 4.1) presented earlier in this chapter will also help you to ensure that particular groups are not over-burdened.

CONCLUSION

The activities in this chapter build on, and are complementary to, the continuous processes of monitoring and review. They help to establish with some clarity what those with a stake in your organisation (including yourselves) want to know, what is already known and where there is a need for further enquiry. These will then need to be prioritised with reference to your Development Plans. Nominal Group Technique can be used for this purpose. Alternatives would be to delegate the task to a representative group, or to circulate a list of possibilities and ask everyone to state their preferences. Any process chosen will need to build some commitment to its outcomes. The focusing and prioritising process should not preclude individuals or groups engaging in their own evaluation initiatives but should ensure that such evaluations complement rather than complicate institution-wide activity.

The focusing process is designed to identify areas that need further enquiry. The choice of focus will often emerge from the continuous processes of monitoring and review going on. However, account should be also be taken of the views and interests of all those with a stake in the organisation. If a large number of areas seem to need further enquiry, priorities will need to be set. There are limits to the amount of time and energy available for such activities. Evaluation activities at organisational, specific-group and individual levels need to be recorded across the whole organisation so that some kind of balance and coherence can be ensured. The discussions needed at each stage of the focusing process should increase interest in evaluation in general and the findings of others in particular. The processes of focusing and prioritising almost certainly save more time than they take. You will find that, as a consequence, there will be a reduction in the volume of detailed enquiry and an expansion of the learning potential of each activity that takes place.

FURTHER READING

References to the purposes or focusing of an evaluation enquiry can be found in Hopkins, *A Teacher's Guide to Classroom Research* (1985) – Chapter 5 on problem formation. Although not specifically concerned with evaluation, some helpful suggestions about ways of exploring issues and considering and tackling problems can be found in Section 2 of Easen, *Making School-Centred INSET Work* (1985).

Chapter 5

Planning and managing the process

Once the focus of evaluation has been decided, it is necessary to give consideration to how the process is to be planned and managed. As was indicated in Chapter 1, evaluation processes can be subject to many pitfalls. The only way to ensure that these are avoided is by planning carefully the work which is needed and ensuring that the plans which are developed are realistic and are effectively implemented. In Chapter 1 we considered evaluation as part of the planning and management cycle in an organisation, but the process of evaluation itself must be carefully planned and managed if it is to be carried out effectively. This chapter explores some of the main issues which this involves.

As Chapter 1 indicated, management involves 'getting things done through and with other people'. This definition has a number of implications and this chapter considers three key issues to which it gives rise. The chapter begins by considering the question 'Who is to be involved in the evaluation process and how?' In doing this, it considers a number of key roles which typically need to be played if an evaluation is to be managed effectively. Involvement in evaluation may be on an individual basis; more commonly, however, many aspects of evaluation are managed in groups. Therefore, the chapter proceeds to a discussion of the important issues of how such groups can be used effectively in the management of evaluation. Finally, consideration is given to the question of how ethical issues should be treated.

DECIDING WHO TO INVOLVE

Although there is often a strong temptation to manage an evaluation yourself, not least because others appear so busy, it will be a rare evaluation process where this is the most appropriate strategy. As Chapter 1 made clear, management is not about doing things yourself, but rather involves bringing together the knowledge, skills and commitment of a group of people to achieve a desired end. This may involve managing a clearly defined team of people who work together on a day-to-day basis. Or it may involve orchestrating the work of a number of individuals and groups whose main link is through you as the overall manager of the process. In either case, the ways in which they are to be involved need thinking through carefully. We need to make clear what we mean by involvement in this context. We are not concerned with the individual's involvement merely as a source of data, for example by filling in a questionnaire or by being interviewed. Our concern is with involvement in the *management* of the evaluation process which, as a minimum, implies having an organised opportunity to influence the nature of the evaluation being undertaken.

There are a number of reasons for involving others in the process of managing an evaluation. You may choose to involve them because they have particular *skills* or *expertise* which will be helpful: this may relate to the subject of the evaluation, or it may relate to some aspect of the evaluation process itself. For example, a particular person may have skills in questionnaire design or in the processing of data on computer.

Second, they may be involved because they have a *stake* which needs to be recognised in the issue that is being evaluated. A Stakeholder Analysis (see Chapter 4) will help to identify individuals and groups whom you wish to involve for this reason. Stakeholders are normally involved in the evaluation process in some way because it is felt they have a right to be, as their interests could be affected by the process or its outcome. For example, a negative outcome of the evaluation could affect an individual's career prospects in the school or college or a department's access to resources. The nature of the stake may of course vary. Sometimes you may feel that an individual's orientation to the issue being evaluated is a good reason to *exclude* that person. This is dangerous, however, and may often be felt to be morally wrong.

Third, involvement may be necessary because a key individual or group has *power* or *influence* which could be used to support or hinder the evaluation process. This is a more pragmatic reason for involvement than the previous one, although it may relate to the same groups. Power or influence here may derive from a variety of sources. For example, it may relate to the control of resources, such as an individual's own time, the time of others, or a financial budget. Or it may relate to the formal authority to sanction or proscribe particular courses of action. Even those who are relatively junior in an organisation have considerable negative power to block or delay, if you are dependent on them to provide critical data for example.

Finally, involvement may simply be *developmental* for those involved. This reason for involving people in management processes is often under-emphasised. Real involvement is a cheap and extremely effective form of management development. Not only does it broaden the range of people with management skills and knowledge of the evaluation process, it also has the potential to widen the constituency of those in the organisation who have an interest in evaluation.

You may choose to involve different people, then, for a number of reasons. Furthermore, the degree of their involvement may vary, with different people involved in different ways at various stages of the evaluation process. For a significant piece of evaluation there will be a variety of possible patterns of involvement, and role analysis of the type described in Chapter 2 then becomes very important. It may be helpful here, however, to identify a number of issues that need to be addressed in determining how an evalu- ation is to be managed:

- Who is to lead the process and what should this involve?
- Who else should be consulted or participate in the management process?
- To whom should those managing the process be accountable and how?
- What external support will be required?

We will address each of these issues now.

Leadership

The effective management of evaluation requires leadership. It is useful here to distinguish between two kinds of leadership role. One is that of *sponsor*. Evaluation needs to be given status in the institution and legitimised by being sponsored, in both word and deed, by one or more senior members of staff. This need not mean their managing the process. However, it does mean their constantly demonstrating and reaffirming that evaluation in general, and this piece of evaluation in particular, is important; and it does mean supporting those who are managing it.

The second leadership role is that of *manager*. One or more individuals will be involved in initiating, co-ordinating, keeping up momentum and monitoring the evaluation process. This does not mean doing it all them- selves, but it does mean *ensuring* that it is done in a way that generates commitment from all those who will be involved. Ideally, the manager(s) should have, and demonstrate, a commitment to the evaluation *process* rather than to any particular outcomes. This role need not be carried out by the same individual(s) who are the sponsors, but it does require status, credibility and personal skills. The manager(s) might be assisted by, and report to, a representative steering group which would oversee and support the on-going management of the evaluation process.

Consultation and participation

It is useful to distinguish between these two terms. Consultation involves seeking individuals' views about an issue *before* making a decision (otherwise it is 'pseudo-consultation'), but without giving those consulted a final say in the decision that is made. Participation, in contrast, gives the participant an equal say in the decision that is reached. Probably more misunderstanding, confusion, frustration and bitterness occurs as a result of poor management in this area than in any other. It is essential, therefore, to establish clearly at an early stage who is to be involved and what the nature of their involvement is to be, and to communicate this clearly. In most cases, the strategy adopted is likely to involve a combination of consultation and participation, but whatever mix is used it is essential to develop a climate in which people feel that their views matter, and that the evaluation which eventually emerges is genuinely a shared product of all those who have been involved.

There are a variety of strategies for involving individuals and groups in the management process:

- through large-group events such as staff development days for a whole school or a cross section of staff of a college;
- through existing teams such as departments or year groups of teachers;
- through the use of *ad hoc* working parties;
- through delegation to individuals.

Each may have a place, depending on the purposes of an evaluation and the particular stage being considered.

There is considerable awareness of the need to consult staff and encourage participation. Sometimes this may be a difficult process but it is also possible to be surprised by the strength of response. The following cameo describes what happened in one large secondary school when staff were invited to participate in whole-school review using SWOT (see Chapter 3).

Cameo

Planning for participation

I used the SWOT exercise at an INSET session with eighty teaching staff of a large comprehensive school, where I was deputy head. We needed to introduce the idea of a review of the curriculum, the organisation of the school, and staff development and motivation. All these were areas identified at a Senior Management Team residential weekend where we had also used SWOT.

I introduced the INSET session with these aims:

- to give staff better understanding and awareness of the opportunities as well as the constraints facing the school in the future;
- to give opportunities for personal involvement in the processes of review;
- to identify routes forward.

I then set the scene in the light of National Curriculum, Appraisal, Local Management of Schools, and TVEI Extension.

We then split into six groups, which we had previously identified, each of which included a member of the Senior Management Team as facilitator. Two groups looked at curriculum, two at organisation, and two at staff development and motivation. Each group was asked to identify its perceptions of the school's two greatest strengths, weaknesses, opportunities and threats. These were then fed back in a plenary. With hindsight, this would have been a good point to pause for reflection and further planning, but we went a stage further.

The final activity for the day was for individuals to fill in a sheet indicating whether they wished to be involved in the review process and in which areas, indicating priority. They were also asked whether they had a particular strength or talent which had so far been ignored by the organisation. The response to this questionnaire was overwhelming, with the majority of staff wishing to be involved. Several areas were given top priority and some staff wanted to be involved in more than one. After some debate we decided to set up six working groups. These were:

- investigating the learning experiences of the Year 10/Year 11 core curriculum;
- school organisation;
- staff development;
- pastoral care of pupils;
- pastoral care of staff.

What lessons did I learn from this? I should have thought the whole process through to a greater degree beforehand. In particular, I should have been clear about what was to happen after the SWOT. It would have been very helpful if I had allowed time for the results of the SWOT exercise to be prioritised into a proper action plan before attracting working groups. The problem was that we had to respond to the expectations I had raised. Feedback after the event also made it clear that some groups had worked more successfully than others. I realised that I should have considered more carefully the selection of group facilitators – were SMT members the most appropriate or the most skilled available?

This cameo is not intended to put you off consultation. However, it is a useful reminder of how easy it is to find yourself in the position of having to cope with more than you anticipated. Careful planning can help you to proceed step by step, to sustain progress and to manage the situation more effectively.

Accountability

The issue of accountability will already have arisen in the discussions about stakeholders in the previous chapter. It is essential at an early stage to consider to whom you are accountable for this particular piece of evaluation and how this accountability arrangement is to operate. There are clearly a number of possibilities:

- Accountability might be to a line manager such as a head of department or headteacher.
- It may be to colleagues through a working party of staff representatives or a staff meeting.
- It may be to some formal group such as the academic board or governing body.
- It may be to some outside agent, such as the Department of Employment or the LEA.
- It may even be to individual clients through a report to parents or to student representatives.

In some cases, the line of accountability may appear to be quite clearly mandated, for example within a TVEI scheme, although in reality even here there may be more fingers in the pie than initially meet the eye. In other cases, there may appear to be no obvious lines of accountability, or they may be multiple and confused. Accountability may involve relationships through which an account is expected, for example to a line manager, a governing body or a funding agency. Or it may involve a relationship where you feel a moral responsibility to *offer* an account although it is not required, perhaps to a staff meeting or to student representatives. You may now wish to consider these issues further by looking at Exercise 5.1.

EXERCISE 5.1

ASPECTS OF ACCOUNTABILITY

Purpose

To enable you to consider the kinds of accountability to which you are, or will be, subject as you manage an evaluation.

Context

An individual or group activity to be undertaken in the early stages of planning an evaluation.

Materials needed

None.

The exercise

Consider the following questions individually or as a group:

- Who has asked that the evaluation be done?
- Who expects to be formally consulted about how it is done?
- Who will expect a report of the outcomes?
- Who has the formal power to distribute rewards or sanctions in response to the outcomes?

External support

It is often useful to obtain some external support in the evaluation process. Such support might be obtained from a number of sources: the LEA, an institution of higher education, or from one of the growing band of private consultants. Where such support is sought, it is important to be clear exactly what attributes are required and what role the individual or group concerned is expected to play. There are a number of possibilities:

- To provide particular expertise which the school or college feels it is lacking.
- To fulfil a 'facilitator' role at key points when staff wish to step back from managing aspects of the process directly.
- To provide a disinterested perspective on the activity or issue being evaluated.

Developing a strategy for involvement

The appropriate pattern of involvement in evaluation will vary depending on the context. For example, a large secondary school or a college will probably have a more complex pattern of organisation for managing an evaluation than a primary or special school. And the pattern will be more complex where the evaluation is concerned with an institution-wide issue than if it is concerned with the work of one department or curriculum area. The important point is that the four key areas of leadership, participation, accountability and external support should all be addressed. In doing this, it is helpful to consider how various individuals and groups are to be involved at various stages that were outlined in the Introduction. These stages are:

- determining a focus;
- preparing plans;
- clarifying purposes;
- determining criteria;
- managing data-gathering;
- producing and reporting results;
- determining and implementing action.

Worksheets 5.1 and 5.2 provide frameworks for considering these issues and developing plans for the management of a particular evaluation activity.

WORKSHEET 5.1

DESIGNING AN EVALUATION PROCESS (1)

Consider who should be involved in the process of evaluation and how this might best be done.

Involvement in evaluation

	Groups	Individuals
Leadership Who? How?		
Participation Who? How?		
Consultation Who? How?		
Accountability Who? How?		
External Support Who? How?		

WORKSHEET 5.2

DESIGNING AN EVALUATION PROCESS (2)

Consider who should be involved in the process of evaluation and how this might best be done.

Stage 1: Determining a focus
   Who should be involved?   How?

Stage 2: Preparing plans
   Who should be involved?   How?

Stage 3: Clarifying purposes
   Who should be involved?   How?

Stage 4: Determining criteria
   Who should be involved?   How?

Stage 5: Managing data-gathering
   Who should be involved?   How?

Stage 6: Producing and reporting results
   Who should be involved?   How?

Stage 7: Determining and implementing action
   Who should be involved?   How?

USING GROUPS

Worksheet 5.1 explicitly and Worksheet 5.2 implicitly draw attention to the distinction between the involvement of people individually and the use of groups in the management of evaluation. Groups, both formal and informal, play an important part in many evaluation activities and can fulfil a variety of functions. For example:

- Those managing the evaluation may be formally accountable to a group such as a steering committee.
- A small formal or informal group may be charged with the day-to-day management of the evaluation process.
- A group may be used to develop ideas about the key issues to be addressed or possible approaches to the problem before a detailed plan for the evaluation is developed.
- Evaluation data may be gathered through group discussion rather than, or in addition to, more individually focused methods such as interviews or questionnaires.
- A staff meetings or a Senior Management Team might be used as a sounding board for the preliminary findings of an evaluation.

Because the composition of these groups and the nature of the task with which each of them is charged is different, each will need to be managed rather differently if it is to be effective. However, a number of important general points can be made about how groups work which will assist in the effective management of this aspect of evaluation.

For many members of organisations, feelings about groups are ambiguous: meetings are regarded as an integral and necessary part of our working life, but they are to be avoided because they are a source of pain. A useful exercise to help you begin thinking systematically about the issue of managing through groups is to take an example of a group situation that went wrong for you, and for most of the other group members, and to consider what it was that caused difficulties. Exercise 5.2 provides a framework for doing this.

EXERCISE 5.2

DIAGNOSING GROUP PROBLEMS

Purpose

To examine the factors which facilitate and hinder the effective working of groups.

Context

This is best used as a group activity, by a group which is involved in a fairly sustained way in the management of evaluation or some other activity.

Materials needed

- Sufficient copies of the Group Problem Worksheet for all members.
- Flipchart paper and pens.

The exercise

1 Individual members think about a recent group experience which is felt to have been ineffective or particularly painful for many of those involved. If possible, an experience should be chosen which was concerned with evaluation or its management. Notes should be made under the following headings:

   - What went wrong?
   - Why did it go wrong?
   - What feelings were engendered in you and (perhaps) the group during and after the group meeting?

   The Group Diagnosis Worksheet should be used for this purpose.
2 Members then share their ideas. If they have all considered the same shared experience, a composite Group Problem Worksheet can be built up on a sheet of flipchart paper.

Points to note

- This exercise can usefully be undertaken by an individual immediately after a group experience. However, it is better used by an established group to examine a recent experience which members have shared. Alternatively, members of a new group or an existing one may wish to reflect on some group experiences which each had elsewhere.
- It is, of course, difficult to have group discussions of this kind. This is why they are so often avoided. However, the process of using the problem classification on the Group Problem Worksheet and taking time to write things down can be very useful in helping group members to share their perceptions of group processes in a structured way.
- A helpful ground rule is always to stick to issues, incidents and kinds of behaviour, and to avoid talking about personalities or seeking to apportion blame.
- If things are really sticky, it may be helpful to ask an outsider who is trusted by the group to help to facilitate the discussion.

GROUP PROBLEM WORKSHEET

	Use of expertise/opinion in the group	Ability to undertake problem-solving processes	Individual needs in the group	Group ability to operate as ensemble
What went wrong?				
Why did it go wrong?				
What were the underlying feelings for you and (perhaps) the group?				
How could the group process be improved?				

You will see that the exercise classifies the factors which affect group effectiveness into four areas. These are:

- the quality and use in the group of members' expertise and opinions;
- the ability of members to undertake proceedings in an orderly fashion in relation to sequence and rational problem-solving;
- the ability of the group to meet individual needs without particular individuals' needs for power and control becoming overriding; and
- the group's ability to achieve a feeling of ensemble not only in relation to purpose but also in relation to their ability to work together.

Your analysis can now related to some of the issues that are commonly encountered by members of groups.

Some common problems in groups

Access to expertise and opinions

Processes of evaluation are sometimes complex and often controversial. They require expertise both in relation to the specific issue or area being evaluated and to the process of evaluation itself. They also require that the full range of opinions on the issues at hand have an adequate opportunity for expression. Yet groups involved in evaluation may be characterised by insufficient, inappropriate or even excess expertise, and the opinions of some members may dominate those of others. In the meeting you have considered were there too many people offering their opinions or expertise? If so, was this because there was nobody in the group with the authority to tell those with excess opinions and expertise to quieten themselves? Or was it a meeting where it was considered legitimate for there to be a free, frank and wide-ranging exchange of opinions and expertise, so that the basic agenda of the group was difficult to change? In either case, dominant feelings may either embody a sense of competition in relation to expertise or opinion and a strong desire on the part of members to put forward their opinions and expertise, or alternatively a sort of insolent submissiveness where members feel they cannot put forward their own case but submit to those who can.

Problem-solving

Each stage of an evaluation will generate problems that need to be addressed and hopefully solved, at least for the time being. Indeed, very often the evaluation process itself may be viewed as one large problem-solving process. Effective problem-solving requires a degree of order. Was the meeting you have considered characterised by disorder and an inability to undertake its work without a decent sense of order and progression? If so, was this because there was nobody in the group who was able to take command of the situation and impose some sort of order and sequence on the group's activities? This could have occurred because the nominated chairperson felt that he or she could not override the wishes of the group not to pursue matters in a logical manner, or, if there was no formal chairperson, because none of the members of the group felt it was legitimate to take some command of the situation, to create some sense of order out of the chaos. In such situations, the dominant feeling may well be one of time-wasting and disillusion with self and/or others; a sense, that there is no one in the group able to take control. There may well be feelings of strong frustration and impotence that members seem to be tossed backwards and forwards with little sense of control or direction.

Individual needs in the group

Because of the ways in which evaluations, or their outcomes, can affect the lives of individuals, people's feelings about the more controversial aspects can run high. It is easy for individuals to feel that their needs are not being ade- quately met, or that they are not being treated with the respect and consideration which they deserve. With reference to the meeting you have been considering, you may ask: was it characterised by certain members dominating the group, placing their needs first, expressing their needs for dominance or control before those of others in the group? If so, was this because there was no mechanism in the group to control the urges for power and dominance of individuals, or were members locked in a collusion of politeness so that these dominant members were 'able to get away with it'? Here, as with the issue of using expertise and opinions, there may be a desire to compete or submit, but when there is clearly an individual bid for power and control, these feelings can be more powerful, so that the tone can be felt to be aggressive, or the degree of hero(ine) worship more marked.

Achieving group ensemble

Although we have suggested that evaluation can act as a focal activity for the members of a school or college, there may be a failure of the group as a whole to establish some sort of agreement about its identity and its reason for being. If so, was this because the members of the group were not particularly well motivated to be there, because they felt that the remit of the group had been imposed on them, or that they were locked into their individual concerns – soloists unable to form an ensemble? In such circumstances, the dominant feeling is often that the group does not meet personal needs and values, that the members of the group are united only by their individuality. This feeling of lack of common purpose can lead to a sense of alienation and purposelessness, so that there can be anger either in relation to other group members or to the 'fates' that placed the member in the situation in the first place. In some cases this can lead to that dangerous feeling among group members that they need to collude with one other to agree to reach a false solution to their problems – where dissent is seen as a problem for the group, so that they only disagree in private or after the meeting.

Some solutions

Analysis of what goes wrong in group settings can throw a great deal of practical light on the successful management of groups in which we work, and also serves to demonstrate that running a successful group requires a great deal of skill. Although the four aspects outlined above are very closely intertwined, we will now explore the criteria for success in relation to each of them.

Access to expertise and opinion

Members of groups concerned with evaluation often have a great deal of expertise, and they may also hold strong opinions. For the group to meet its purposes successfully, there clearly needs to be a forum for the sharing and dissemination of this expertise and for the airing of opinions. When a person is performing in the 'expert' role there is a need, on the one hand, for a certain orderliness in the presentation of material and, on the other, for an ability to notice the non-verbal signals of members of the group in order to avoid negative consequences of the arousal of submissiveness or competition. At a group level, the key need is for the development of a culture that emphasises what might be termed 'candid supportiveness', and this may require a long period in which people can develop trust in one another. A crucial determinant for success is the ability to bring in the expertise of all members of the group – particularly the more junior ones who may have very close contact with what will and will not work – and the ability to get some people to reduce their contribution without the annihil- ation of their confidence to contribute ever again.

Problem-solving

Although groups that engage in 'a free and frank' discussion over a wide range of topics can be enormously enjoyable, it is probably the case that feelings of success in most evaluation meetings require a sense of order, so that decisions are made and agreements are secured. The classic sequence in relation to this process is shown in Figure 5.1, although a route such as this is clearly only one amongst many. What seems to be important about successful groups is that they make a decision about how they are going to work and then stick to it. If people feel a need to depart from this agreed method, that is best made explicit, and becomes an agreed departure from the 'normal' way of working. What matters here is a sensitive awareness of the value of conformity to routine aspects of the activity of the group where, for example, conformity prevents time-wasting and enables the group to get on with its work.

Individual needs in the group

As we saw in relation to access to expertise and opinion, a key feature of successful groups lies in their ability to create a culture which is supportive of all members of the group. When this has been managed, there is usually a reduction in the need to compete at personal levels. At a personal level, it means that members may have to manage deep antipathies towards other

Figure 5.1 The problem-solving process

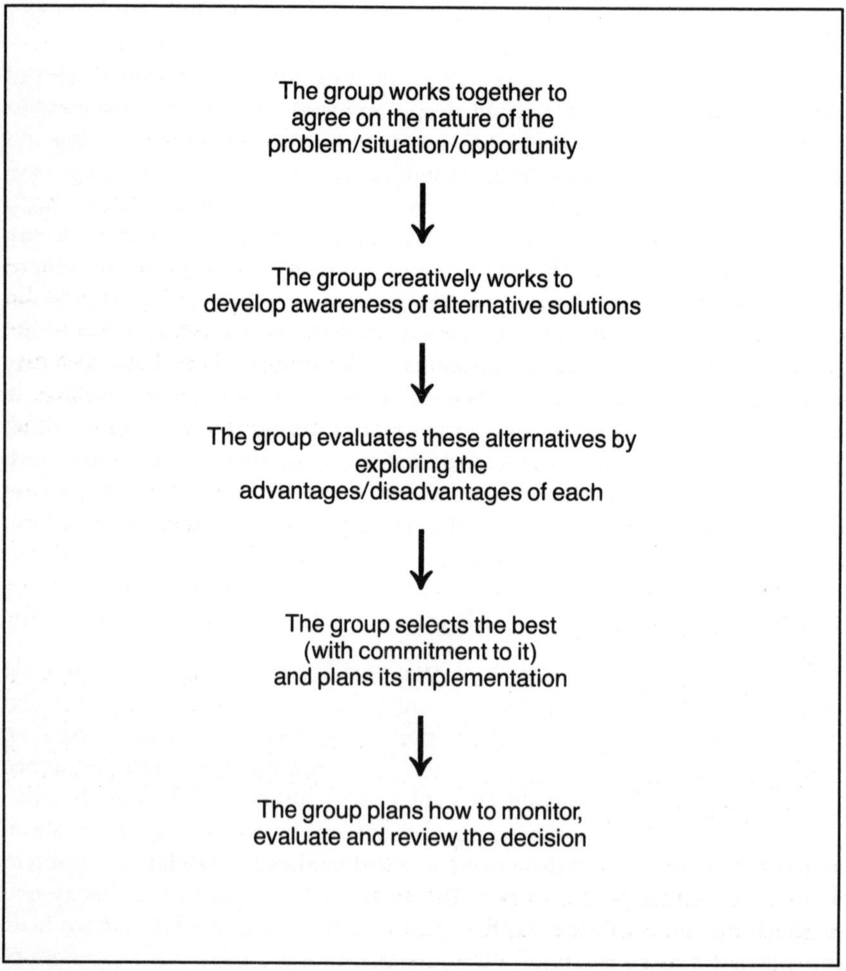

The group works together to
agree on the nature of the
problem/situation/opportunity

↓

The group creatively works to
develop awareness of alternative solutions

↓

The group evaluates these alternatives by
exploring the
advantages/disadvantages of each

↓

The group selects the best
(with commitment to it)
and plans its implementation

↓

The group plans how to monitor,
evaluate and review the decision

members of the group so that they do not engage in 'negative listening' – that is, listening merely in order to contradict or deny. A key issue here is that the goals of the group are seen as being of such high value to the school or college that they transcend interpersonal difficulties. In this respect, the more senior members of the group have a crucial function in acting as role models in terms of standards of behaviour appropriate to the situation. In groups that are most successful in these terms, individuals find membership challenging and refreshing, fulfilling a need for some control over and satisfaction in the task; fulfilling a need too for the good company of a group of interesting colleagues.

Achieving group ensemble

An important aspect of managing a task group of the sort associated with evaluation is that such groups are often relatively short-lived. To develop a sense of ensemble, all groups need to go through a number of stages. From initial formation, they need to pass through a stage where individuals are attempting to assert their identity in relation to the group and other group members, to a sort of truce where members feel able to get on with the work in hand but not with very high commitment to the group and its goals. Finally, an effective group will eventually achieve a sense of being a high-performance, ensemble group. If a group reaches this level of being – and by no means all groups do – a problem may arise when the group completes its purpose but has a strong drive to maintain its existence because of the sheer pleasure of membership. The key to successful ensemble lies in the creation of effective basic assumptions in the group. These basic assumptions are embodied in agreements about how people are going to behave in relation to one another. They are not easily broken promises, but rather involve deeply embedded commitments to the purposes of the group and the creation of realistically supportive relationships among members. Again the role of group leaders, formal or informal, is crucial here in setting the conditions for decent membership of the group in relation to the avoidance of collusive politeness, the development of creativity as a basic assumption, and the placing of a proper value on the strengths that different people bring to the group.

Another aspect of effective group working is the ability of a group to ensure that the sorts of roles that are essential for its effective operation are present and are allowed to operate. The work of Meredith Belbin and his colleagues (Belbin, 1981) suggests that if groups are to work effectively a number of such roles need to be fulfilled:

- to orchestrate the group's personal resources towards its task;
- to drive and shape the work of the group;
- to generate lots of ideas for the group;
- to do solid reliable work for the group;

- to create and maintain harmony in the group;
- to get the group to complete its task on time;
- to keep a check on the group's progress and achievements;
- to look for resources for the group.

Unfortunately, in groups where the worth of all these roles is not recognised, there can be a tendency for members to personalise issues and even to develop positive dislikes for others who operate in rather different ways. For example, people who generate many ideas will often express the feeling that people who want to achieve completion are essentially 'boring'; and the latter will accuse the former of 'only' becoming involved when the task is interesting and of losing interest when the 'hard work' needs to be done. Belbin's message is that we need to respect each other's potential contribution in a full way, that each can make a genuine contribution to the fulfilment of the group. Second, all the roles are needed in the group and groups become less effective when one or two roles come to dominate. The key issue is to achieve the balance. These issues are addressed further in Exercise 5.3.

EXERCISE 5.3

CONSIDERING GROUP ROLES

Purpose

To enable a group to reflect on its group management skills and to develop a plan of action for improving its effectiveness.

Context

This is an activity for a group that is involved in a fairly sustained way in the management of evaluation or some other activity.

Materials needed

Sufficient copies of the Group Roles Worksheet for all members.

The exercise

1 Individual group members are asked to reflect on their knowledge of the members of the group and to complete the Group Roles Worksheet.
2 The group then shares their comments from the third column and discusses why the group exhibits particular strengths or weaknesses.
3 Attention is then given to how the group's performance might be improved.

Points to note

- This is a potentially sensitive exercise. That is why group members are encouraged to share their perceptions of the *group's* strengths and weaknesses rather than those of individual members.
- Nevertheless, the exercise requires a degree of both knowledge and trust and should therefore be carried out in fairly confident groups. Where a new group is forming, it will be more appropriate to use Belbin's original questionnaire (Belbin, 1981: 153–8) which depends on self-assessment and is relatively non-threatening.

© Routledge 1992

GROUP ROLES WORKSHEET

Group roles	Who performs this role?	How are they responded to and valued?	Does performance of the role need strengthening/ weakening?
Orchestrating group resources			
Driving and shaping			
Generating lots of ideas			
Getting on with the job			
Creating and maintaining harmony			
Getting the group to finish its work			
Checking progress and achievements			
Generating resources for the group			

© Routledge 1992

What we have tried to suggest in this section is that many of the dis-illusionments that people have with group working are brought about by the feeling that groups 'just happen' rather than being actively managed. If group working in evaluation is important, then the key issues that need to be managed centre around ensuring that the goals of the group are expressed and accepted, that the culture of the group is realistically supportive, and that membership of the group is seen to have significant pay-offs for all its members.

ETHICAL ISSUES

The final matter to be addressed in this chapter is the ethical dimension of evaluation. Evaluation is a value-laden and political activity which takes place in value-laden and political contexts. Consider the following examples and questions:

- As a result of going on a course, a headteacher decides to invite a team of outsiders to provide a Curriculum Day in January before the start of the spring term. In general, staff do not appreciate the choice of date or of topic. They are also tired of being subjected to their head's enthusiasms. The LEA requires that all Curriculum Days are evaluated and provides a standard questionnaire for such purposes. *Can such an event be evaluated in a way that is fair to the contributors?*
- An LEA decides to retain a proportion of the general INSET budget in order to launch an LEA initiative. Not everyone agrees that this is the best use of this resource. Schools and colleges are dissatisfied with their budgets and are suffering from 'innovation fatigue'. This project is to be staffed by seconded teachers. *What success criteria should be set in such circumstances and by whom?*
- In the process of evaluating a curriculum change, pupils are interviewed, questionnaires are circulated and classrooms observed. Although the evaluation is focused on the curriculum, it becomes painfully clear that some teachers are delivering the new curriculum more effectively than others and that one person in particular is having real problems. *How should these findings be handled? Who has a right to know what in this situation?*
- Your head or principal is taking an MEd. She asks if she can observe in your classroom as part of her study on gender differences in teacher/pupil interaction. *Which factors would influence your response? What guidelines would you want to, or could you, establish before any observations took place?*

The first two of these examples highlight the power/political dimension of evaluation and the risk of bias. In the first, there is a potential for staff to use the questionnaires to vent some of their frustration with the head, perhaps inadvertently damaging others in the process. Similarly, in the second case, the seconded teachers would find themselves affected by circumstances for which they were not responsible. Any evaluation process would need to acknowledge this situation. It is interesting to note how seldom short-course evaluation questionnaires raise the issue of any responsibility participants have for the success or otherwise of what takes place. Similarly, the success of external projects is dependent on the soundness and appropriateness of the initiative, the quality of the project workers, and the response of those in individual institutions. A balanced evaluation would acknowledge the perspectives of participants or recipients (including pupils), providers and, when possible, outside observers of some kind.

The third and fourth examples expose the issue of confidentiality. This is a serious issue from which personal feelings, prejudices or bias must be excluded. For example, your feelings about what should be done with the information about the teacher in the third example might be different if you knew that he or she was going through a painful divorce, rather than if the teacher were known to be a 'clock watcher' who had resisted every change introduced into the school. Your relationship with your head or principal and the level of trust between you would almost certainly influence your response to the request in the fourth example. However, *ad hoc* value judgements do not provide a sound basis for dealing with the dilemma between the 'public right to know' and an individual's right to privacy and confidentiality. What is to be observed or studied, what is going to be reported, in what form, when and to whom must be clearly established from the very beginning of any process. What is agreed should be recorded and circulated to everyone concerned. Never assume that because someone was at a meeting when something was verbally agreed that this is enough. Remember it is difficult to disagree with a general trend, status can be a particular problem, and someone might even not have been listening at the time.

No matter how collaborative and shared the evaluation process is, it is still essential to ensure that individuals are not damaged, but this does not mean that difficult matters are not addressed. For example, it is possible to describe the teaching styles and approaches that are proving most useful in the context of a new curriculum development without identifying who is, or is not, using them. Steps may need to be taken to help individuals who are experiencing difficulties, but these need not – indeed should not – be made public in any way. It is important to remember that pupils also have rights to privacy and confidentiality. Reporting includes what is *said* as much as what is *written*, and the same ethical code must be applied. Both written and verbal reports should focus on issues not individuals.

You may find it useful to return to the 'Why? What? How?' exercise at the beginning of Chapter 2 and work through each of the areas in the context of a post-evaluation experience, thinking specifically about the ethical issues (which will include the political dimension).

Reflection 5.2

Why?   What?   How?   Who?   When?   So What?

For example:

Why?   Was there a political dimension to the evaluation: for example, whose interests were helped or hindered?

What?   Why was this particular area or development chosen?

How?   Was a particular result hoped for and a method chosen in the light of this?

Who?   Who decided who was involved and why?

When?   Was there any desire to block, slow down or conversely bias resources towards a particular development that influenced the timing of the evaluation?

So What? Were powerful individuals or groups able to block or promote the findings of the evaluation?

How far does this experience match up to House's statement?

> Contrary to common belief evaluation is not the ultimate arbiter delivered from our objectivity and accepted as the final judgement. Evaluation is always derived from biased origins. When someone wants to defend something or to attack something, he often evaluates it. Evaluation is a motivated behaviour. Likewise the way in which the results of an evaluation are accepted depends on whether they help or hinder the person receiving them. Evaluation is an integral part of the political processes of our society.
>
> (House, 1973: 1)

An ethical approach to evaluation will acknowledge and take into account the power/political dimension. However, it will not promote the interests of the powerful at the expense of others unable to protect themselves. A commitment to evaluation includes a commitment to take action as a result of the insights gained. The more open, shared, consultative and involving the process, the more possible it is to address these issues.

FURTHER READING

More information on the use and workings of groups can be found in Handy, *Understanding Organisations* (1986b, Chapter 6), which considers the purposes of groups and the factors which determine effectiveness. *Superteams* (1986), by Hastings, Bixby and Chaudhry-Lawton, offers an up-beat approach to the selection, development and deployment of high-performing teams. In *Management Teams, Why They Succeed or Fail* (1981), Belbin suggests that, to be effective, groups and teams need to combine different personalities with different operating styles. The book contains the well-known questionnaire on group roles. The issue of negotiation is dealt with in vigorous style in Fisher and Ury, *Getting to Yes* (1981). The book offers guidance on negotiating in situations where 'they' are more powerful, and places emphasis on learning how to invent options.

Ethical issues are mentioned in most books on evaluation and are explored in some detail in Adelman, *The Politics and Ethics of Evaluation* (1984). Lawton deals with the politics of curriculum evaluation in Chapter 3.1 of McCormick *et al.*, *Calling Education to Account* (1982). Easterby-Smith *et al.* consider ethics and the politics of management in business and industry in Chapter 4 of *Management Research* (1991). Another interesting read is Holt, *Evaluating the Evaluators* (1981) in which the author challenges the whole notion of evaluating performance. On the basis of evidence from both Britain and North America he suggests that such processes can undermine teachers' confidence and impoverish the curriculum.

Chapter 6

Resourcing the process

Even the simplest piece of evaluation needs to be resourced. Consideration needs to be given to what financial expenditure will be required and whether a budget is available for this. There may be a need for particular materials or equipment: perhaps large amounts of paper for printing questionnaires or a computer for processing results. Commonly, however, the prime need is for time, particularly that of people who are already busy. It is because time is commonly the main resource needed that insufficient attention is often given to the careful planning of how an evaluation is to be resourced. However, other costs, too, are often forgotten. The cumulative result is that the evaluation is carried out inadequately or is not completed at all.

This chapter outlines an approach for thinking about the resourcing of evaluation. Its underlying theme is that effective management requires clear thinking and forward planning. It does not require sophisticated technical skills, although the section on networking at the end of the chapter is likely to be of most interest to those planning a fairly complicated evaluation. The chapter is in two parts. The first considers the issues of *costing* (the process of determining what resources are required) and *budgeting* (the process of ensuring that they are actually made available). The second considers the *scheduling* of activities over time.

COSTS AND BUDGETS

Common errors in the early stages of planning are to underestimate the true costs of carrying out an evaluation through all its stages or to fail to take the actions which are necessary to ensure that all these costs are budgeted for. Managing the resourcing of evaluation involves essentially three stages:

- identifying the *resources* which the evaluation process will require;
- assessing the *costs* which these imply; and
- ensuring that these costs will be met (*budgeting*).

The resources required to carry out an evaluation will be of three types. First, people's time will be required. This will include the time of those managing the process through all its stages; but it will also include the time of those who provide data by filling in questionnaires or being interviewed. Second, various kinds of equipment, materials or services will be required (for example, for designing, printing and posting questionnaires or to support group discussion). Finally, the evaluation process may need to make use of space, perhaps for offices or for meetings.

Some of these resources will require additional financial expenditure, for example, for materials, for postage for questionnaires, to pay for part-time clerical assistance, or for a fee for an outside facilitator. Some of the most important costs, however, will not be financial ones at all. The most obvious example here is the time of staff whose main work is not concerned with evaluation. Teachers or lecturers may agree to be interviewed in their non-contact time or office staff may type up questionnaires in their normal working time.

The central concept which links these various elements of cost is that of *opportunity cost*. Opportunity cost can be defined as the value of the best alternative which is given up by using resources in one way rather than another. Thus money used for postage is not available for other desirable expenditure, and time spent on managing evaluation or filling in question-naires cannot be spent teaching or on curriculum development.

An opportunity cost perspective draws attention to a number of key con-siderations in the management of resources. First, it is important to be *totally resource conscious* and not just *budget conscious*. Budget consciousness implies a concern primarily with financial expenditure. Local management of schools and colleges and the financial accountability arrangements embodied in schemes such as TVEI are currently causing those with managerial responsibilities to become acutely aware of financial costs in a way which is quite new. Such awareness is important. However, it is also important not to lose the broader resource awareness which has traditionally underlain processes of staff deployment and timetabling: an awareness that all decisions to use resources in a particular way involve sacrifices, whether or not money expenditure is in-volved. In schools and colleges only some managers – often the more senior ones – control financial budgets. But everybody incurs costs by virtue of the choices they make about the use of their own time and of the demands they make on the time of others. For an activity like evaluation, which often operates at the financial margins of the organisation, such costs can be quite significant.

An initial costing of an evaluation, therefore, may well not be expressed primarily in financial terms. It will begin by identifying all the resources which are likely to be required to carry out the evaluation effectively; and it will then attempt to measure these in whatever currency seems appropriate (person-hours, £s, etc.). This should lead naturally to a consideration of how the resources are to be made available, and hence to a consideration of opportunity cost. You can use Worksheet 6.1 to explore the opportunity costs of an evaluation with which you are involved.

WORKSHEET 6.1

PREPARING AN OPPORTUNITY COSTING

Take each stage of the process of evaluation which is being planned
and complete the following in as much detail as possible:

Resources required	Quantity (in person hours, £s, etc.)	Opportunity cost (what will need to be given up)
People		
Equipment, materials and services		
Space		

© Routledge 1992

Consideration of what needs to be given up to ensure that the necessary resources are available leads to a second point about opportunity cost. Costs are often distributed among individuals and groups who are affected by a particular decision in a way which makes many of these costs all but invisible to those who are managing the process. Thus sending out a questionnaire or some other request for information may require little effort (its opportunity cost may be low to the sender), whereas to provide a good-quality response may be an extremely time-consuming business. Too often those managing an evaluation process take insufficient account of the fact that 'there is no such thing as a free lunch' – someone, somewhere, will have to pick up the bill.

At first glance this may not seem to matter. Why not load costs on to others if this is possible? The answer is embodied in our third point. People's behaviour is heavily influenced by their personal perceptions of opportunity cost. If a person is asked to fill in a time-consuming questionnaire without being convinced of the value of doing so, the result will be a small number of returns or a very quick response which gives little attention to the quality of information being provided. It pays, therefore, in assessing the costs of an evaluation process, to attempt to identify these as comprehensively as possible, whoever bears them. Consider Reflection 6.1.

Reflection 6.1

Return to Worksheet 6.1 which was concerned with identifying opportunity costs. Have any been omitted because they are borne primarily by individuals or groups who have not been considered in the costing process, e.g. pupils or students, parents, employers or others outside the school or college? If so, add them to your table.

One final point needs to be made about the opportunity cost perspective. Although an evaluation may entail considerable costs, and may therefore not seem to be worth the effort, there will also be opportunity costs associated with *not* undertaking it. These are the likely benefits which will arise for the school or college as a result of the evaluation. Benefits are usually less tangible than costs, but it is necessary to consider them alongside costs by asking the following questions:

- What benefits are expected from the evaluation?
- Who is likely to receive them?
- What steps need to be taken to maximise the likelihood that they will occur?

The first two questions should have been considered already, and Chapter 4 in particular is relevant here. The third question is addressed in Chapter 9.

Analysing costs in this way provides an excellent basis for budgeting. For this budgeting involves not only assessing what resources are needed but also the implementation of strategies to ensure that they will be available. This involves answering four questions. Two of these have been addressed already:

- What resources will be required?
- What will need to be given up to ensure that they can be made available?

The other two questions are:

- Who is in a position to ensure that the required choices are made?
- How can they be encouraged to make the necessary choices?

Figure 6.1 outlines a possible analysis of the costs associated with using a questionnaire for parents. Such an analysis may suggest that the opportunity cost of this method is too high: consider what other methods might enable you to find out what you need to know at less cost, rather than abandon the effort.

SCHEDULING THE EVALUATION

An important aspect of planning an evaluation concerns the management of resources over time. Even if the necessary resources are costed accurately, there will still be problems if insufficient time is allowed to carry out key tasks or if they are scheduled for times when the people who need to be involved are heavily committed elsewhere. An essential part of the planning process, therefore, involves producing a realistic implementation schedule. Frequently this does not occur:

- Insufficient time is given to discussing evaluation plans with those whose co-operation is necessary, with resulting lack of understanding or commitment.
- Meetings are arranged when key people are not available.
- Insufficient time is left between meetings to enable key issues to be reflected upon, or necessary information to be gathered, or action to be taken.
- Plans are not made to ensure that secretarial or clerical staff are available at the times when typing, mailing or collation must be done.
- Insufficient time is allowed for respondents to return questionnaires and non-respondents to be followed up.
- Over-ambitious interview schedules are arranged with a large number of interviews squeezed into a short period of time, when interviewers and interviewees have other commitments.
- Adequate time is allowed for data-gathering, but the time needed to collate and analyse the results is underestimated.

Figure 6.1 Costing a questionnaire for parents

Resources required:
● time of planning group to prepare questionnaire;
● secretarial time to type up questionnaire;
● cost of postage, including stamped addressed envelopes;
● parents' time in filling in questionnaire;
● time, including possibly computer time, to process results.

What will need to be given up?
● teaching staff time:
  ◆ less teaching, preparation or marking?
  ◆ other uses of 'management time'?
  ◆ own time?
● secretarial time:
  ◆ other use of secretary's time?
  ◆ other uses of funds used to buy in secretarial support?
  ◆ teacher time?
● parents' time: personal time?
● financial expenditure: other uses of funds?

Who can ensure choices are made?
● teaching staff time: the individuals themselves;
● secretarial time: whoever is responsible for determining priorities in secretarial workload;
● parents' time: parents, influenced by their perceptions of 'worthwhileness' of exercise;
● finance: controller of relevant budget.

How can they be encouraged to make the choices?
● In each case an appropriate strategy of persuasion, or occasionally direction, will focus on the priority to be given to the exercise or the value the individuals concerned may gain from it.

- No account is taken of the timing of a key meeting, with the result that feedback misses it and is out of date by the time the next meeting comes round.

Effective scheduling needs to take account of three points in particular. First, estimates of the time required to complete tasks must be realistic. Second, it is important to take account of the fact that, even if *your* time will be devoted solely to the evaluation process, that of others almost certainly will not. Third, it is important to ensure that sufficient time is allowed at key points in the process for taking stock and, if necessary, replanning. Many an evaluation has come unstuck because the need to keep *doing* has pushed out the time required for *thinking*. This is another reason why we have continually attempted to de-emphasise the issue of gathering data in this book: if earlier stages in the process have not been addressed effectively, it will be too late to deal with problems arising at the data-gathering stage.

In many evaluation situations, an awareness of the need to ensure that activities are realistically scheduled – together with a commitment to act on that awareness – will be enough. Sometimes, however, it may be helpful to deal with the issue of scheduling more formally, especially when a large or complicated piece of evaluation is being planned. The rest of this section outlines a particular technique – called *networking* – which can help you to do this.

Networking

Networking is a tool for planning any complex task which comprises a number of activities which are interrelated in the sense that some need to be completed before others can start, while others can be undertaken simultaneously. For example, a questionnaire must be designed – and possibly piloted – before it can be sent out. Permission may need to be sought from parents before children can be interviewed. An appropriate programme must be chosen or written before data can be processed using a computer. To analyse complex tasks of this kind, three key pieces of information are necessary.

First, a complete list must be produced of all the activities which need to be undertaken from the beginning to the end of the evaluation. This list must be as detailed as possible. It may be helpful to start with the stages we have used in this book:

- determining a focus;
- preparing plans;
- clarifying purposes;
- determining criteria;
- managing data-gathering;
- producing and reporting results;
- determining and implementing action.

These stages are defined much too broadly, however. Each will comprise a number of activities, each of which will require time in its own right. For example, the stages of gathering, processing and feeding back data might involve the following activities if it is decided to use an interview method and feed back through a seminar:

- decide what information is required;
- decide on method of gathering data;
- decide method of data processing;
- design interview schedule;
- determine sample;
- inform interviewees of purposes of interview and arrange interviews;
- brief interviewers;
- conduct interviews;
- process data;
- write report;
- type and reproduce report;
- circulate report;
- plan feedback seminar;
- advertise feedback seminar;
- run seminar.

Each of these activities will take time. How *much* time is the second piece of information required. This will depend very much on the situation: the complexity of the task involved and the other pressures which may be expected to arise during the process. To estimate the time which is likely to be necessary, start by considering how much time is likely to be necessary if all goes well. Then consider *who* will be involved in this particular activity and whether they have other commitments which might cause delays in the process; and *when* the activity is likely to be undertaken and whether this will mean that specific events that may cause delays, such as public holidays, will occur at that time.

Finally, information is necessary on which activities must necessarily be completed before others can begin. These are known as 'predecessors'. For example, in the case above, it is clearly necessary to decide what information needs to be collected before designing the interview schedule and, possibly, before selecting the sample. The interview schedule must be designed before the interviewers are briefed, but it may not be necessary to design it in detail before informing the interviewees and arranging interviews, although the sample must be chosen before this can occur.

The results of the information obtained so far can be presented in a table of the type shown in Figure 6.2. It will be seen that seventeen discrete activities have been defined, starting with deciding what information is required and ending with running the seminar. Once such a table has been produced it should be the subject of critical scrutiny. It might be appropriate

Figure 6.2 Gathering and processing data: key activities

Activity	Estimated time	Predecessor(s)
1 Decide needed information.	2 weeks	–
2 Decide data-gathering method.	0.5 weeks	1
3 Decide data-processing method.	0.5 weeks	2
4 Determine sample.	0.5 weeks	2
5 Design interview schedule.	2 weeks	3
6 Inform interviewees/arrange interviews.	1 week	4
7 Brief interviewers.	1 week	5
8 Conduct interviews.	3 weeks	6,7
9 Process data.	4 weeks	8
10 Write report.	4 weeks	9
11 Type and reproduce report.	2 weeks	10
12 Circulate report.	1 week	11
13 Reading report.	2 weeks	12
14 Plan structure of feedback seminar.	6 weeks	2
15 Plan content of feedback seminar.	3 weeks	10,14
16 Advertise feedback seminar.	3 weeks	15
17 Run seminar.	0.5 weeks	13,16

to subdivide some activities further. For example, the early decision stages might involve organising a series of meetings. Furthermore, the estimated times and the predecessors may be the subject of debate. When we are considering plans for the future, the element of uncertainty and judgement will always come into the picture; and an analytical process such as this can be extremely helpful in clarifying our thinking. Worksheet 6.2 provides a pro forma for you to undertake this kind of analysis for yourself. A column has been added for any notes about particular stages: for example, key assumptions underlying the estimates or potential difficulties which might render them unreliable.

WORKSHEET 6.2

ACTIVITY SCHEDULE

Activity	Estimated time	Predecessor(s)	Notes
1			
2			
3			
4			
5			
6			
7			
8			
9			
10			
11			
12			
13			
14			
15			
16			
17			
18			
19			
20			
21			
22			

Continue on separate sheet

It is possible to take this analysis further. The information in the table can be transferred to a chart which plots the various activities over time. Such a chart is shown in Figure 6.3. This has been drawn up by placing those activities with no predecessors at the left-hand side and then adding activities to the right of their predecessors. Since all its predecessors must have been completed before an activity can start, any activity will be scheduled to commence immediately on completion of that predecessor which finishes *latest*. If there is more than one predecessor, the one which finishes earlier is projected forward as a dotted line as far as the point at which a succeeding activity begins.

A number of points can be noted from Figure 6.3. First, the time needed to complete the whole process from deciding what information is needed to running the seminar is 23.5 weeks – considerably less than the aggregate

Figure 6.3 Diagram of activities

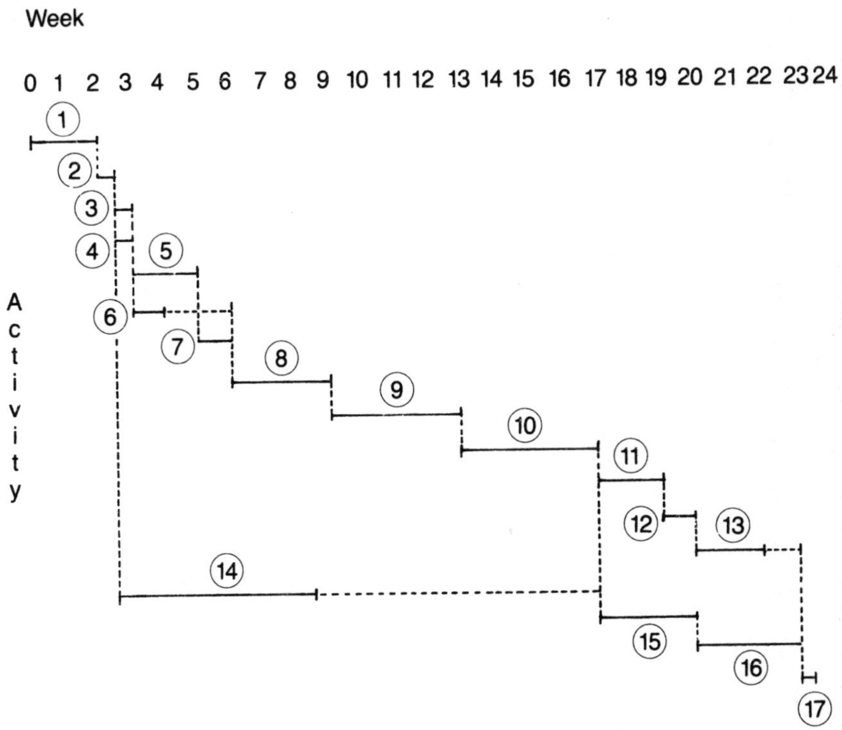

time of all the activities (36 weeks). This is because some activities can be carried out 'in parallel', that is to say simultaneously. Second, some activities, such as 6 and 14, are succeeded by dotted lines. This implies that, if they are delayed, this will not delay the completion of the overall process provided the delay does not exceed the period represented by the dotted line. In other words, there is some 'slack' in this part of the process. Conversely, some activities have no slack associated with them. If their completion is delayed, the whole process will take longer than has been planned for. These activities are said to be on the 'critical path'. In this case, the critical path lies through activities 1–2–3–5–7–8–9–10–15–16–17.

This kind of analysis is extremely helpful in planning and resourcing the evaluation process. For example:

- It is important to ensure that activities lying on the critical path keep to time if the overall process is not to be delayed.
- The timing of non-critical activities can be adjusted to help spread the workload.
- Where a number of activities need to be carried out in parallel, it may be necessary to draft in additional help if they are all to be completed on schedule. Otherwise the overall process will be delayed.
- The creation of a 'real time' schedule, by adding dates to the week numbers, enables us to see whether the planned schedule is consistent with other pressures and demands such as holidays or the timing of key meetings.

Beyond this, carrying out an analysis of this kind in a group can be extremely helpful for clarifying assumptions about how the evaluation process is to be carried out and what its major logistical requirements are. It forces us to make our assumptions explicit and therefore to test them against those of others. Furthermore, once the plans have been prepared, the schedule can be used to monitor progress and see whether we are keeping to schedule or whether corrective action needs to be taken. It is not difficult to translate the time schedule into an action planning chart of the kind illustrated in Worksheet 6.3.

Worksheets 6.2 and 6.3 can be used to apply these ideas to your own evaluation project. The method of analysis presented here is relatively simple, although it should be adequate to meet the planning requirements of most evaluations undertaken in schools and colleges. A variety of more sophisticated techniques are available, however. References relating to these can be found below.

WORKSHEET 6.3

ACTION PLAN

Activity	Scheduled completion date	Resources required	Responsibility of:

FURTHER READING

Some of the main ideas outlined in this chapter are discussed in more detail in Simkins, *Economics and the Management of Resources in Education* (1981). The approach to scheduling outlined in the last part of the chapter is dealt with in more detail in Lockyer, *Critical Path Analysis and Other Project Network Techniques* (1991).

Chapter 7

Using success criteria

In Chapter 2 we made mention of terms such as success criteria, performance indicators and target setting which have recently gained currency in the world of education. The observation was also made that this kind of language is traditionally associated with the culture of commerce and industry, and is viewed with suspicion by many educationalists. Those who hold this view argue that this kind of language implies an emphasis on formal accountability, on a product-centred view of the task at hand, and a preoccupation with quantifiable findings, whereas educational organisations are dealing not with a product but with the complex process of educating and developing people which cannot be represented in such relatively simple ways.

There are many who view this apparent culture clash as irreconcilable. However, such a view often represents more a rejection of the language being used than a desire to be uncritical or unaccountable. Good professionals are invariably looking for evidence of success and indicators of their level of performance. In simple terms, they constantly pose the question 'How are we doing?' This question in turn implies a need for clarity about what we are trying to achieve and about how we shall know whether we have achieved it. This may lead to the design and use of fairly hard, quantitative 'performance indicators'; often, however, this will be inappropriate and softer approaches will be necessary. Whatever particular method is used, however, it needs to be based on a systematic approach. This chapter attempts to provide this. It begins with a cameo which illustrates some of the issues involved. It then proceeds to outline a series of questions which need to be answered as success criteria are developed and used. This leads to an examination of the relationship between the information with which people are provided and how they behave. The chapter concludes with some suggestions for ensuring that the best use is made of success indicators in the evaluation process.

DESIGNING AND USING SUCCESS CRITERIA AND INDICATORS

All evaluation is in some way comparative. Either explicitly or implicitly, information gathered through on-going monitoring processes or from specific pieces of investigation will incorporate ideas about the standards or criteria against which performance should be judged and about the kinds of information which represent evidence of success or otherwise in achieving these standards. This is the world of performance indicators. These may be specified in a fairly 'soft' or subjective way, or they may be embodied in apparently 'harder' and more objective measures. Hopkins and Leask offer the following definition of a performance indicator:

> A performance indicator is a statement against which achievement in an area or activity can be assessed; they are also useful for setting goals and clarifying objectives. For some performance indicators, a brief statement is sufficient; for others the statement should be more specific and refer to supplementary processes which would give a measure of depth, quality and/or commitment in a particular area. In our view there is a place for both quantitative and qualitative indicators.
>
> (Hopkins and Leask, 1989: 6–7)

The development and use of success criteria and indicators is not necessarily a complex technical task, although there are many examples of performance measures in education which do require a good deal of specialist knowledge for their application and interpretation. Consider the following cameo.

Cameo

Success criteria for careers education and guidance

We came together as a group of teachers involved in Careers Education and Guidance (CEG) as a result of a joint LEA/Careers Service conference. The LEA and Careers Service were jointly launching a CEG Policy Document and the *National Curriculum Document 6* (National Curriculum Council, 1989), establishing CEG as a cross-curricular theme, had just been published. We were pleased to feel that the importance of CEG had been recognised, but during the day had become increasingly anxious about the size and nature of the task we appeared to be facing. It seemed sensible to go on meeting as a group to pursue this problem further.

At our next two meetings we reviewed the ever-growing amount of documentation relevant to CEG. For example, we found *Towards a Skills Revolution* by the Confederation of British Industry, *Skills 2000* by the Trades Union Congress and the Government White Paper on Employment (Department of Employment, 1988) had many implications for both careers education and guidance. We considered the implications of CEG becoming a cross-curricular theme, realising that we were going to be engaged in a major management task. Teachers on A and B allowances, some relatively young and inexperienced, shuddered at the thought of taking particular heads of departments to one side to discuss how their approach to pupils and their lesson content might help or hinder the CEG work carried out in other contexts. Even those with the status of head of careers were aware that this was regarded as a lowly position by some colleagues, secure in 'high status' subjects. We became rather depressed. Our task seemed to be becoming bigger and more complex by the minute.

Then one person came forward with a suggestion. Why didn't we try to identify some targets or success criteria towards which we could work, taking the four areas of 'opportunity awareness, transition, decision, self awareness' – so familiar to careers teachers – as our starting point (Law and Watt, 1977). Consideration of these areas led us to begin to identify possible indicators of success. These included:

- *Pupil destinations.* The careers service provided valuable information. We needed to look at this and see if it was possible to make judgements about the quality of the decisions pupils were making about their futures.
- *The quality of pupil action plans.*
- *The ability of pupils to rationalise and explain their choices to others.* We could, for example, ask for feedback from careers officers about how pupils respond to their careers interviews.
- *Evidence of pupil self-esteem and self-presentation skills.* This might be obtained through considering their behaviour in mock interviews.
- *The quality of the careers library.* Is it well stocked and up to date? Does it avoid or negate gender stereotyping? Is it well used? Could untidiness be an indicator of success?
- *The number and quality of work experience placements.* We could use evidence from pupils in debriefing or review sessions after the placements. Some people realised at this point that their pupils' work experience took place too late in the summer term to allow immediate debriefing and began to wonder whether this detracted from the experience.

- *The quality of applications for jobs and training post-16.* We realised that feedback from the colleges was readily available as college staff were part of the group. It is also relatively straightforward to get feedback from YTS schemes, but it is more difficult from employers. We realised that we were not logging the phone calls and other informal feedback that we already receive.

As the discussion progressed, we realised that our approach was not incorporating the curriculum dimension of CEG. So we began to identify some further criteria in this area:

- Is Careers Education and Guidance a *part of pupil entitlement?*
- Is there *coherence and development* in CEG from Year 7 to leaving school?
- If Careers Education and Guidance are two discrete elements, is there a *programme to bring them together?*
- *What is taught* in the context of CEG across the curriculum? Where, to whom, how and when? (Two people decided immediately that a curriculum audit might be an urgent priority for their institutions.)

Once we had concluded that there were many possible and attainable success criteria and that some, if not all, were readily to hand, we began to feel much more in control of the situation. We agreed that each individual would work with colleagues in each institution to decide on relevant starting points. We recognised that we had not yet considered other important groups, such as parents and governors. We agreed to continue to meet, to bring back information and learn from one another's experience.

This cameo demonstrates the value of the idea of success criteria in providing an impetus and a framework for clarifying our thinking about what our purposes are and how we can know whether, or to what degree, we are achieving them. The group in the cameo clearly found this to be the case, but they did so very much through a process of trial and error. Such learning processes can be extremely valuable. However, if success criteria are to be of maximum benefit, they need to be developed and used in a systematic way which takes account of the pitfalls that can arise. A systematic approach can best be developed by working through a number of key questions in relation to a programme or activity.

Question 1: what is it trying to achieve?

This is the central question, and will require considerable thought and discussion. It needs to be addressed within the context of the specific purposes for which the evaluation is being undertaken. So, for example, the criteria will be very different if the main concern is to monitor the implementation of a project over time than if it is to assess the impact of a change in teaching method on students' learning. The group working on CEG began their search for success criteria by identifying the key areas of opportunity awareness, transition, decision and self-awareness. Only later did they add the area of curriculum. They could usefully have spent more time at this stage, ensuring that all the relevant 'performance areas' for the programme had been identified, and determining one or more 'focusing' questions for each one. Two examples of approaches to the identification of performance areas are given in Figures 7.1 and 7.2. One is taken from the school's sector, the other from further education.

It will be seen that the two approaches differ substantially in their emphasis. That proposed for schools explicitly identifies three performance areas and defines a focusing question for each one. In contrast, the Joint Efficiency Study moves straight to the specification of six performance areas: although these are based on two core performance areas, 'efficiency' and 'effectiveness'. The study defines efficiency as the relationship of inputs to outputs and effectiveness as the extent to which objectives are being achieved. Thus criteria 1 to 4 broadly relate to the area of efficiency and 5 and 6 to that of effectiveness.

There are other differences. The school criteria make no reference to resource utilisation or cost whereas three of the further education (FE) criteria, with their concern for efficiency, do. In contrast, two of the school criteria are concerned with process whereas none of the FE criteria is. And, whereas the FE criteria are all relatively straightforward to define and easy to quantify, two of the school criteria are quite difficult to represent other than in a qualitative way.

Figure 7.1 Sheffield University school success criteria

1 *Academic progress*
 What proportion of pupils in the school have made above average levels of academic progress over the relevant time period?

2 *Pupil satisfaction*
 What proportion of pupils in the school are satisfied with the education they are receiving?

3 *Pupil–teacher relationships*
 What proportion of pupils in the school have good or 'vital' relationships with one or more teachers?

Source: Gray and Jesson (1990)

Figure 7.2 The Joint Efficiency Study's success criteria for further education

---

1 *The staff:student ratio* based on full-time equivalent (fte) student and academic staff numbers.

2 *Non-teacher cost* per enrolled student.

3 *Cost per fte student* enrolled on a course.

4 *Completion rates* for students enrolled on courses, and the cost per fte student completing a course.

5 *Rates of target qualifications* gained for students enrolled on a course, and the cost per qualified fte student.

6 *Rates of employment or progression* to further and higher education for students completing appropriate courses.

Source: DES (1987), The Joint Efficiency Study

These differences, though important, should not be allowed to detract from the main point, which is that any success criteria should be based on an analysis of what the key dimensions of achievement are. Only when this is done is it safe to proceed to a consideration of more specific indicators of success.

Question 2: what would be appropriate indicators of success?

Having identified our area of concern, we need to identify one or more phenomena about which information can be gathered and which will help us to answer our chosen question: what would indicate success in this particular area? The group considering CEG brainstormed some answers to this question, but it is not entirely clear how their indicators of success were systematically related to their selected performance areas. For example, what does 'the quality of the careers library' relate to? Perhaps another performance area: 'level of resourcing'? And 'opportunity awareness' is not obviously included among the indicators, although it might be an aspect of 'the quality of pupil action plans', if the meaning of 'quality' here were specified more clearly.

An example of how broad performance areas can be translated into more specific success indicators is the 'Quality of Learning and Teaching Profile' developed by the Scottish HMI in relation to further education (Scottish Education Depart- ment, 1990). This translates five areas – relevance, access, responsiveness, appropriateness and standards – into seventeen 'quality statements' (QS) (see Figure 7.3).

Figure 7.3 Quality of Learning and Teaching (QLT) Profile

Relevance
QS1   There is a planned portfolio of programmes which is broadly consistent with the identified needs of clients.
QS2   The overall content of each individual programme is suited to its aims and purposes.
QS3   Programme content is accurate and up-to-date in its treatment of employment practice and new technology.

Access
QS4   Potential clients receive clear, accurate, and comprehensive information about programmes on offer and have the opportunity to clarify their goals in order that students enrol for a suitable programme.
QS5   The prior learning of students, whether certificated or experiential, is adequately taken into account.
QS6   Circumstantial restrictions on access, such as those arising from the timing and location of courses, are minimised.

Responsiveness
QS7   Innovative programmes or modifications to existing programmes for employers and community users are provided with a minimum of lead time.
QS8   There is liaison and collaboration with employers and community users in the delivery of programmes.
QS9   Students have access to sources of information, advice, and support which assist them to meet their learning needs, cope with difficulties and progress satisfactorily from a programme.
QS10   Programmes are negotiable and components are selected to meet individual needs.
QS11   Students are able to progress at their own pace.
QS12   Clients have the opportunity to evaluate provision.

Appropriateness (of learning and teaching approaches)
QS13   There is a climate of purposefulness and rapport, and a concern for individual student achievement.
QS14   The learning resources and environment are well planned and organised with regard to the accomplishment of learning outcomes.
QS15   Learning and teaching methods are appropriate to learning outcomes, emphasise student activity and responsibility, and are varied.

Standards
QS16   Assessment approaches cover all the learning outcomes and performance criteria and are applied to the work of all students.
QS17   The standards, as set out in descriptors, are correctly applied and systematically moderated.

Note: Terminology tends to vary among different kinds of educational provision. In reading these quality statements 'programme' should be deemed to include 'courses', and 'learning outcomes' to include 'outcomes' and 'learning objectives' and so on.

Source: Scottish Education Department (1990)

It is important that a systematic framework is developed for thinking about performance, so that all major performance areas are defined and suitable indicators are developed for each. This might be done in a number of ways, depending on the programme or activity being considered. The QLT Profile is just one approach. Another classification which is often advocated is that of 'input', 'process' and 'outcome'. Each of these three dimensions focuses on a different aspect of provision. *Input* concerns the scale and appropriateness of the resources devoted to a programme. It includes such considerations as expenditure, costs and the appropriateness of teacher skills. *Process* is concerned primarily with the quality of inter-actions between, and experiences undergone by, those involved in the programme. It might include, for example, the degree of active learning undertaken by pupils or the range of teaching methods used on a course in further education. Finally, *outcome* concerns the results of the programme – learning achieved, entry to further education or work, and so on. In each of these areas it is possible to think of indicators of success which are both quantitative and qualitative. Each of these three areas can be developed in a variety of ways, depending on the objectives and priorities of the programme under consideration. Such an approach can be used at a variety of levels from the individual activity or programme to the whole institution. An example is given in Figure 7.4.

As our discussion of the CEG case suggested, the definition of per-formance areas and the derivation of indicators for each can best be considered as an iterative process. The systematic identification of per-formance areas can provide a framework for deriving indicators appropriate to each (for example, using the QLT Profile or the input/process/output model); on the other hand, the generation of a large number of indicators can lead to the refinement of performance areas or the identification of new ones. You may now wish to apply this approach to a programme with which you are familiar by undertaking Exercise 7.1 or using Worksheet 7.1.

Figure 7.4 Success indicators for a Careers Education and Guidance programme

	Quantitative	Qualitative
Inputs	Is CEG part of entitlement? Time devoted to CEG, by class No. of work experience placements Size of careers library	Teachers' commitment to CEG work
Processes	What is taught in CEG across the curriculum, to whom and when (Curriculum Audit).	Quality of work experience placements Coherence and development in CEG provision Integration of CE and G
Outcomes	Pupil destinations (work and further education) Pupil satisfaction questionnaire Log of feedback from employers and colleges	Quality of pupil action plans Careers officers' feedback on pupil interviews Pupil performance in mock interviews

EXERCISE 7.1

GENERATING SUCCESS INDICATORS

Purpose

To enable participants to develop a clear understanding of the success indicators that should be applied to an activity or development as part of the evaluation process.

Context

A group planning a development, or, more specifically, one that is charged with determining how it should be evaluated.

Materials needed

Flipchart and pens.

The exercise

1 The group begins by brainstorming answers to the following question:

> What observable phenomena would indicate to us that the activity or programme we are considering was successful?

In this context, 'observable' simply means that it is possible to collect relevant evidence, for example by observation, interview, discussion or the analysis of documents or statistics. The evidence might be quantitative (for example, test or exam results, costs, or attendance rates) or it may be qualitative (for example, teachers' and students' perceptions of aspects of the teaching/learning process). Try to generate as long a list as possible. Record everything.

2 Discuss the list as a group. Remove items where there is obvious duplication; refine statements where they are unclear.

3 Group the remaining indicators into performance areas. Give each area an agreed name.

4 Review the picture which emerges:

- Do the performance areas which have emerged represent adequately all the major dimensions along which the programme should be judged, or are there important dimensions missing? For example, is the resource dimension adequately covered? Or that of client or stakeholder satisfaction?

- Is there an adequate spread of indicators across all the performance areas? If not, can you identify any additional indicators in the areas which are under-represented?
- In the light of the picture which is emerging, do any of the indicators need further refining?

Points to note

- In undertaking the exercise it is important to follow the rules of brainstorming strictly. The group should sit in a circle with one member acting as recorder using a flipchart:

  ♦ *Don't judge:* Let all ideas come without comment.
  ♦ *Go wild:* No matter how crazy or unique the idea seems keep it for consideration. You can always reject it later.
  ♦ *The more the merrier:* It's quantity not quality that counts initially.
  ♦ *Interrelate:* Combine ideas to generate new ones, new avenues to explore further.

(Leigh, 1983: 105)

WORKSHEET 7.1

A FRAMEWORK FOR GENERATING SUCCESS INDICATORS

Consider a programme with which you are concerned. Individually or as a group, develop a set of success indicators using the framework outlined below.

	Quantitative	Qualitative
Inputs		
Processes		
Outcomes		

Question 3: how should data be gathered and processed?

There are usually many ways of gathering and processing data on a particular phenomenon. This may involve measuring things. Consider academic achievement, for example. One possible measure of this is examination performance, perhaps in GCSE, or test results. Is it sufficient to measure the number of passes, or passes at a particular level, or should different weightings be applied to different grades of pass? If the latter, what should the weightings be? As a measure of efficiency of staff utilisation, too, the SSR can be measured in a variety of ways: for example, at different times in the year, or by weighting part-time students in particular ways. Where such choices exist, different measures are likely to show different patterns of performance.

To choose a suitable way of gathering and processing data we may need to refine our criteria of success. For example, is 'success' enabling a high proportion of less able students to obtain passes at GCSE, or is it maximising the number of students who obtain passes at grades A and B? The former would best be assessed by a simple measure of total passes; the latter would need the results to be weighted heavily in favour of the higher grades. A department which performs well on one criterion may not do so on the other, and vice versa.

Statistics of examination results, of staff deployment or of anything else, are not the only kind of data which might be collected as indicators of success, however. In its work on the Quality of Learning and Teaching Profile, HMI suggest ten evaluation instruments (EIs) which combine a variety of interviews, questionnaires and recording schedules (Scottish Education Department, 1990: 20). These are:

EI 1   User Survey (postal questionnaire)
EI 2A   Student Survey: guidance (questionnaire)
EI 2B   Student Survey: learning and teaching (questionnaire)
EI 2C   Student Survey (interview)
EI 3A   Staff Survey: guidance (questionnaire)
EI 3B   Staff Survey: learning, teaching and assessment (questionnaire)
EI 4   Programme Analysis (recording schedule for analysis of programme documentation and interview findings by a team of evaluators)
EI 5   Module Analysis (recording schedule for analysis of 'extended' modules and findings from discussion by evaluators)
EI 6   Analysis of Student Work (recording schedule for analysis of assessed student work by evaluators)
EI 7   Analysis of Teaching (recording schedule for analysis of findings arising from observation of learning and teaching in classrooms, workshop, etc. by evaluators)

These evaluation instruments are then related to the seventeen quality statements as shown in Figure 7.5. Evidence from instruments such as these is just as valid as more traditional statistics – indeed it may be more so for particular purposes. Data from such sources will still need to be aggregated in a suitable way, however, to produce usable information. A more extensive discussion of data-gathering methods is to be found in Chapter 8.

Question 4: with what can the results validly be compared?

However well the success criteria have been designed and however well the data have been gathered and processed, information about performance in relation to a particular development at a given point in time is of little value on its own in answering the question 'How are we doing?' It has to be placed in comparative perspective. The statements 'We're doing OK' or 'We could do better' implies the existence of some standard against which performance is being judged.

It is common to use three main types of standard for making judgements about achievements:

- *Comparative*. How are we doing in comparison with similar developments elsewhere?
- *Progress*. How are we doing compared with how we have done previously?
- *Target*. How are we doing compared with a specific standard or target(s) which we have set ourselves, or which others have set for us?

Each of these approaches has its attractions. Comparison with similar programmes elsewhere ensures an outward-looking approach to evaluation and guards against parochialism. An emphasis on our own progress demonstrates the importance of development and potentially can be extremely motivating. The development and utilisation of specific targets encourages the development of clear links between plans and performance assessment. Perhaps the best advice is to use a combination of all three approaches in an attempt to get the best of all worlds.

Question 5: what other information is necessary to put the results into context?

The availability of information which can be used for comparative purposes, while essential, may not be sufficient to enable appropriate conclusions to be drawn from evaluation data, however. The question still remains: 'Is the comparison valid?' or 'Is like being compared with like?' There may be many reasons why a comparison with similar developments elsewhere may not be valid. Differences in examination performance, for example, often reflect differences in student ability rather than teaching quality; or perhaps a relatively low SSR reflects the need to teach a higher than average proportion of students with special needs in small groups. Our own progress over time may have been affected by staff shortages or a changing student profile. And

Figure 7.5 The quality statements addressed by each evaluation instrument

Quality Statement (abbreviated)	Evaluation Instrument									
	1	2A	2B	2C	3A	3B	4	5	6	7
Relevance										
QS1 Relevant portfolio of programmes	✓		✓				✓			
QS2 Appropriate programme content	✓		✓	✓		✓	✓	✓	✓	✓
QS3 Accurate, up-to-date content	✓		✓			✓		✓	✓	✓
Access										
QS4 Appropriate pre-entry guidance	✓	✓			✓					
QS5 Recognition of prior learning			✓	✓			✓			
QS6 Circumstantial restriction on access minimised	✓		✓	✓	✓		✓			
Responsiveness										
QS7 Innovative programmes provided quickly	✓						✓			
QS8 Collaboration with employers in programme delivery	✓		✓	✓			✓			
QS9 Appropriate continuing guidance		✓			✓					
QS10 Programme re-negotiation		✓			✓		✓			
QS11 Self-spaced learning		✓			✓			✓		
QS12 Evaluation by clients		✓			✓		✓	✓		
Appropriateness of learning and teaching methods										
QS13 Purposefulness and rapport; concern for individual achievement			✓	✓		✓		✓		✓
QS14 Appropriate learning environment and resources			✓	✓		✓		✓		✓
QS15 Appropriate learning and teaching methods			✓	✓		✓		✓		✓
Standards										
QS16 Comprehensive assessment approaches						✓		✓	✓	
QS17 Correct application of standards; moderation						✓	✓	✓	✓	

Source: Scottish Education Department (1990)

the targets we have set, or been set, may have been based on quite unrealistic expectations deriving from experience in very different circumstances.

It is essential that performance assessment takes account of such qualifications. It is important too, however, that they are used in a sensible way. Too often in education it is argued that our achievements cannot be assessed because our situation is unique. Interestingly, uniqueness is more often claimed to excuse apparently poor performance than to explain good! Where there are concerns about comparability, a number of strategies are possible:

- Use statistical techniques to attempt to take account of the sources of difference. For example, it may be possible to take account of differences in student ability in comparing examination results.
- Seek other comparators. For example, look for schools, colleges or departments whose characteristics most closely resemble your own. Or alternatively, move to a self-determined progress or target model rather than an externally imposed comparative one.
- Seek a wider variety of information which captures different aspects of achievement.

The discussion and development of these kinds of approaches not only increase the likelihood of drawing valid conclusions; they also enhance in a more general sense our understanding of the problem of assessing 'success'.

Question 6: what conclusions can legitimately be drawn?

We can now begin to put the elements of the development and use of success indicators together. These elements are:

- identification of *performance areas*, with one or more focusing questions for each;
- identification of a number of *success criteria* for each area;
- determination of the *kinds of data* which need to be collected and analysed to present evidence in relation to the chosen criteria;
- determination of the basis on which the level of performance is to be judged (the basis for *comparison*);
- consideration of any *particular circumstances* which may need to be taken into account in interpreting performance.

Figure 7.6 shows the process of analysis for two very different areas of concern.

Figure 7.6 Developing and using success criteria

	Example A (Primary school)	Example B (Further education)
Performance area	Pupil-centred learning	Efficiency of staff utilisation
Success criterion	Pupil–pupil co-operation	Staff:student ratio
Data collection	1 Observation schedule 2 Teacher interview	Annual Monitoring Survey data
Comparator(s)	Progress over time	1 DES target 2 Other similar colleges
Contextual factors	Class sizes have increased	The college's work is biased towards staff-intensive subjects

Worksheet 7.2 comprises a pro forma which can be used to carry out a similar exercise for a programme with which you are concerned.

Once the analysis gets to this point, conclusions should be emerging. However, at this stage it is worth reviewing the process which has been undertaken so far:

- Have the correct areas of performance been identified?
- Have criteria been identified which adequately represent these areas?
- Have data been gathered and processed in appropriate ways to assess achievement against these criteria?
- Have comparisons been made with the right things?
- Has account been taken of particular circumstances that may limit the validity of comparisons?

It may be helpful to draw up in relation to each of these questions a list of the strengths and weaknesses of the process through which success criteria have been defined and in relation to which evidence has been gathered.

WORKSHEET 7.2

ANALYSING PERFORMANCE

Performance area:

Success criteria	Data collection methods	Comparators
1		
2		
3		
4		

Contextual factors:

While doing this, it is desirable to consider how far the information which has been obtained meets a number of basic quality tests:

- Is it *relevant* to the focusing question or questions? It is too easy to collect information on the basis of convenience or cost rather than in relation to clearly defined questions. There is also a danger of collecting far more information than is necessary to form judgements about the performance area in question. It is essential, therefore, that the most rigorous standards of relevance be applied. With resources scarce, it is not acceptable to collect information because it appears 'interesting'.
- Is it an *adequate* response to these questions, in the sense that it reflects the full range or complexity of the issue or does it present a limited view? We have already pointed out the danger of omitting important performance areas from the analysis. This is particularly likely to occur if only one stakeholder is involved in the discussion. For example, teachers may give quite a low priority to assessing the efficiency of a programme in which they are involved; conversely, administrators may not always be too concerned about educational quality provided the resource sums look right.
- Is it *valid*, in the sense that it adequately represents what it is supposed to represent? Perhaps the biggest, and most common, criticism of the performance indicators approach to collecting evidence for evaluative purposes is that quantifiable measures tend to drive out the less quantifiable dimensions of performance, and that the essence of educational quality cannot be captured by such measures either at all (the extreme position) or alone. One problem here is that quantified and standardised measures are much easier to treat comparatively, and external comparison is an important dimension of accountability in education.
- Is it *reliable?* Would similar conclusions be drawn if the information was obtained by somebody else or by some other method? This is a tricky area. Again, quantitative indicators are often more reliable than more qualitative ones, although as the previous paragraph suggests, their reliability may be bought at the expense of their validity. Where reliability is a problem, there is advantage in using more than one kind or source of data in relation to a particular criterion. The idea of 'triangulation' which this involves is addressed in Chapter 8.

Worksheet 7.3 provides a framework for analysing the quality of the information which has been collected.

WORKSHEET 7.3

THE QUALITY OF PERFORMANCE INFORMATION

Performance area:

	Strengths of information	Weaknesses of information
Relevance		
Adequacy		
Validity		
Reliability		

Question 7: what action follows?

In Chapter 3 we referred to the four ways in which information might be managed. Briefly, these were using information *symbolically,* or as a *score-card,* or in an *attention-directing* way, or for *problem-solving.* Information arising from monitoring and evaluation processes, including that relating to success criteria, can serve any of these four purposes. It is often tempting to concentrate on collecting and providing symbolic and scorecard infor-mation, especially where this is sufficient to ensure a quiet life! However, such an approach is not consistent with the kinds of values outlined earlier. It will do little to encourage and facilitate processes of development and even the accountability function will be quite restricted. Performance information, if it is to be of value, must be attention-directing and it must be supplemented by processes which ensure a problem-solving approach to the identified areas of concern. Such a philosophy, however, is not a cosy one. It challenges and it may threaten. It is essential, therefore, to consider carefully the behavioural implications of information management.

INFORMATION AND BEHAVIOUR

A key characteristic of the management of information is that it affects behaviour. Often its effects are intended – when, for example, a teaching approach is changed in response to negative feedback by students. Frequently, though, the methods used to collect or disseminate information have behavioural consequences which not only are unexpected but are the exact opposite of what was hoped for. It is essential, therefore, that those responsible for developing and using success indicators concern themselves not merely with the *technical* adequacy of their information – in terms of its relevance, validity, reliability and so on – but also with the *behavioural* appropriateness of the methods they are using to manage the evaluation process. Questions of perception, expectation and motivation are just as important as those of research design.

Individuals view information management processes, including monitoring and evaluation, in terms of its impact on themselves and their work. They attempt to interpret the purposes of those who are managing the process and they also attempt to envisage the likely consequences of these processes for their position in the organisation. They may accept the 'official' view about these things. Or they may develop their own alternative under-standings on the basis of their previous experiences or their perceptions of how the process of monitoring and evaluation is proceeding. For those managing evaluation, therefore, it is important that the 'style' adopted is consistent with the philosophy espoused. Often this is not the case, and then a number of possible behavioural consequences follow. This can be illustrated by the kinds of responses which may arise in relation to success indicators whose design or use have been ill-judged (Lawler and Rhode, 1976, Ch. 6) Some responses are legitimate, although they are not in the best interests of the organisation and were not intended by those designing the evaluation process. For example:

- Individuals may respond in a *rigidly bureaucratic* way, changing their behaviour uncritically in response to the type of performance implied by the indicator. The often-cited fear of 'teaching to the test' is a good example of this.
- They may adopt *strategic behaviour* designed to make them look good in terms of the indicator. This may involve spending up at the end of the financial year on anything which is available, when 'spending to budget' is an indicator of success and funds cannot be carried over. Or it may mean limiting examination entries to the most able students to ensure a good pass rate.

Other responses are normally considered to be illegitimate, but may still be engaged in by those who feel their interests are threatened:

- *Reporting invalid data* which puts the performance of an individual or group in a good light. An example of this might be the marking of absent students as present on class registers when attendance is used as an indicator of success.
- Attempting to *subvert* the whole information-gathering process by ridiculing it, overloading it and so on.

Such responses arise because information is often used in situations where conflicts of interest exist and people are conscious of the potential impact of information on key decisions. These concerns can be addressed in part by ensuring that indicators cannot easily be manipulated in these ways – the design issue. But this is not always possible, especially where, as is often the case in education, the factor which is being assessed is complex. Furthermore, there is always the danger of a vicious cycle setting in, with 'unacceptable' responses giving rise to tighter restrictions, which lead in turn to new methods of getting round the system being invented. Most of these examples relate to the use of success indicators for accountability purposes alone. Where the developmental dimension dominates, the dangers are fewer, but still they cannot be ignored. People may have differing views about what comprises desirable development. In these circumstances it is necessary to think about the behavioural as well as the technical dimension of information management.

MANAGING SUCCESS INDICATORS

If success indicators are to be used effectively, a number of issues need to be considered carefully before the process of designing them begins.

1 Keep them simple and clear

Success indicators can be developed at a number of levels and in a variety of ways. At the level of the organisation, it is possible to develop very long lists, such as the list of school performance indicators promulgated by the DES (DES, 1989) or the indicators developed by the Department of Employment for evaluating TVEI (Employment Department, 1991). The general consensus, however, is that such lists are of limited use except as stimuli to creative thinking. The aim should be to develop a relatively small number of indicators which capture the key dimensions of success for the programme or activity which is being monitored or evaluated.

The argument for simplicity, however, should not be used as an excuse for unjustifiable reductionism. For example, unadjusted examination scores do not 'speak for themselves'; and examination success will rarely be acceptable as the only dimension of performance which needs to be measured. The point being made here is about obtaining a realistic focus, not an inappropriate oversimplification.

2 Set them after discussion

The best success indicators are those which have been developed by or in partnership with those who work in the area where performance is to be assessed, or who have an interest in the area. Such a process ensures that the indicators have credibility and authority, and this in turn reduces the likelihood that the undesirable consequences outlined above will occur. Success indicators developed in this way will:

- be built upon the educational objectives of the programme which is to be assessed, although they may also take account of externally determined requirements;
- take account of local circumstances, although they will also take account of good practice in comparable circumstances elsewhere to ensure that expectations are not set unrealistically low (or high!).

Put another way, success criteria should take full account of what a programme is trying to do and the circumstances in which it is being done, but they should also put performance in the broader context of the expectations of others and the experience of what is being achieved elsewhere. Those running a programme are key stakeholders, but they are rarely the only ones.

3 Ensure openness

It is important that all those stakeholders who have a legitimate involvement have a shared understanding about the kinds of information that is being gathered and the purposes for which it will be used. This is not always the case. There is a need to be clear about:

- what criteria are to be used;
- why they were chosen;
- what information is to be collected in relation to them;
- how the outcomes of the process will be used.

Information about these things should be communicated in ways appropriate to the particular audience. This is not always easy, especially if the indicators involve a good deal of technical calculation or analysis. It should always be possible, however, with sufficient thought.

4 Use the indicators for developmental purposes

The driving force for the development of success indicators is commonly that of accountability. Those who manage us, or from whom we obtain resources, commonly set the pace or call the tune when indicators are being designed. Even when we take the initiative, it is because we wish to pre-empt the issue before others set the agenda for us. It is highly desirable, however, that indicators are viewed from a developmental perspective whoever takes the initiative and whatever the prime motivation for their development. The intelligent use and interpretation of information about performance can be a powerful influence for change and development.

It is important, therefore that the use of success indicators is seen as an integral part of the monitoring and evaluation *process*, not simply as a parallel activity which is necessary to meet external requirements.

5 Keep them under review

Success indicators may be used for monitoring and/or as part of a review or in-depth investigation. In either case, but particularly for monitoring, it will probably be appropriate to use the same indicators for a period of time, perhaps for a number of years. This has advantages. Not least, a consistent time series of information enables progress to be charted in a helpful way. On the other hand, there is always the danger that the same information will continue to be routinely gathered, despite the fact that objectives have been modified or external factors have changed so as to render any comparison of performance meaningless. It is important, therefore, that the success indicators being used are reviewed regularly

At this point it may be profitable to return to the Stakeholder Analysis, first introduced in Chapter 4, by looking at Exercise 7.2. This exercise, instead of merely identifying the stakeholders and what their expectations might be in relation to a given development, tries to determine what their criteria for success might be. We have also made the assumption that the Stakeholder Analysis 1 (Exercise 4.1) has already been carried out. However, it is possible merely to identify the stakeholders without exploring their expectations in any detail.

EXERCISE 7.2

STAKEHOLDER ANALYSIS (II)

Purpose

To enable participants to explore the success criteria which a programme's key stakeholders apply to it.

Context

A group exercise to be undertaken by a team planning an evaluation.

Materials needed

Copies of Stakeholder Worksheets 2 and 3.

The exercise

1 Identify, either in small groups or as individuals, which groups you consider to be the key stakeholders in a particular development.
2 Then write down, on Stakeholder Worksheet 2, the five or six major stakeholders identified and consider what *success criteria* they might use and what *indicators of success* you think they might look for. Keep this as practical as you can.
3 When this is complete, break into larger groups if possible and, from the lists you have compiled, select perhaps four success criteria and four indicators which you think best reflect the wishes, and the needs, of those with a stake in the development.
4 On Stakeholder Worksheet 3, write down the title of the development or activity and your final lists of success criteria and indicators of performance.

Points to note

- More details about the stakeholder concept can be found in Chapter 4 and Exercise 4.1.
- Obviously, the number of people involved will have a bearing on how this exercise is tackled. For example, it could be carried out by a small group or by a larger group, in which case a good deal of sorting will need to take place. The facilitators will need to adapt the exercise to their particular circumstances.

- The nature of the people involved will also influence how the task is carried out. If there is a mix of professionals and lay people, then it may be better initially to place parents with parents, governors with governors, and teachers with teachers. After that, the groups can be mixed up for the second part of the exercise.
- If you are dealing with a large group, a subgroup might be delegated to undertake the task of drawing up a final list of criteria and indicators. In other words, the exercise is used to canvass opinion and provide a long-list for final consideration.
- If possible, try to carry out this type of exercise before the development begins. It is better to consider your criteria for success and indicators of performance at the planning stage before the development begins.
- Stakeholder Worksheet 3 could be used as a working summary document for your institutional planning for evaluation. It could include such areas as Work Experience, Records of Achievement, Academic Performance or a Staff Development Programme.

STAKEHOLDER WORKSHEET 2

Stakeholder	Success criteria	Indicators of Performance

STAKEHOLDER WORKSHEET 3

Development/activity	Success criteria	Indicators of Performance

© Routledge 1992

CONCLUSION

This chapter has been rather different from most of the others. Some readers will consider it more 'technical', more concerned with content than process. Some will have been reinforced in their concerns about the dangers of adopting approaches to evaluation in education which are too hard-nosed and which embody dangers of serious misuse. As Mrs Angela Rumbold, Minister of State, said in introducing the DES's list of performance indicators for schools in 1989:

> Those of us advocating the use of performance indicators in education must always attach a 'Government Health Warning'. Considered in isolation they are open to misinterpretation and misuse and can damage the health of a school.
>
> (*Education*, 8 December 1989)

We share these concerns. The view that all indicators should carry a 'health warning' is a valid one, and we have tried to indicate in this chapter the kinds of issues that such a warning might address. However, it is also our view that in a world where legitimate pressures for accountability in edu- cation are increasing, it is important that educators are as clear as possible about what they are trying to achieve and the ways in which they wish to demonstrate success. Such clarity is not just valuable in rendering an account, however; it can also provide the basis for gathering information which can really contribute to successful development. The links between evaluation and change will be considered in Chapters 9 and 10. First, we will consider in more depth the range of methods which can be used for gathering information for evaluation purposes.

FURTHER READING

A good deal, of varying value, has been written on performance indicators. For colleges of further education, measures of effectiveness and efficiency are discussed in the DES publication *Managing Colleges Efficiently* (1987) which is a seminal document. The work by Scottish HMI, *Measuring Up: performance indicators in Further Education* (1990) deals with such indicators in a more practical way. The Further Education Unit (FEU) gives a further interesting approach in *Towards an Educational Audit* (1989), and for those in higher education, Cave *et al.*, *The Use of Performance Indicators in Higher Education* (1991) is an important resource.

The schools sector is perhaps less well served in this area. The DES, in *Education*, 8 December 1989, provides a long shopping list of indicators and useful discussions are to be found in the Employment Department's *Guidance on TVEI Performance Indicators* (1991) and the Society of Chief Inspectors and Advisers' *Evaluating the Educational Achievement of Schools and Colleges* (1989). For more critical discussion of the whole area, try two journal articles: Gray and Jesson, 'The negotiation and construction of performance indicators: some principles, proposals and problems' (1990), and Hopkins and Leask, 'Performance indicators and school development' (1989).

Chapter 8

Collecting the data

As we said at the beginning of this book, it may be surprising to find the chapter concerning collecting data appearing so late in the proceedings. However, it cannot be stressed often enough that if information is collected without the thought and action described in the previous chapters, time and effort is likely to be wasted. Many people in schools and colleges have stories to tell of a piece of evaluation that was carried out without sufficient thought and planning and of the frustration and disappointment which was experienced later as a result. This chapter will assume that the issues raised in the previous chapters have been carefully considered. If you have opened the book here to look for guidance on specific methods, please look at the rest of the book before leaping into action.

The chapter offers some guidance on the management of the process of collecting data before outlining in more detail the most commonly used methods. As well as giving some guidance about each method, we list the advantages and disadvantages of each. All methods have their strengths and weaknesses, and some methods are more appropriate in certain circumstances than in others. Unlike the other chapters, this one does not include exercises, as exercises on methods would be inappropriate for this book. However, guidance on further reading is given at the end of the chapter.

CHOOSING A METHOD

The methods of evaluation described are as follows:

- questionnaires;
- interviewing;
- observation;
- documentary evidence;
- visual evidence.

You may also wish to reconsider review sessions of the kind described in Chapter 2.

As part of the process of considering the most appropriate method of evaluation to use in the light of your preliminary work, it is helpful to ask the following questions:

Can this method provide the information we are looking for?

This question applies both to the method you choose and the way in which you apply it. Do you need, for example, a comprehensive overview of the whole staff's reaction to your institution's use of Curriculum Days? If so, a questionnaire may be the obvious method. However, it is very important to establish the detail and depth of the proposed questionnaire. If, on the other hand, you seek insight into the way staff identify their development and training needs, you may need a strategy which involves some in-depth interviewing or a well-structured review meeting that facilitates reflection.

Will this method be acceptable to the people who will be involved?

The reasons that make a method acceptable or unacceptable are varied. Staff would, for example, probably be annoyed if each brief INSET experience was accompanied by a lengthy questionnaire. There is a limit to the number of lessons pupils or students would wish to review. Some methods pose more difficulty than others. For example, most people enjoy being interviewed unless they suspect an underlying motive. Classroom observation is more difficult. If there is any suspicion of undeclared appraisal, for example, there will be problems. In general, the more those who will be taking part in an evaluation activity can be involved in its planning, the more likely they are to find the methods acceptable.

Have we time to plan and apply the method properly, including the necessary analysis of the data collected?

Managing time is as crucial in the area of data collection as in any other. It is essential to be aware from the beginning that the data you collect must be analysed and fed back to any interested parties or stakeholders. The time this takes is often underestimated. How many piles of questionnaires lie in cupboards awaiting the time for their analysis? We wrote in Chapter 1 of the line between evaluation and research. Any evaluation exercise must be feasible within the time and resources available, and at the same time be sufficiently rigorous to provide valid evidence on which to base future decisions. It is helpful to build up smaller pieces of evidence step by step, perhaps using different methods until enough is available.

Is any equipment or back-up support needed and, if so, is it available?

This is a basic question but one that is sometimes not asked. Necessary support is sometimes underestimated. Secretarial support may be assumed without thought for the increased workload or the need to abandon other work if the evaluation work is undertaken. The inclusion in some way of all those who will be involved in an evaluation can prevent a project foundering because a crucial group has not been consulted.

SAMPLING

Sometimes you may want to gather information about a large group of people: for example, all teachers in a particular pyramid, cluster or consortium, or all the pupils or parents in an institution. It would be possible to do this by sending to everyone a focused questionnaire with few or no open questions. However, although this would enable you to gain an overview of perceptions, this might not provide the richness of data that you require. If you need more detailed insight into a particular group's perceptions, you will need to devise ways of selecting a 'sample'.

First, you will need to decide how many people it would be desirable and possible to include. It is generally accepted that a group of at least thirty is necessary if you want to be able to generalise beyond the group involved in the evaluation to the whole group that they represent. However, you may prefer to start with a smaller group and see how your findings relate to your expectations, only moving to a larger group if it is clear that you need more information. You may feel pressured by colleagues to take a larger sample than is necessary. If you need to get into technical debate on these issues, you will find some useful references at the end of the chapter. It is always sensible to make the size of your sample clear and never to make claims that cannot be justified.

The sampling methods you are most likely to consider are as follows:

- *Random sampling*: choosing a sample completely at random, for example, by taking names out of a hat or rolling a dice.
- *Systematic sampling*: names are taken according to some kind of a system, for example, taking every seventh name from an alphabetical list.
- *Stratified sampling*: this involves first subdividing the original list into categories according to, for example, gender or age. Before sampling within each of these groups, you might want to select a representative cross section based on different kinds of criteria, such as length of time in teaching (for teachers), year group or class (for pupils), or part of the catchment area or age of child (for parents). It is important to identify only the factors which are essential, otherwise you will be complicating the sampling procedure unnecessarily.
- *Convenience or opportunistic sampling*: start with the most available people and continue until you are sure that patterns of response are clearly emerging.
- *Deliberate or purposive sampling*: here you decide for some reason that a particular group or individual is appropriate for your purpose. For

example, it might be legitimate to choose to interview all members of a group which is generally accepted to be representative of staff as a whole. Another example would be the selection of a particular child to be shadowed for a day when the purpose of the exercise is to gain an insight of the more general pupil experience. In this latter example, the child or student is the vehicle for the evaluation rather than its subject, and it is helpful to choose a pupil who can cope with such an event. It is not, however, legitimate to choose subjects in this way because you want to bias the findings of the enquiry in any way.

The sampling method needs to be made public and may need to be agreed by the potential subjects. Even when this happens, it is interesting to note how difficult it is for some people to believe they have been selected by chance. It is not uncommon to find individuals either pleased or suspicious that they have been 'chosen'.

PILOTING

Whichever evaluation method you use and however you sample, you will find it helpful to *pilot* or trial the method with a few people first. Otherwise you may find yourself asking the 'wrong' questions, perhaps ones that bias your respondents to a particular answer or that different people understand quite differently. Asking questions plays a part in most evaluation methods. The way in which you ask them will influence the answers that you are given – the data that you collect. For example, your intention may be to discover the effect on classroom practice of a particular project. You may decide that you need brief answers that will provide statistical information and ask a closed question:

'Are you changing your teaching style to promote more active learning?'

However, asking the question in this way may imply that this is the desirable action and may influence the reply that you are given. Less indication of the desired reply is given by:

'Can you describe the effect, if any, on your teaching style?'

If you want responses that are easy to analyse, you could provide a list of possibilities. For example:

'Please tick which of the following teaching styles you prefer.'

or

'Please indicate in which circumstances you use the following teaching styles.'

Alternatively,

'How have you been affected by your involvement in . . .?'

leaves the answer completely open.

Different styles of questioning are appropriate in different circumstances. A questionnaire circulated at the end of a period of development may be designed to provide statistical evidence of the proportion of staff that fall into previously identified categories and hence pose deliberately closed questions. A review session or in-depth interview may use open-ended questions so that all possibilities can be explored. The time available for both the collection and the analysis of data may encourage questions that are focused but also open to more extended answers. The way that people respond to you will also be affected by the way you behave, and this factor is raised at several points in the guidelines that follow on each of the main methods of data collection.

QUESTIONNAIRES

The circulation of questionnaires is the method most widely used in large-scale surveys and for this reason may be the most familiar. This can lead to questionnaires being the first and perhaps only method considered for gathering information. The method is adaptable and can be used in a variety of ways. However, its advantages and disadvantages must be carefully weighed.

Advantages

- Questionnaires can provide an overview and can be particularly useful at the beginning of a process of evaluation in order to reveal the broad span of opinion or activity before deciding which aspects to consider in more depth. At a later stage the proportions of those holding particular perspectives can be clarified.
- They enable everyone to feel that their opinion has been sought and that they have contributed to the debate.
- They enable comparisons between groups and individuals.
- They can be anonymous, which may be important in some circumstances.
- They are flexible. They can be used for a broad survey or as a method of quick review at the end of a session or lesson.
- They can provide quantifiable data.

Disadvantages

- Designing questionnaires is difficult but crucial, particularly in a postal survey where it is not possible for respondents to check what is meant by a particular question.

- You will only be given the answers you ask for. Important issues may be missed or obscured, even if you add 'Is there anything else you would like to say?' as the final question.
- Analysis of the data can be difficult and time-consuming, particularly if the questionnaire is lengthy or where open-ended questions are used.
- The choice of a response scale – for example 'Strongly agree . . . strongly disagree' – may lead to an averaging of responses. The broader the scale, the more likely this is.
- Because questionnaires are impersonal, we may lack information that sets responses into context. For example, anxiety about an imminent set of redeployments may affect morale and therefore responses but not be revealed through the questionnaire.
- Recipients may feel that questionnaires are an imposition, a bore or difficult to fill in, and this may affect the response rate.

Guidelines

- Decide exactly what it is that you need to know that the questionnaire *can* reveal. Do not try to make the questionnaire cover absolutely everything.
- Decide what format you will use, for example:

  ◆ A series of questions with yes/no answers, e.g.

     'Were you given enough information before coming on the course?'
     Yes/No

  ◆ A response scale, e.g.

     'Did you find the session . . .
        very useful/useful/adequate/not useful/useless'

  ◆ Open-ended questions, e.g.

     'Please indicate your reaction to today's programme.'

  The first two of these can be combined with more open-ended questions such as 'Please explain' or 'Please give reasons'.

- Whatever the format, the wording must be clear. Check for ambiguities by piloting the questionnaire with a small number of colleagues or pupils.
- Consider the order of the questions. Is it logical? Will it influence responses?
- Consider whether the questionnaire looks inviting. Would you want to fill it in?
- At every point in the design process, consider whether you will be able to handle the information that will be generated. If your time is limited, do not try to oversimplify complex issues into yes/no questions that will conceal as much as they reveal. If you need more in-depth information,

go for a more open-ended questionnaire with a smaller group of people, or consider another method of collecting the information.

- If you decide that you need to carry out a large-scale, postal questionnaire it is useful to know that it may well involve the sending of two or three reminders before you reach a 70 per cent response. On average, you can expect a 40 per cent response from your first mailing, an additional 20 per cent from the first reminder, a further 10 per cent from the second and 5 per cent from the third. This has clear implications for the timescale involved. An internal questionnaire, for example to all staff in a college, may not present the same problem, particularly where the staff have some understanding of the reason why the questionnaire is being used.

INTERVIEWING

Although interviewing is widely used as a research technique and by external evaluators, samples tend to be small, so few teachers may be familiar with this method. Interviewing can be approached in a number of ways, varying from being used as a verbal questionnaire, perhaps with pupils whose reading and writing skills are limited, to an open-ended conversation between colleagues. However, as a method of evaluation, interviews are usually structured in some way around particular questions, although interviewees may, and do, choose to range beyond the questions in their answers.

Advantages

- Interviews can provide rich data and give considerable insight into perceptions and attitudes.
- Misperceptions or misunderstandings about what is being asked can be recognised and dealt with at the time.
- It can be rewarding to be interviewed. The interviewee has an opportunity to express opinions, clarify ideas and to feel that these are valued.
- The interview can prove a learning experience for both parties.

Disadvantages

- Interviews are time-consuming at all stages. It is difficult to deal with more than a small sample.
- The breadth and amount of data may make interpretation and analysis difficult.
- The interviewer's style and status may influence the response. This can prove problematic if several interviewers are involved or when teachers interview pupils.
- There is a danger of bias, both in the way that the interview is conducted and in the way that comments are recorded.

- The interview itself cannot be anonymous. If quotations are used in a report they may be identifiable, even if the speaker is not named, particularly within a group who know each other well.

Guidelines

- Unless you have unlimited time available it is best to structure your interview. Decide what it is you want to know and devise the questions that will elicit this information.
- Think carefully about the ordering of the questions.
- Decide how you are going to record the interviews. Both the use of a tape recorder and the writing of notes can be off-putting to the interviewee. The tape recorder has the advantage of enabling the interviewer to focus on listening and asking supplementary questions, but the recording has to be transcribed in some way later. Transcribing is a lengthy process. It is estimated that one hour of tape takes up to 8 hours to transcribe in full. However, it is unlikely that an evaluation exercise would require such detail. It may be enough to make notes of what is said, with the occasional literal transcription if you want illustrative quotes for a report. Again there is a danger of bias. If you make notes, you may decide to write down as much as possible and hope you can read it later; or you may opt to note only major points. You may attempt to devise a checklist against which to record – this may be difficult to devise and use. Alternatively, you may choose to make no notes until the end, when you and the interviewee decide together what to record.
- Before you begin to interview it is helpful to tape record (or video!) yourself interviewing a volunteer colleague or student. You can then consider your style of interviewing. For example, do you dominate the conversation? Do you influence responses by making judgemental statements or by your expression?
- It is helpful to give the interviewee a copy of your questions or to explain the areas that you intend to cover before the interview takes place.
- In the interview situation, make sure that the interviewee is feeling relaxed. It is helpful to be in comfortable surroundings without too much background noise. Stress that you will turn the tape off or stop writing if the interviewee asks you to. Do not launch abruptly into your questions. Within limits, allow the interviewee to stray from the topic if necessary. Do not ask questions that have already been answered, except to ask if there is anything else to add. Finish by asking 'Is there anything else you would like to say that I haven't given you the opportunity to say?'
- In some circumstances it may be helpful to interview a small group together. Pupils in particular often feel more confident in this setting. Both tape and written recording is more difficult in this situation. Agreeing

together what points to record at the end may be the most practical approach in these circumstances.

OBSERVATION

Classroom observation is becoming more commonplace in schools. Activities such as pupil tracking are used to help teachers gain insight into the pupils' experience of schooling. Paired teaching, with an element of mutual observation, is a useful strategy in considering the issue of teaching and learning styles.

Advantages

- Observation can take into account and record group processes.
- Observation can provide insight into events as they happen.
- Quantitative observations can sometimes challenge our existing perceptions and assumptions.
- It is a flexible technique. For example, teachers can observe their own classrooms, engage in paired observation as equals, or act as participant or outside observers.

Disadvantages

- Observation provides a 'snapshot' of an event. It is hard to establish how typical this is.
- The presence of an observer often influences what happens.
- It is impossible to observe everything all of the time. Open observation can be confusing and closed, checklist observation may limit what is seen.

Guidelines

- It is important to establish the purpose and focus of the observation before deciding on the method you will use. For example, if the purpose is to see whether a teacher is spending more time interacting with particular pupils, a tick-list tally may be enough. However, if you want to establish what effect this is having, it would be inappropriate and inadequate.
- It is essential to negotiate with anyone involved in being observed why the observation is taking place, what will be observed, how and for what purpose. It is important to honour this agreement and not to be drawn into discussion of issues outside it with those involved or with anyone else.
- An observation checklist can be helpful, but if it is too complex or too simple you may spend more time trying to decide where to put your ticks or comments than actually observing.

- There are other ways of reducing the problem of how much to observe. It is possible to focus on a small number of pupils or participants. For example, pupil tracking often involves one pupil. Timing the observations is an alternative. Note what is happening at specific intervals. These may be more or less frequent according to whether you are an outside observer or participant.
- Be careful to note what you actually see, not what you assume to be happening. This is surprisingly difficult. Look through your notes carefully afterwards to check for assumptions.
- If your agreement includes checking your perceptions with those involved afterwards, be tactful. Do not say 'You should have . . .' or 'Why didn't you . . .?' Again, feed back what you saw not what you assumed or felt about it.
- Perhaps more than any other method, observation takes practice. Be sure to include time for this in your estimate of the time involved.

DOCUMENTARY EVIDENCE

There are many sources of information about developments and initiatives. There is often a considerable amount of documentation available and this can provide evidence of the way that a project (and thinking about a project) develops over time. Documentary evidence can be of several kinds: for example, initial proposals, on-going reports, such as curriculum statements and materials, letters, diaries and journals. The latter can be personal and confidential reflections, open accounts of what is taking place or individual or shared 'critical incident diaries' in which interesting incidents are recorded as they happen.

Advantages

- Documentary evidence can be relatively easy to collect.
- Examination of written materials will form an essential part of an evaluation of curriculum developments.
- Reports, materials, minutes and some letters are public documents and, if this is so, confidentiality is not a problem.
- Documents can provide evidence of what happened in the past which can be compared with individual recollections.
- Letters, diaries and journals can provide insight into the development of perceptions over a period of time.
- Diaries and journals in particular provide an opportunity for the writers to reflect on, and make sense of, what is happening and therefore contribute to the learning process and the way a project develops.

Disadvantages

- Because documentation may be partial, or part of the writer's desire to influence rather than record, it may distort or conceal aspects of a development.
- Letters, diaries and journals may be confidential documents and therefore not available to others.
- Reports, materials and minutes may be rather dry, 'safe' documents which contain no hint of important aspects of a development such as the feelings generated or the intensity of the debate.
- There may be a large amount of documentation available which may be tedious and difficult to analyse.

Guidelines

- Always check the confidentiality status of documents before using them, particularly if you wish to use extracts in a report.
- If documents such as diaries are confidential, this may be overcome by asking diarists for an account they are prepared to share that is based on their journals.
- Analysis of curriculum materials may take the form of:

  goal analysis – listing stated or inferred aims and objectives;
  content analysis – for example, listing concepts, analysing tasks, locating instances of bias;
  textual analysis – examining the nature of the argument, examples and conclusions;
  readability – the reading level required.

  (McCormick and James, 1988: 271)

PHOTOGRAPHS AND DRAWINGS

Visual evidence such as photographs or drawings can often capture particular aspects of what is happening and offer new illumination.

Advantages

- Photographs and drawings can offer illumination of a project or of perception in a way that is quite different from other methods of evaluation. For example, on a management course, groups of headteachers were asked to draw how they saw themselves in their role. The resultant images of jugglers, plate spinners, lion tamers, load bearers and a smiling face with a tearful image inside provided rich insight into their perceptions.

- These methods can complement and enhance other forms of evaluation.
- It is possible to collect a good deal of visual evidence in a short period of time.
- They capture the moment and feelings that might later be forgotten.

Disadvantages

- Photographs can provide only limited evidence. There is no evidence of what is said, for example. It is also difficult to establish how typical the moments recorded were.
- There is subjective photographer bias in both what is photographed and how the film is printed. For example, a small part of a photograph can be blown up and offer a particular view which the whole photograph would not substantiate.
- The presence of a camera may affect the behaviour of participants.
- Drawings may be difficult to interpret without an explanation from the artists.

Guidelines

- Photographs are difficult to anonymise and therefore their use should be cleared by the subjects.
- Visual evidence is most likely to be used to bring life to some other form of evidence.

MANAGING THE COLLECTION OF DATA

Whichever of these methods you choose, do not get carried away. References to the dangers of being overwhelmed by data have recurred throughout this book. Collect moderate amounts of information; only seek more if you find the evidence confusing or contradictory. If the evidence is inconclusive, check whether this is enough to know or whether it is necessary for you to know more. One school wanted evidence of the value to pupils of work experience. They examined the Project Trident questionnaires already completed by pupils and extracted the relevant information. They involved one form of fifth-formers in a structured review of their experiences. They collected further evidence from the English GCSE assignments of another form based on the same topic. From these three different sources they were able to build a picture of the meaning pupils made of their experiences that had both breadth and depth but which had involved only a manageable amount of time.

This is an excellent example of how to collect an amount of information that is manageable yet sufficient to provide consistent and useful evidence. This had been achieved by:

- Devising economic methods of gathering information: using existing sources (the questionnaires and the English assignments) and reviewing and analysing the responses of pupils in one class.
- Collecting the data in different ways: questionnaires, written assignments and shared review.
- Collecting the data from different samples: the questionnaire covered all pupils; the assignments were from one class; and the review process involved another.

Incidentally, these teachers were impressed by the quality of work produced in these evaluations and began to wonder why pupils produced lesser offerings in other circumstances.

The technical term for collecting data in a variety of ways and from more than one sample is 'triangulation'. As with these teachers, if you can find three different ways of looking at an issue and come up with coherent findings, you can be fairly sure that these will provide valid evidence on which to proceed. Economic triangulation of this kind can be very helpful. Wherever possible, combine methods and work with others. The following cameo illustrates the further advantage of working with colleagues from another or several other institutions in evaluating an issue of common interest.

Cameo

Evaluating across schools

Phase 1

Small teams of staff from six schools came together out of a keen interest in investigating the processes of evaluation. After a fair amount of negotiation amongst them, it was decided to take Equal Opportunities as a shared area of study. There was, in a workshop setting, discussion amongst the members of what it was that each school would want to look at, and the ways in which they wanted to do it. There was also a great deal of discussion as to the *meaning* of Equal Opportunities. This discussion was of very great importance because it was clear that there were not only different definitions to discuss but also very different values.

Phase 2

Back in the schools, staff made more detailed decisions about what they were going to do and the types of information they would seek.

Some schools used qualitative methods, such as conversational interviews; others relied more on quantitative methods such as structured
interviews and questionnaires. Some schools chose only to interview
teaching staff; others conducted interviews with staff and students.
When students were involved, this sometimes involved individual
interviews and sometimes the use of single- or mixed-sex group
settings. In all cases the evaluation strategy was one developed by the
team. This development of the strategy was undertaken with maximum
flexibility. Although the evaluators knew where they were ultimately
going, it was important to be flexible about methods and about choices
as to whom to interview. For example, in one school the decision to
interview some of the youngest pupils was taken late in the day, when
it became apparent from other interviews that there was an important
group of people whose views had not been taken into account.

Another key aspect of the strategy was the planning of people's
availability for the projects. This was particularly important because the
project had to be fitted into the normal extremely busy course of life in
the schools. Decisions had to be made that reflected the need for
economy in time management.

Phase 3

At a second workshop some three months later, there were presentations of the outcomes of the research and discussions about how
the work that the research had initiated would be continued.

In all the presentations there were a number of powerful suggestions made about the future development of Equal Opportunities in
the schools. This confirmed that, for this group, this had been a useful
way of undertaking the evaluation. All the groups had found 'doing'
evaluation interesting and involving. Each team explained to the others
what it had done. In all the presentations there was an awareness of
both the strengths and weaknesses of the evaluators in terms of competence, and a number of them identified areas where they wanted to
develop skills. Although they had all identified time as a critical
pressure on them, they also suggested that projects such as this helped
to embed evaluation as a 'normal' activity in the school.

The group also identified gains in such areas as:

- development of team approaches in doing the evaluation;
- developing new patterns of consultation in the school;
- using the evaluation to take a fresh view of existing data resources
  in the school;

- enlarging competence in the management of evaluation in a broader sense.

A common by-product of doing the evaluation was an enhanced understanding of management issues in the schools themselves. In one case there was also enhanced understanding of the political issues in the school. Related to this for the teacher who was acting as change agent, undertaking the evaluation itself, especially in the interview situations, was a useful way of raising awareness. It was suggested by more than one of the members that this way of doing evaluation opens up the possibility of debate about areas that some members of staff felt were settled. This was seen as positive. In some cases the evaluation also involved interviews with the pupils/students in the school. This served either to reinforce an already existing culture of openness in the school, or was seen as contributing to its creation.

The school team in this cameo were given some support in the process by being brought together initially to carry out the work and by the structuring of the two whole-group meetings. Such support in providing a framework for action is helpful but not essential. There were key events in each of the three phases described above which are replicable in other situations.

Phase 1

- Deciding on the focus of the evaluation.
- Discussing the nature of the topic.
- Making initial decisions about where and from whom information would be collected.

Phase 2

- Considering in more detail, developmentally and flexibly, the people who would give information and the methods of data collection.
- Considering the different phases of the evaluation, starting with a general picture of the issue that was the shared focus of study, checking out others' perceptions, and establishing which findings are trustworthy.
- Deciding how best to use the evaluators' time. This included the development of a team spirit amongst those involved.

Phase 3

- Sharing with colleagues at two levels: actual *outcomes* in relation to the issues studied and evaluated, and what the *process* of evaluation itself had revealed about schools in general, about doing evaluation and about team work.

- Establishing the 'next steps' in the development of evaluation processes.

One of the benefits for the participants in this activity was the legitimate 'time out' from their individual schools during which they could reflect, plan and test out these plans with others grappling with similar situations. This process enhanced the learning about their shared focus of interest and about pupils, parents, teachers and schools as organisations. This juxtaposition of things that are in common and things that are different is very helpful. Whenever you have the opportunity to work collaboratively in this way, take it and use it to the full.

The second cameo covers a rather different aspect of managing evaluation, that of the need for both formative and summative evaluation of a fixed-term project. A seconded team of primary teachers wanted to evaluate their work for two reasons. First, they wanted to ensure that they learned as much as they could in a short period of time; and second, they felt themselves to be highly accountable because of the nature of their work.

Cameo

Evaluating a primary project

As a project funded by an LEA at a time of financial restraint, we were aware from the beginning that our work would be subject to a good deal of scrutiny. This awareness gave an extra edge to our keenness to evaluate our work as we went along. Most of the team were primary class teachers, seconded for two years, and new to working with teachers across an authority in this way. We needed feedback on how well we were doing, but we also knew that we had a very large task, introducing our project to every primary school in the city. We did not want to spend more time evaluating than doing.

We were helped by meeting with the INSET evaluator at an early stage and discussing all the ways in which we could be building up evaluation activities, procedures and evidence as we went along. We realised that we needed to keep a detailed record of the schools we visited, the courses we ran and all other activities as part of organising our workload and setting priorities. We also needed this information to report to our steering committee. We wanted to ask teachers to fill in brief questionnaires at the end of any INSET sessions we provided. We wanted to know how well we were meeting their expectations and to get information which would help our future planning. We would, as a matter of routine, keep minutes of our team and steering committee meetings. We were already setting ourselves targets or aims as part of the process of clarifying what we had to do, and were in the process of

---

clearing these with the same committee. We agreed to meet once a term to review our progress against these targets.

During the second year of the project, we spent some time considering what progress schools might reasonably have made. We drew up a list of questions about the number of schools and classes that were putting the work of the project into practice and identified what we felt to be key features that we might expect to see. Inevitably we had felt more welcome and been more involved in some schools than others and we needed to build up an authority-wide picture. We visited every school during the last term of the project and were able to gain the answers to our questions. This turned out to be a most cheering experience. We had worried about getting accurate information and did not want headteachers to tell us what they thought we wanted to hear. However, we found that we were presented with work stimulated by our project, that other teachers came to talk to us or invited us into their classrooms and, best of all, that even schools where we felt there had been little response were becoming involved.

With the help of the INSET evaluator, we found we were able to bring the wide variety of evaluation evidence we had collected quickly and coherently together. We were fortunate in that she undertook to carry out any further analysis that was needed and to write the final report. That report also included a summary of the comments from the minutes of governors' meetings about the impact of the project in schools. The project was a major LEA initiative and we were pleased to see that it had been generally welcomed by governors.

As a high-profile project, we frequently felt rather vulnerable. The self-evaluation activities that we undertook helped us in two ways. First, they provided us with useful information that enabled us to make changes as we went along and therefore improve the quality of our work. They also meant that we felt more confident because we could answer questions that were raised. For example, one INSET session did not go particularly well, for a variety of reasons, but we had the evidence from our course questionnaires that this session was the exception rather than the rule.

During the two years, we built up a considerable amount of useful information about our progress. We had a record of all the work we had undertaken and all the review meetings. We were able to produce some statistical evidence from the INSET questionnaires and the interviews in schools. The additional information from the governors' reports was very useful and relatively easy to obtain. The most surprising discovery was that evaluation did not have to take over our lives. Almost all the evidence that we collected was a necessary part of doing the job.

This cameo illustrates the benefits of careful planning. Through monitoring key information, carrying out regular reviews and pursuing more in-depth enquiry when necessary, this team of teachers was able to collect a considerable quantity of valuable information in a manageable way. The information was also of different but complementary types, thus helping to provide comprehensive and broad-based feedback and the basis for an interesting report.

ANALYSING THE DATA

Once the data has been collected, sense has to be made of it if it is to be turned into usable information. This requires a process of analysis: sorting and collating the data and reducing it to manageable proportions. This must be done with care not to distort or bias the results. An impressionistic account is not enough, but it is as important with analysis as with anything else to know when enough is enough. Analysis can be carried out by an individual or by a small or even large group. In a group review, for example, everyone is involved in making sense of the information, and this may include pupils or students. However, in this instance, the issue is the analysis of data gathered through the methods described in this chapter. Analysis by an individual or small group will be discussed, followed by a process for involving a larger group.

If the information you have collected is in the form of tick-box responses, the task is one of counting. If the material is more open, start by reading everything through twice. If, despite all the warnings, you have large amounts of material, read a quarter or a half of what you have twice. This may seem a time-consuming process. It may make you panic a little, but this will pass. As you read you will find that certain points or issues are beginning to recur. Do not try to make too much sense too soon, and continue to read until you have finished this task.

Then, as a group or individually, begin to draw up a set of categories that covers the issues you have begun to identify. See if you can apply these categories to the questionnaire, interview or observation data that you have. As you progress, you may find you need to add new categories or perhaps reduce your original list. For example, 'talking to friends', 'repeatedly sharpening pencil', 'reading a comic', may all be subsumed into 'off-task activities'. Keep modifying until you have a workable set. This process is seldom as difficult as it may sound. Categories and patterns emerge quite quickly. You may notice with interviews, for example, that people are making a point more or less eloquently, but it is essentially the same point.

Once your categories are clear, go through your information again to note the span and recurrence within each category. If you come across individual exceptions, note these if you wish, but make sure you note them as such. You may want to make a straightforward tally, for example:

Pupils use the term 'boring' to denote:

too difficult	~~1111~~ ~~1111~~
too easy	111
covered in another subject	~~1111~~
not relevant	11
not interesting	~~1111~~ 1

You may want to do something more complicated – for example, to check if there is a connection between staff responses to a particular question and the number of years they have been teaching. If there is a connection, it is probable that this too will emerge quite quickly. If there is no evidence in the first ten to fifteen replies, then abandon the search. If your original sample is too small to enable such an indication to be firmly established but suggests there may be a connection, you will need to devise a larger-scale process which can test this hypothesis.

This sorting and analysing process can be carried out by a larger group. It may be helpful or desirable to work in this way. For example, a group which has planned a Curriculum Day, or a year group which has been evaluating pupil responses to a curriculum initiative, may wish to take part in making sense of the information. It may be advisable to involve a key group of individuals in the process in order to increase their interest in, and understanding of, the findings. Of course, such groups may feel they are very happy, indeed anxious, to delegate this responsibility to others. Some tasks, however, such as analysing a large number of questionnaires or flipchart feedback sheets, may be difficult for an individual to handle on his or her own.

If you can gather together a group of perhaps six to ten participants to analyse a large number of items, split these evenly among the group:

- If there are tick-boxes to tally, each person records their scores for the first question. If there are more open-ended questions, each individual reads the answers to the first question and writes down a brief summary of the responses. It is possible to add one or two representative quotations to the summary if you want some 'colour' for the final report.
- Each person then reads their summary out loud in turn. Check for apparent inconsistencies. Are some responses being biased by the summarisers or is this just a bunching of particular kinds of replies?
- Continue this process until all the questions have been analysed in this way.
- Each person then collects the summaries for a particular question or questions and produces a final summary of these, including quotations if desired. These are also read aloud to provide a final opportunity to check the balance of reporting.
- These summaries can be put together to form the basis of a report with, perhaps, the inclusion of an agreed introduction and conclusion.

Whether you have analysed your data on your own or as a group, always conclude by discussing, or thinking about, what you have learned about evaluation as well as what you have learned about the issue under review. What have you learned about the method you used, about constructing a questionnaire, carrying out and recording interviews or observations, for example? What makes analysis easy? What makes it difficult? What is lost or gained in each of these two situations? What will you do differently next time?

CONCLUSION

This chapter has outlined the main evaluation methods, highlighting the advantages and disadvantages of each, and described some ways of analysing results. Throughout, the emphasis has been on making the process as rigorous as necessary and no more. It is very important that you do not distort or bias the findings from enquiry of this kind. There is always the danger of discrediting both the process and yourself (or selves). This can happen accidently, through rushing the process or through deciding early on what the results are going to be. If you were sure from the beginning what your findings would be, you would not really need to carry out the enquiry. Perhaps even more importantly, in effect you would be wasting everyone's time and losing the potential of learning from the process. It is very helpful for everyone to be aware that effective evaluation must hold the potential of surprise.

FURTHER READING

The matters dealt with in this chapter are developed in greater detail and with many practical examples in two books by authors with a good deal of personal experience of educational evaluation: Hopkins, *A Teacher's Guide to Classroom Research* (1985), and Walker, *Doing Research* (1985). The specific issue of research methods for managers in general is explored in Gill and Johnson, *Research Methods for Managers* (1991) and Easterby-Smith *et al.*, *Management Research* (1991).

If you are interested in moving more towards the 'research' end of the continuum described in Chapter 1, the three following books take very different approaches. Cohen and Manion, *Research Methods in Education* (1989), works through research methods systematically and in some detail, stressing the importance of a thorough and scientific approach. Burgess, *Field Methods in the Study of Education* (1985), contains a series of chapters on qualitative and ethnographic methods such as observation, photography, action research and case study. In Reason and Rowan, *Human Inquiry in Action* (1981), you will find forty chapters challenging these more traditional approaches to research (for example, Torbett on 'Why educational research is so uneducational') and placing new emphasis on collaborative and participative approaches.

Chapter 9

Changing practice

Chapter 1 suggests that a key characteristic of evaluation is that it should contribute to decision-making. If evaluation is to fulfil its purpose, and to be seen by busy practitioners to be worth the time and effort, it must make some kind of difference to what happens next. Sometimes evaluation processes do not contribute in this way. This may be for several reasons, for example:

- The process concludes with recommendations requiring resources that are not available.
- The evaluation has not addressed the central questions.
- Key people have not been involved in the process and are not committed to taking any action as a result.
- The evaluator(s) does not have, or does not present, convincing data with which to back his/her recommendations.
- A powerful individual or group does not wish to make the changes indicated: the micro-politics of the organisation get in the way.
- The evaluation has highlighted issues which indicate some unpalatable and difficult conclusions. Learning in such situations is seldom an easy or straightforward matter.

Spending hours, or even weeks, finding out something that others do not want to hear about is deeply frustrating. The earlier chapters of this book are designed to help you to minimise the first four of the problems outlined above. These matters are most directly the responsibility of those carrying out an evaluation.

This chapter opens by taking the process a stage further, through considering helpful procedures for feedback, reporting and the presentation of findings and recommendations. Although this chapter occurs towards the end of the book, it has already been acknowledged that thinking about feedback cannot be left to the end of a process of enquiry. The emphasis on the involvement of key others throughout is part of the informing process. However, it is necessary at this point to consider the specific issue of feedback in some detail. Attention is then turned to the last two of the issues listed above. First we offer some approaches for dealing with the micro-politics of your organisation, and then, lastly, we consider the factors that influence an individual's willingness to learn.

FEEDBACK AND REPORTING

Part of the process of planning an evaluation enquiry is to be clear from the beginning what will be reported, to whom, when and in what form – although, of course, this may be renegotiable if necessary. Stakeholder Analysis (see Exercises 4.1 and 7.2) is useful in this context. Those who are interested in results fall into two broad groups:

- participants in the enquiry, or, indeed, the monitoring or review;
- other interested parties.

It is always important to remember that *all* those who have been involved in some way are likely to be interested in the consequences. It is surprising how often pupils are forgotten in this context. They may be interviewed or fill in questionnaires and then never hear about what has happened as a result.

Reporting can be divided into two types:

- regular, formative feedback and reporting;
- summative, more formal reporting.

In both of these it is important to remember the ethical issues raised in Chapter 5. This means that, whatever the form of reporting, it is better to stick to issues not personalities and to try to design your feedback to share the learning in a way that raises the general commitment to take appropriate action as a consequence.

Formative feedback and reporting

To participants in the evaluation

Although those involved in an evaluation process will be aware of what is taking place, this is not usually enough. On-going reporting needs to be formalised to some degree in order to ensure clarity about what is happening and what is being learned. This can be carried out in several different ways. For example:

- brief minutes of meetings circulated to all participants and filed;
- keeping a common, open, evaluation diary in which those involved in different aspects of the evaluation write regular brief reports;
- regular, brief and well-structured meetings for review or exchange of information, the conclusions of which are recorded in written form;
- involving the whole group in analysis and writing up the findings as described in Chapter 8. It is interesting how often involvement of this kind increases interest in the implications of the analysis.

It is important to hold the balance between recording more than is necessary and recording so little that valuable on-going insights are lost. Keep it brief, keep it to the point, but keep it.

To other interested parties

Here there are two main problems. The first is that of identifying who the interested parties are. Some indication of this was given at the beginning of Chapter 6. Basically, other interested parties can be of three types:

- *Contributors to evaluation*: those who were observed, for example, or whose opinions were sought but who were not part of the evaluation team. Pupils and students often – perhaps too often – fall into this category, but so could many other groups, such as local employers.
- *Agents of accountability*: those requiring evaluation to be carried out and expecting to be informed of results. External funding agencies such as the Department of Employment, the DES or the LEA are the obvious examples here, but specific pieces of evaluation may be commissioned by groups such as governors or a cluster or pyramid working party.
- *Other supporters or interested groups*: those who are not involved in commissioning, carrying out or contributing to the evaluation but who are nevertheless interested in the results. These might be other staff, parents, governors or other institutions, and they may or may not be in a position to respond to the implications of any findings.

Having identified the groups that might want or need to know, it is necessary to address the second problem – how to keep these groups sufficiently informed without overwhelming them. This informing process can also be carried out in several ways:

- All or any of the suggestions above can be made available to others as a matter of course, perhaps to the senior management team, or on request.
- Representatives of the evaluation group, or even the whole group, could give regular or occasional verbal feedback to interested groups.
- Short regular reports could be included in other meetings, such as staff or governors' meetings.
- Brief written reports can be circulated at intervals or be available at a recognised spot such as a notice board.

Different reporting styles will be appropriate for different groups, but whatever the style, it is as important not to overdo the reporting as it is to neglect it. Never-ending streams of information will be off-putting; and you may be met with enquiries as to whether or not you have too much time on your hands. Of course, not everyone will read or hear what you say, but communication is a two-way process and your main responsibility lies in making information available and doing so in an accessible way. It may be necessary or helpful to have conversations with individuals or groups before or after an informing meeting in order to head off difficulties or to pick up and smooth ruffled feathers after the event. Of course, those most directly involved will ideally have been participating in the process. However, it is possible for individuals or groups to find it quite difficult to be presented with a report on developments being carried out in another part of the school or college. For example, in a school, if one year group is reporting on findings about pupils' reactions to new teaching and learning styles, this may be perceived as threatening by other year groups who are resisting such developments.

This kind of on-going feedback and reporting is an integral part of the evaluation process. You will need to spend some time thinking about what you have learned about feeding back and the process of communication at the end of any such experience. Verbal reports in particular can be seen as part of an on-going evaluative conversation, from which both the presenters and questioners of reports can learn. On-going findings will, to some extent, be tentative and open to question, but anyone who challenges these findings should be encouraged either to provide different, valid evidence of his or her own or preferably to join in the process of enquiry.

Summative or formal reporting

Formal written reports are not automatically necessary; even if desirable, they do not always need to be lengthy. If you know or think that you are required to produce 'a Report' check with the individual or body that requires it as to what exactly is needed. Written records have the advantage of providing a permanent record and appear in some way to be more authoritative. However, no matter how brief, elegantly written, well-produced and inviting a report may be, it may very well be put on one side for further reading only to be submerged by subsequent documents. It is, therefore, helpful to complement written reports with verbal reports to interested groups with an opportunity for discussion.

If you are writing a report, give details of how information was obtained and from which groups. If you are using quotations or examples based on individuals' views or experience, check that they are happy with this. You may have been given a general clearance by all those involved, but check again if you think there is any chance of a problem. A particular turn of phrase may be recognisable: for example, in a situation where people know each other well. It is important to make the data on which you base any conclusions or recommendations quite clear and to be careful never to make claims that your data cannot substantiate.

You may need to acknowledge the limitations as well as the strengths of your enquiry and point to areas where further investigation may be needed. Keep your report brief and to the point. If you are required to produce a lengthy document, it is very helpful to produce a two- or three-page summary to accompany the longer version or for wider circulation. The audience for whom the report is written will influence its style and possibly its content, but remember that once a written document is produced it might end up anywhere. This does not mean that you should only produce anodyne, safe documents, but it does mean that it is foolish to write a report that could easily be misinterpreted in a damaging way.

If you back up the report with its verbal presentation to interested groups, each presentation can be geared towards its particular audience. It is helpful, if possible or practicable, to talk to small rather than large groups and this is also less stressful for the evaluators. It will generally be helpful to decide as a group where your particular strengths lie. Some people write or talk more easily than others. Perhaps one or two people will decide to take the main responsibility for writing a report, others for talking to specific groups, and others for offering feedback and support. Remember, it is difficult if not impossible for a committee to write a report.

Effective reporting is a key element in influencing future action. Throughout the verbal or written report, the 'tone' is as important as the content. One strategy for raising difficult points is to present the data in a balanced and unemotional way and then pose some key questions rather than make recommendations. However neutral and objective you set out to be, you may find that you begin to feel quite strongly about the import of the data you have gathered. Whether or not your feelings are involved in this way, you will certainly feel responsible for putting the points across effectively. The more open and collaborative the process of enquiry has been, the more people will feel that they have a stake in the findings. Quite often changes will have been made well before the final reporting stage. The skill in on-going and final reporting lies in highlighting success and raising difficulties in a way that others can hear and accept. Otherwise those who see themselves as having been found wanting may put all their energies into rejecting the process, the recommendations, and the evaluators' right to make them.

In your own institution you should be aware of sensitive matters, vulnerable groups, hidden agendas, interpersonal or intergroup alliances or conflicts which might influence the process of reporting and the response. Understanding and handling these micro-political dimensions is another key area in ensuring that any evaluation enquiry is used to good purpose.

CHANGING PRACTICE

Whatever the nature of the evaluation that you are managing, it is a mistake to assume that your objectives, your expectations, or your values will be shared by all of those with whom you will have to work. It may be the case that there is a good deal of consensus about these things, and that this consensus will be translated into commitment, but this is often not the case. It cannot be assumed that all the members of an educational organisation, let alone its diverse external constituencies, share a common view about purposes, priorities or practice; and if they do not, their responses are likely to be coloured by their perceptions of the likely impact of the evaluation on their interests. Even the most well-planned change can go wrong if insufficient attention is given to the micro-political forces at work. These forces can be examined by considering two key variables: orientation and power.

The *orientation* of individuals and groups to any particular change can vary considerably. Some will support it and others will resist it. And the degree of support or resistance may vary from the essentially passive to the extremely active. A major determinant of levels of support and resistance among those affected by a proposed change will be their perceptions of how their interests are likely to be affected. Ball (1987) distinguishes between three kinds of interests which teachers, in particular, hold. *Vested interests* arise from the rewards associated with an individual's work: in addition to such obvious concerns as salary and career prospects, they include such things as the facilities and materials available to do the job and 'territory' such as office or classroom space or a defined part of the curriculum. *Ideological interests* relate to personal values and philosophical commitments: for example, to mixed-ability teaching or to enhancing access to further and higher education. Finally, *self-interests* relate to an individual's sense of identity and aspiration to be a particular kind of teacher: for example, a subject specialist or a facilitator or an enforcer of discipline. These interests will deeply colour individuals' views about what is desirable and what is undesirable in their organisations; the differences which arise are the stuff of micro-politics.

Differences in orientation towards a change, however, only represent half of the micro-political picture. Individuals and groups also differ in their ability to influence situations: they differ in the *power* available to them. Power is the ability to influence people and situations: to cause individuals to act and things to happen which would not have happened if the power had not been applied. There is an enormous literature on the sources and uses of power in organisations. There is general agreement, however, that power can derive from a number of sources. The most important of these are:

- *Expertise*: the possession of specialist knowledge or skills.
- *Control of information*: the ability to obstruct or direct information flows to ensure that particular items reach, or do not reach, particular individuals or groups.
- *Control of rewards and resources*: the ability to allocate resources such as finance, status or career advancement.
- *Formal authority*: the occupation of a formal position in the organisation which entitles the incumbent to expect others to comply with his or her directions or requests.

- *Physical force*: the ability to coerce others by physical punishment or restraint.
- *Personality*: the possession of personal characteristics which cause others to identify with an individual's views and purposes.

All of these sources of power can be seen in operation in most educational organisations, but the most significant are usually those of expertise and formal position, with the latter being reinforced by the control of information and rewards to which it gives rise.

Before considering any change, it is useful to map the forces which are likely to be at work. To do this, undertake Exercise 9.1.

EXERCISE 9.1

MICRO-POLITICAL MAPPING

Purpose

To enable participants to identify the orientation of members of the organisation towards a proposed innovation, their potential influence, and the implications of these factors for possible implementation strategies.

Context

This activity can be undertaken individually, but it is best carried out by a group which has an interest in the process of implementing a proposed change which has arisen as the result of an evaluation.

Materials needed

Copies of Worksheets 1 and 2. Flipchart paper and pens.

The exercise

1 Participants identify individually all those individuals and groups who are likely to be involved in the change or to be affected by it.
2 For each individual and group identified, participants list on Worksheet 1:

   • their perceptions of the interests of the individuals and groups they have identified and consider how these are likely to be affected by the proposed change; and
   • their main sources of power.

3 Individuals now come together and discuss their analyses, agreeing, for each individual and group they have considered, a view about:

   • their *orientation* to the change in terms of positive support, neutrality or resistance;
   • their *power* to support or resist the change.

This is done on Worksheet 2, which should be reproduced on a piece of flipchart paper. It can be seen that this worksheet enables the various individuals and groups who have been considered to be placed in four quadrants:

- powerful and supportive;
- powerful and resistant;
- weak and supportive;
- weak and resistant;

5 The group now considers what the picture looks like. Is there a critical mass of support necessary to implement the change? Where do key individuals and groups appear?

6 Consideration can now be given to how each group should be treated in order to enhance the chances of achieving a successful change. For example:

- Can the powerful supporters be engaged to persuade the powerful resisters to become more supportive, or at least reduce their resistance? This is particularly important if you are not one of the more powerful!
- Can those who are supportive but weak be empowered? For example, can groups in this quadrant be brought together to reduce their isolation and develop a mission or sense of identity? Can they be given 'voice': for example, through the opportunity to speak at a staff meeting? Can individuals' status be raised by giving them a post of responsibility, even a temporary one?
- Can the weak supporters work on the weak resisters? Attempts by powerful supporters to persuade weak resisters may generate a sense of pressure or coercion and make things worse.
- Is understanding a problem for resisters? If so, how can understanding of the proposed change be increased?

Points to note:

- This activity can be done by an individual, but it is much more valuable if done as a group. In the latter case, it is helpful if individuals spend 10–15 minutes working through stages 1 to 3 on their own before coming together and comparing notes.
- Participants should be encouraged to employ the classifications of interests and power which are used in the text, namely:

  - vested interests, ideological interests and self-interests;
  - expertise, control of information, control of rewards and resources, formal authority, physical force and personality.

- Issues relating to orientation and power should be treated as problematic rather than objective. Different members of the group may have different perspectives on these issues and these differences need to be explored in detail as the micro-political map is constructed.

MICRO-POLITICAL MAPPING: WORKSHEET 1

Group	Interests	Sources of power

MICRO-POLITICAL MAPPING: WORKSHEET 2

ORIENTATION

	Strong resistance	Neutrality	Strong support
Powerful			
P			
O			
W			
E			
R			
Weak			

Micro-political mapping of the kind explored in Exercise 9.1 is likely to give rise to a more general discussion about the factors that inhibit or facilitate change. Such factors may arise from the particular orientations of individuals or groups; but they may also arise from other factors. For example, there may be insufficient time or resources available, or there may be external pressures which make change essential. An example is given in Figure 9.1. Taken together, the various forces in operation in the situation might be thought of as being in dynamic equilibrium. In other words, at any point in time there is a balance of helping and hindering forces which causes the situation to be as it is; but this point of balance of forces is constantly changing as some forces become weaker, others become stronger, and new forces enter the equation. The management task is to work on the helping and hindering forces so that the situation changes in desired ways. A useful exercise for exploring these factors is 'Force Field Analysis' (Exercise 9.2).

Figure 9.1 Increasing parental involvement: a Force Field Analysis

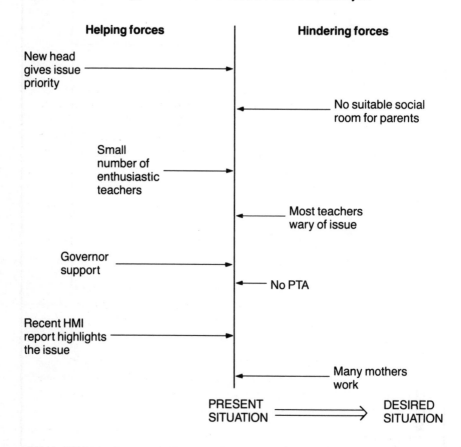

EXERCISE 9.2

FORCE FIELD ANALYSIS

Purpose

To enable a group to examine those factors which are likely to facilitate and inhibit change as a basis for developing a plan of action.

Context

For maximum value, this exercise must be undertaken by a group, preferably comprising those who will have to manage the change which is being considered.

Materials needed

Flipchart paper and pens.

The exercise

1 Choose a problem which has been identified as a result of an evaluation activity. Specify as clearly as possible the nature of the problem and the factors which seem to be at work.
2 Consider what would be a desirable situation to aim for. What would be the characteristics of the situation which you would wish to move towards?
3 Brainstorm (see Exercise 7.1) as long a list as possible of:

   • those factors which are likely to *help* or move the situation towards the desired state;
   • those factors which are likely to *hinder* or stop movement in the desired direction.

   Make sure that you have included:

   • the motivations and attitudes of individuals and groups involved;
   • current policies and procedures in the organisation;
   • external pressures of various kinds.

4 Draw a map of the forces you have identified, similar to the one given in Figure 9.1. Indicate your assessment of the relative strength of the forces by the lengths of the lines. In this exercise use longer lines for the stronger forces.

5 Now consider the strategies which might be used to change the patterns of forces to encourage movement in the desired direction. In particular, how might the hindering forces be reduced or the helping forces enhanced? You need to think about:

- Which forces are easiest to influence?
- Which forces are likely to have the greatest impact if modified?
- Which helping forces might set off countervailing hindering forces if tampered with?
- Can new helping forces be identified and utilised?

6 Finally, translate the outcomes of your analysis into an action plan identifying the phasing of activities and the resources required. Worksheet 6.3 will be helpful for this.

Points to note:

- In considering strategies, it is desirable to give priority to strategies that are likely to reduce the hindering forces without damaging the helping forces. The latter are then likely to grow under their own impetus.

The following cameo describes the way in which staff in one secondary school ensured that evaluation did influence practice. Through being clear about their *purpose*, being aware of the *micro-political context*, thinking carefully about *process* and how to handle *feedback*, they were able to influence significantly what happened next.

Cameo

Designing evaluation to bring about change

The school is an 11–18 comprehensive with 1,514 students. Records of Achievement (ROA) had been fully established in all years for 12 months and there was a growing awareness of their potential to have an effect upon teaching and learning styles that went far beyond reporting progress to parents or to employers.

It had become clear that those departments which had adapted their assessment processes to fit in with the high level of self-assessment that went into the ROA welcomed the change and felt that the effect of the ROA was beneficial. However, this was not true of all departments. In those areas which saw the ROA as solely a substitute for the reporting system, and thus 'bolt-on' extra work, things were not going so well.

Our TVEI targets for the first year of Extension included the intention to identify those areas where there were problems so that help, advice and support could be given. Thus, the evaluation task we set about was to look at departmental assessment and marking policies and strategies, and how these tied in with ROA.

We were concerned that the audit should not be seen as further evangelising by the ROA Steering Committee, particularly now that the principle that the control and running of ROA was in the hands of departments and pastoral teams had been largely accepted. It was decided that it should be done through the Curriculum Development Group, a relatively new body elected from different constituencies in the staff, who were awaiting new Schemes of Work before embarking on a full-scale curriculum audit.

The Curriculum Development Group agreed that we would devise a questionnaire that would lay stress upon those aspects of assessment that ROA had strengthened, for instance, targeting, self-assessment and positive reinforcement. We would also support the questionnaire with an individual interview with a member of the department, normally its head. From the beginning we wanted the evaluation to fulfil several aims, the most important being that the process should be at least as useful as the product. The questionnaire had been designed quite specifically to promote discussion about the relationship between marking and assessment and ROA; in effect it was a questioning of existing practice. We felt that an individual interview would enable discussion around the subject to take place and this, too, could affect perceptions. It would also ensure that we got closer to what actually happened – because claims could be questioned – than would a questionnaire on its own.

Whilst everything written about evaluation seems to stress the importance of the purity of evaluation – that we should not confuse evaluation with influence – if you are going to put a lot of energy and time into something, you need to get more out of it than a set of results. In effect, we wanted to be in a position where, even if we had thrown away the results once we had got them, it would still have been worthwhile.

The other broken rule was in the fact that we were not sure exactly where we were going or quite what we were going to do with the results. It was very much a process of feeling our way step by step and always hoping that the next stage would manifest itself when we got there! This may not be the ideal but it was very much in the tradition of active learning and we did learn!

We didn't throw away the results! The interviews took place and the results were very encouraging. The effect of ROA on departments' marking and assessment strategies was more developed than we had perceived. More important was that the process excited a discussion in several departments preceding and following the interviews, as did the interviews themselves. This resulted in a number of departments re-examining their practice. The results were fed through to the ROA Steering Group who used them to begin the process of formulating a school marking and assessment policy that was able to take account of where we were and, at the same time, move us on a stage. They were also fed back to departments so that they could formulate strategies for meeting the targets that they had identified in the questionnaire.

What had we learned about evaluation?

- The value in using existing structures to give it legitimacy and ownership.
- That when it was integrated with current concerns, the 'spin-off' in terms of affecting change was more marked.
- That you could take into account multiple outcomes without devaluing the evaluation.
- That a stage-by-stage feeling your way through the process may be against the rules but it was a good way to learn!

It is clear from this account that the intention was that this evaluation would influence practice. The 'So What?' question from the 'Why? What? How?' exercise (Exercise 2.1), was very much in the consciousness of those initiating this evaluation. In this situation, feedback and the reporting of findings was an integral and natural part of the proceedings. Representatives of all areas affected by the evaluation were themselves part of the process. Keeping in touch with developments through the representative, and receiving more formal feedback of the findings from the interviews, was relatively straightforward. Each department was interested in receiving the feedback on its own development and was predisposed by the process to want to take this further.

The evaluation team were also careful to take into account the micro-political context in which they were working: for example, in asking the Curriculum Development Group to help design and carry out the evaluation, they paid close attention to process throughout. They were also very clear about their purposes, recognising that they had several. These included:

- To relate the process to the TVEI requirement to set and meet targets, thus meeting both accountability and development needs.
- To establish the effects of developing Records of Achievement on departmental marking and assessment policies.
- To increase such effects by asking questions that stimulated recognition of the consequences for more traditional forms of assessment of the approaches developed through ROAs.
- To increase the evaluators' own understanding about both ROA and evaluation through some active learning.
- There was a hope, at least, that any new awareness raised by the evaluation process might lead to more general effects on teaching and learning styles.

All of these purposes were achieved. There was, however, a further significant effect of the evaluation that may not have been anticipated. Stimulated by the findings of the evaluation process, the ROA group began the process of formulating a school marking and assessment policy. This link into policy-making is not always easy to achieve and we will return to it in Chapter 10.

It is interesting to note that this event has a logic and order that the author of the cameo makes clear emerged in retrospect rather than being pre-planned. However, there was from the beginning a desire and intention to learn as much as possible from this experience. Easterby-Smith (1986: 12–17) suggests three general purposes for evaluation: *proving, improving* and *learning*. There is often a hope that an evaluation will *prove*, or sometimes that it will *disprove*, the worth of an initiative. However, except in the least complex of situations, such proof may be difficult to establish for 'proof', like beauty, often lies in the eye of the beholder. *Improvement* is perhaps less problematic, and formative evaluation has a key part to play in ensuring that continuous improvement is taking place. Here the problem is to ensure that incremental improvement is not disguising fundamental problems. Are you asking, 'How can we do this better?' when you need to be asking, 'Should we be doing this at all?' It is more unusual for *learning* to be an explicit aim of an evaluation activity, and Easterby-Smith suggests that such instances necessitate a truly collaborative approach by 'evaluators' and 'evaluated', which may be most difficult to achieve when external evaluators are involved. Nevertheless, explicit or not, a desire to use evaluation to inform future action – to change behaviour – requires learning of some kind to occur. The general import of this book is that certain ways of planning, carrying out and reporting evaluation are more likely than others to enable this to take place. However, such learning cannot be guaranteed. There are blocks to both individual and organisational learning that can get in the way. The final part of this chapter considers the issue of personal learning; that of organisation learning will be explored in Chapter 10.

LEARNING TO LEARN FROM EVALUATION

Learning, other perhaps than that which involves merely committing to memory, is an active process. It involves making meaning or sense of experience in the light of present understanding, which is in itself dependent on previous experience. Learning is, therefore, also provisional and open to future development. The latter factor is important because, if an idea, an opinion or a behaviour is not open to revision, it becomes a stereotype, a prejudice or a fixed habit and a block to future learning. It might be expected that as teachers are daily involved in the processes of teaching and learning, they will be particularly 'good' learners, but sadly there is no evidence to suggest that this is so. Teachers share the general human defences against learning and, therefore, even when an evaluation has been carried out with consummate skill and care, its findings may still be rejected.

It may be helpful to spend some time reflecting on your own approaches to learning by working through Exercise 9.3.

EXERCISE 9.3

REFLECTING ON LEARNING

Purpose

To help you identify the factors which help or hinder your learning.

The exercise

1 Think about a time recently when you feel that you learned something about yourself as a teacher, or about an aspect of your work, and answer the following questions:

   - What did I learn?
   - How did I learn it?
   - Which factors helped me to learn?
   - What changed as a result? (How did I know that I had learned something?)

2 Now think of a time when you resisted learning – for example, not accepting suggestions from a course or a colleague – and answer these questions:

   - What did I resist learning?
   - Why did I resist it?
   - Which factors hindered my learning?

3 Finally, summarise the factors that help and hinder learning, remembering to include the factors within yourself as well as those outside. Use the attached sheet.

Points to note

- Sometimes you will find that the same factors – for example, 'pressure' – can help or hinder learning in different circumstances.
- This exercise can also be carried out in a pair or a group of up to about eight. In this case spend 10 to 15 minutes working on the first set of questions on your own and then take it in turns to share your comments as a group. Repeat this process with the second part of the exercise before drawing up a common list of factors that help and hinder learning. When using the exercise it can be interesting to note all the different ways in which we learn.

FACTORS WHICH HELP AND HINDER LEARNING

	Helps	Hinders
Within self		
Other factors		

Helps and hindrances

Both the factors that help and those that hinder are important in the context of bringing about change. The aim must be to maximise the former and minimise the latter. We all have blocks to, and defences against, learning which come into play, sometimes despite the best of intentions. Some blocks to learning have been identified in the section of this chapter concerned with micro-politics; however there are perhaps more deep-seated factors to contend with. In considering this matter, it is important to recognise that defences to learning are not automatically a 'bad thing'. It is not possible for all our beliefs and behaviours to be open to constant review. Teaching is a demanding and active occupation: it is necessary to build up a pattern of working and to develop tried and tested ways of responding to the complexities of classroom life in order to cope. These are defences against potential chaos and as such can be functional. However, to be effective such defensive strategies must remain open to review. The complexities of the processes of teaching and learning preclude simplistic answers: the difficult trick is to hold a balance between order and openness. The consequence of too much certainty is rigidity; that of too little is confusion. Those who are resisting learning are raising their defences and they are the people who have to take these defences down. One of the problems of education emerging into the political limelight is the pressure for imposed change at a very rapid rate. Some people cope with or even welcome such changes, but others find that they strike so hard at their whole conception of teaching and what it means to be a teacher, that they suffer considerable stress or even leave the profession. This is not a new phenomenon: some secondary teachers did not, for example, welcome or cope with the change to comprehensive education.

Types of learning

Some kinds of learning are easier than others. Those that are the most difficult are ones that threaten our view of ourselves as people and those which threaten our competence. Teaching is a very personal occupation with criticism of 'me' as a teacher feeling very much like criticism of 'me' as a person. For some, it is a conflict with their value system that is the most painful. For others, it is the threat to their competence. Reviewing curriculum materials, for example, is therefore likely to prove less difficult than reviewing teaching and learning styles, unless someone has tied his or her professional identity into the former.

It is also helpful to consider Argyris and Schon's (1974) distinction between two kinds of learning – single and double loop. Single-loop learning is of the incremental kind described in the context of 'improvement' above: 'How can we do this better?' In contrast, double-loop learning poses the question: 'Should we be doing this at all?' A practical example is that of an infant school where teachers and school meals supervisors were finding children's behaviour at dinner time very problematic. They were attempting to solve the problem case by case and by blaming the children's parents for their behaviour. The new head, however, saw the problem as a symptom of a more widespread malaise and was able to use it to focus on and improve generally negative relationships between adults and children in the school. Single-loop learning is more straightforward, and therefore easier, than double-loop learning, although it may prove more problematic in the long run. Argyris suggests that professionals have the problem of being very proficient at single-loop learning, having done a good deal of it in order to gain their professional qualifications. He suggests that, when single-loop learning does not solve the problem, this experience, added to a high need to feel competent and a consequent fear of failure, leads them to move not to double-loop learning but to 'defensive reasoning and the doom loop'. These lead those who are feeling threatened to disproportionate despair and a displacement of blame on to those around them (Argyris, 1991: 99–109).

Implications for processes of evaluation

What then are the implications of these factors for the process of evaluation? First it is helpful to recognise that such matters are endemic and not, therefore, the prerogative of certain particularly difficult characters within your organisation. It may also be helpful to acknowledge that you are unlikely always to 'win them all'. This statement is not intended to relieve you of all responsibility. Of course you should always set out to develop a process that will win as many as possible, indeed to create winners rather than losers. However, many discussions become bogged down by focusing on the most awkward individuals and worst case scenarios in ways that sap energy in a most unhelpful way. Exercise 9.1 will have helped you to identify the most positive places in which, and people with whom, to start, but it is important to think beyond the individuals concerned to the whole organisation. Just as some schools exclude more pupils than others, some institutions seem to contain or create more difficult adults. Whilst some people may be difficult wherever they are, many are actually responding to the culture around them. The more threatening the environment, the higher the defences and the lower the morale.

This brings us back to the perceived purposes of evaluation. If staff, or others, perceive the process as one of identifying problem areas in order to establish blame, they will respond very differently than if they perceive it as an opportunity to establish training needs. If they are used to senior management behaving autocratically, they will find it hard to believe that the canvassing of staff views will have any chance of influencing what happens. For example, in one secondary school, staff were asked to consider new timetabling proposals through a lengthy consultation procedure. Although the decision on which procedure to adopt was based on the response of the majority, the staff believed that this had only happened because it reflected the views of the head, although these had not actually been made public. Conversely, in a similar situation in another school, the head made his views quite, but not aggressively, clear during the process of data-gathering and subsequently gracefully accepted a different decision which was preferred, and well argued, by the staff.

Demonstration of a willingness to learn from experience and to consider the views of others is part of the process of developing a learning culture. The actions rather than the exhortations of heads, principals and senior staff are of course very influential, but, in general, the more people who demonstrate an openness to learning, the more such openness becomes the norm. The most will be learned from evaluation when most of those involved have a commitment to such learning. The matter can therefore be seen as both an individual and organisational responsibility. The issue of how to create a learning culture and become a learning organisation is taken up in the next chapter.

FURTHER READING

You will find a useful model for reporting, which distinguishes between 'minor' and 'major' evaluations in Chapter 9 of Caldwell and Spinks, *The Self-Managing School* (1988). There is a large literature on the management of change. A straightforward introduction is *Managing Organisational Change: a practitioner's guide* (1982) by Elliott-Kemp. Much more substantial is Fullan, *The New Meaning of Educational Change* (1991), which provides a comprehensive and relevant review of current thinking albeit from a North American perspective. If you want to read more widely in this area, Mercer, *Striving for Effective Change in the Education Service: a guide to the literature* (1988), provides a useful introduction.

Some of the ideas in this chapter are taken further in Ball, *The Micro-Politics of the School* (1987), in which the author challenges some of the existing forms of organisational control in schools through looking at such issues as leadership, headship, resources and relationships and the politics of gender, career and change.

Chapter 10

Evaluation and organisational learning

The last, and probably most difficult, stage of managing evaluation is that of moving beyond the implications for the immediate area involved and towards influencing the whole organisation. Evaluation is seldom made use of in this way. In general there is considerable evidence that, whatever the rhetoric, there are enormous pressures towards the marginalisation of evaluation activities. Evaluation seems to be managed more effectively at a micro level (that of the individual teacher or small team) than at the macro level (that of the whole school or college or the wider system). This often proves frustrating for those directly involved and prevents the wider institution from benefiting fully from those activities. Individual pieces of evaluation are set in motion, carefully planned and carried out, but if the conclusions that are drawn require changes beyond the immediate area of enquiry, they are seldom acted upon. The wider organisation finds it difficult or impossible to respond, and the learning remains localised. This not only limits the learning potential of each activity, it also influences the status of evaluation as an activity. Those whose wider insights are ignored or denied will approach the next evaluation task with less commitment and lower expectations than before.

It is not only learning from evaluation that has little impact on the wider organisation. It has long been recognised that the emphasis on individual development, that has often been the basis of training or staff development in education and elsewhere, has had little effect on the wider organisation, however powerful an experience it may be for the individual. You may well know, or be, a teacher who has experienced long-term secondment, for example, and who returned refreshed and invigorated to the school or college only to be submerged back into the past, disappointed to find that no one else appears to be at all curious about what has happened and what has been learned. As Argyris and Schon (1978: 9) have observed:

> It is clear that organisational learning is not the same as individual learning, even when the individuals who learn are members of the organisation. There are too many cases in which organisations know less than

their members. There are even cases in which the organisation cannot seem to learn what everybody knows.

This chapter considers the link between evaluation and organisational learning. It opens with a brief overview of the operational and strategic planning that must underpin evaluation activities, then it returns to the issue of organisational culture first raised in Chapter 2. Not all cultures are as open to learning as others. Does your organisation's culture acknowledge that it is possible to learn a great deal from mistakes, for example? Is there a strong emphasis on right answers? Is it assumed that those in the most senior positions are the ones who identify the problems? Is there a collegial approach to problem-solving? The learning climate within an organisation will influence not only what is evaluated and how, but also how the findings are received and what is learned from the experience. We offer a diagnostic tool based on the work of Roger Harrison to enable you to diagnose your organisation's culture and to consider the implications. We then conclude with an exploration of recent thinking about how it may be possible to become a learning organisation and the role that evaluation can play in this process.

OPERATIONAL AND STRATEGIC MANAGEMENT

Throughout this book there has been an emphasis on both the operational and strategic dimensions of management, although these have not always been clearly delineated as such. In considering the management of evaluation, it is useful to distinguish between these aspects of the process. The operational dimension is broadly concerned with the effective management of the details of the evaluation process itself, whereas the strategic dimension is concerned with the broader management structures and processes which provide a framework for, and support or constrain, the operational processes. In moving from the micro to the macro level of managing evaluation, it is necessary to pay attention to both operational and strategic issues.

Operational questions

At the operational level, three major concerns are relevant. First, it is essential that *planning and prioritising* is undertaken adequately before the evaluation process begins. The plans which are developed need to include provision for the following:

- An *initial audit* of existing evaluation activities, including those of monitoring and review. This process identifies and acknowledges strengths, raises confidence and establishes realistic starting points.
- Clarifying the *purposes* of evaluation on the basis of a realistic assessment of the roles and expectations of those involved.

- Establishing reasonable and attainable *success criteria* and targets, which are neither too demanding nor so unchallenging that low expectations are simply confirmed.
- Designing methods of *data collection* and analysis which balance such conflicting demands as validity, reliability and economy.
- Planning for *effective feedback* that will ensure that action is taken as a result. Although this appears at the end of the cycle, in practice attention has to be paid to it throughout the whole process. For example, if senior management is asked initially to mandate an evaluation but then hears nothing until presented with a report with implications for their own practice, it is more than possible that the report will be 'shelved'.

If these questions are not thought through in advance, practitioners often rush into the later stages and begin to collect more data than they can manage, only to find that it does not address the questions they need to answer. In addition, colleagues may be irritated by the processes rather than interested in the results. Chapters 3 to 8 dealt with these stages in some detail.

Second, adequate attention must be given to *the management of resources, especially time.* Without this, evaluation activities have a tendency to expand exponentially through such factors as costly data collection methods, insensitivity or lack of co-ordination in the demands placed on colleagues, or quite simply, through not knowing when to stop. Issues of resource management were considered in Chapter 6, although many other aspects of the argument in this book have important resource management implications.

Finally, consideration needs to be given to the application of *generic process skills* to the management of evaluation. These skills include self-management, the management of groups or teams, and management upwards, downwards and across the management structure. As argued in Chapter 1, although evaluation can be more or less well managed within all kinds of organisational structures, the less the institutional emphasis is on tight hierarchical functions the more generally effective the process is likely to be. References to generic process skills are made at various points in this book, particularly in Chapter 5. It is hoped, however, that the various exercises described in the book will provide the tools that will enable managers to involve others effectively in all stages of the evaluation process.

Strategic questions

While the basis of effective management of evaluation will always lie at the operational level, it is not enough to stick at this level. These day-to-day operational issues must be set into the strategic context. Here, four key areas can be identified.

First, there is a need to be clear about *roles*. Role ambiguity and conflict emerges at all levels in the evaluation process, not only in balancing the demands of evaluation against other demands, but also, for example, in balancing the demand for support against the demand to inspect or hold to account, or demands from below versus demands from above. In the context of TVEI, for example, individuals sometimes feel some conflict between their role as a member of a cross-cluster group and their role as a representative of a particular school or college. This conflict is experienced most particularly by headteachers who are perhaps most aware of the competitive pressures. Chapter 2 considered the question of role in some detail.

Second, a clearer understanding of the *power and status* of individuals and groups and the influence patterns that result is essential if evaluation is to be managed effectively. The issue of power and influence arises in all kinds of ways in evaluation processes, and consequently has recurred in this book. One way of looking at the issue is in terms of stakeholders, as explored in Chapter 4 and again in Chapter 7; another is in terms of micro-political mapping as described in Chapter 9.

Third, *structures* can be both facilitating and restraining forces. For example, in one school the strong departmental structure combined with a difficult relationship with the head had become both an important source of power for individual heads of department and a block to cross-institutional change. However, in other schools and colleges existing elements of the structure (such as curriculum or staff development groups) provided an effective route for establishing evaluation activities. The effective development and management of networks is a key skill.

Finally, the idea of *meta-evaluation* (Kemmis, 1986: 132) is a useful one. This is the process by which evaluation activities themselves are subjected to evaluation. Systematic, regular review of the whole process of evaluation – what it has cost, what its results have been, whether these have been worth the effort – is necessary but seems to occur only rarely. Yet it is extremely important. Only by reviewing the evaluation process itself can it be improved and the resources devoted to it justified. A positive meta-evaluation can do much to ensure that evaluation processes in general are actively supported as worthwhile. Harlen and Elliott (1982) provide a useful checklist for meta-evaluation (see Figure 10.1).

These strategic dimensions are crucial and provide the framework within which evaluation has to be managed. There is, however, still another level to consider. Operational and strategic thinking will be influenced by the wider culture of the organisation. For example, the problem of role ambiguity will be addressed quite differently in an organisational culture which is steeply hierarchical than in one which supports collegial relationships. Approaches to evaluation will reflect organisational culture in a way that is very illuminating and it is worth considering this issue in some depth.

Figure 10.1 Questions for reviewing (evaluating) evaluations

1   Did the evaluation serve to inform the decisions or judgements for which it was originally intended?

2   What decisions have been taken as a consequence of the evaluation?

3   Was the evaluation task interpreted and carried through consistently as intended?

4   Was the information which was gathered appropriate to the purpose of the evaluation?

5   What steps were taken to allow for bias, unrepresentativeness, and low reliability in the information gathered?

6   Were the actual evaluators in the best position to carry out the evaluation?

7   Were the methods used appropriate to the kind of information which was required?

8   Were the methods systematic and explicit?

9   Did those involved in supplying the information approve of the methods used for collecting it?

10 Was there sufficient time allowed in the evaluation for the necessary data to be collected?

11 Was the evaluation carried out at the best time to serve its purpose?

12 What were the side-effects, positive and negative, of the evaluation process?

13 Were satisfactory procedures used to protect the interests of those who supplied information?

14 Were the criteria by which judgements or decisions were made appropriately drawn and explicitly stated?

15 Was the evaluation reported in a way which communicated effectively with the intended audience?

16 What reactions did the report provoke in the participants and in the decision-makers?

Applying these questions to some examples of completed evaluations can be a useful planning exercise for anyone contemplating an evaluation. In most cases it is necessary to follow up initial answers with the further question 'if not, why not?' Reasons are not always accessible but raising the question brings to light issues which should often be considered *before* and not just after an evaluation is carried out.

Source: Harlen and Elliott (1982: 303–4)

UNDERSTANDING THE EVALUATION CULTURE

As we have seen, although in theory evaluation is securely placed within learning or planning and developmental cycles (see, for example, Kolb 1983; Hargreaves *et al.* 1989: 14), in practice it more commonly occurs at the margins or in isolated patches. Systematic evaluation as an integral part of developmental planning is not a well-established feature of most institutional cultures. When teachers and others discuss, plan and reflect upon the management of specific evaluation activities, a preoccupation that tends to surface concerns the nature of their institution or LEA, and what they perceive to be possible or not possible within it. Individuals and groups are aware that although it is important to understand and acknowledge their institutional culture, it is also possible to influence and change it.

We discussed culture at some length in Chapter 2. Here we will consider a rather different way of understanding it, using a perspective developed by Roger Harrison (1987). Harrison suggests that there are four dominant 'cultures', or 'ideologies', to be found in organisations. These will powerfully affect responses to such tasks as monitoring, review and evaluation. It is important to remember that the vast majority of schools and colleges are a mixture of these four models, but one may well predominate. In carrying out evaluation in your school or college, it is helpful to understand the dominant and other cultures and how you stand in relation to them. Exercise 10.1 helps you to do this. It would be helpful for you to do this exercise before reading on.

EXERCISE 10.1

DIAGNOSING CULTURES OF EVALUATION

Purpose

To enable you to examine the values and assumptions which under-lie your organisation's approach to evaluation and to consider how far these match your own.

Context

This exercise is best undertaken by a group, although it will be of interest to individuals as well.

Materials needed

- Sufficient copies of the Instruction Sheet, Questionnaire and Scoresheet for all participants;
- Flipchart paper and pens.

The exercise

1 Hand out the Instruction Sheet, Questionnaire and Scoresheet to participants. Ask them to follow the instructions. The process of filling in the questionnaire and scoring will normally take 15–30 minutes.

2 When all participants have completed the task, enter their results on a piece of flipchart paper designed as follows:

	Power	*Role*	*Task*	*Support*
Organisational reality				
Preferred situation				

It is a good idea to record each individual's highest score (using + signs) and lowest score (using – signs) for the two stages of the exercise.

© Routledge 1992

3 Discuss the pattern that emerges. If the group is large, divide it up into sub-groups of about six.

Points to note

- A wide-ranging discussion normally results from this exercise. Points which might be covered include:

  - Is there a major discrepancy between the perceived reality and individuals' preferences? If so, why might this be the case?
  - If there appears to be one dominant culture, or preference for one dominant culture, what are the implications, given that some mix of cultural elements is desirable, if adequate evaluation policies and processes are to exist?
  - Are there differences in perception between people who hold different positions in the organisation? For example, do those in more senior positions have a preference for the power culture while staff generally have a higher task preference?
  - What developmental needs are suggested by the analysis?

- Identifying your organisational culture has two main purposes:

  - to increase awareness of the context in which you are working;
  - to raise the possibility of designing evaluation activities to influence the culture towards becoming more open to learning, if this is felt to be necessary.

DIAGNOSING CULTURES OF EVALUATION: INSTRUCTION SHEET

You are first invited to think about how your own school or college characteristically handles evaluation activities; and then to think about how ideally you would wish such things to be handled. For this exercise, do not just think about formal evaluation processes: consider also all those informal activities through which the performance of individuals, groups and the organisation as a whole are assessed.

How to complete the questionnaire

You will see that the questionnaire comprises eleven sets of statements with four statements in each set. There are two columns for you to fill in a score against each statement. In each column in turn, and for each set of four statements, score 4 for the statement which most closely approximates your assessment, 3 for the next closest, down to 1 for the statement which is least appropriate.

First complete column 1 for your assessment of *how evaluation activities are characteristically managed in your institution*. When you have completed column 1, do the same thing for column 2, this time in relation to *how you think evaluation should ideally be managed*: again score 4 for the statement which is closest to your preference down to 1 for your least favoured approach.

How to score

When you have completed the questionnaire, transfer your scores to the scoresheet and total the columns. You will see that you have to do this twice: once for column 1 of the questionnaire and once for column 2. The highest total in column 1 of the scoresheet indicates your perception of the dominant culture of evaluation in your organisation and that in column 2 indicates your preferred culture.

DIAGNOSING CULTURES OF EVALUATION: THE QUESTIONNAIRE

	Your organisation	Own preference
1 The person responsible for leading the processes of evaluation:		
1.1 Believes that he/she must deal with those involved in a strong, decisive and firm, but not arbitrary, way.		
1.2 Believes that he/she must apply the 'rules' in a fair and impersonal way.		
1.3 Believes that he/she is only the first amongst equals in relation to the achievement of high-quality evaluation.		
1.4 Believes that he/she must act in ways that create networks of support among the people involved.		
2 Individual staff members responsible for undertaking evaluation:		
2.1 Believe that they should be loyal to the decisions of the evaluation leader.		
2.2 Believe that they should act within the formal guidelines and procedures laid down.		
2.3 Believe that it is important to contribute productively and flexibly to the needs of the task.		
2.4 Believe that they should work co-operatively and supportively with others involved in the evaluation process.		
3 High-quality achievement in evaluation implies:		
3.1 Meeting the expectations of senior staff in the conduct of evaluation		
3.2 Understanding the roles, rules and procedures of evaluation and sticking to them		
3.3 Getting on with the job in ways which respond innovatively to new needs as they arise		
3.4 Developing a great deal of sharing and consensus in the evaluation process.		
4 As far as students or pupils are concerned, evaluation is used as:		
4.1 A way of distributing rewards and punishments to individuals.		
4.2 A way of ensuring that rules and procedures are adhered to.		
4.3 A means of achieving dialogue with the staff about their (the students' or pupils') achievements.		

4.4 A non-competitive device to encourage students or pupils to discuss with each other issues relating to their work.

5   In the school or college, evaluation takes place in a context where:

5.1 Rights and privileges are accorded to individuals on a personal basis: there are heroes and villains.

5.2 Rights and privileges are distributed in a formal way according to well-understood rules of propriety.

5.3 Rights and privileges are not really a matter of concern.

5.4 There is a conscious discounting of the concept of rights and privileges: there are neither heroes nor villains.

6   *Evaluation is used in the school or college as a means of control and influence through:*

6.1 The personal distribution by the most senior members of the staff of rewards for achievement.

6.2 The impersonal exercise of rewards and punishments, for example by the publication of results and outcomes without any personal comment.

6.3 The corporate expression of success in relation to agreed objectives.

6.4 Stressing that quality of performance in the school and college can only be achieved through mutuality and collaboration.

7   *Staff responsibilities for carrying out aspects of evaluation in the school or college are distributed on the basis of:*

7.1 Decisions made by the most senior members of staff on the basis of their aspirations and judgements.

7.2 The formal rules, structures and systems currently in operation.

7.3 The expertise that is available, irrespective of individuals' formal roles or seniority.

7.4 A desire to create patterns of co-operation that cut across traditional boundaries.

8   *Good performance by students in the school or college is valued because it is seen as* :

8.1 A way of enhancing the prestige and status of the institution.

8.2 The outcome of a contract that implies that the school or college provides high-quality resources, and the students, for their part, provide high-quality work.

8.3 The successful culmination of a journey towards a jointly agreed task.

8.4 Proof that we really only can conduct life through processes of co-operation and support.

9   *When there is conflict about an aspect of evaluation, that conflict is usually resolved by:*

9.1 The intervention of senior members of staff, even though these people may not always be well informed in relation to evaluation.

9.2 Adherence to the rules of the school or college, and by the allocation of formal roles with responsibility for conflict resolution, even though this may mean that important issues are avoided.

9.3 By full discussion of the issues concerned in the conflict, with the possibility that there will not be a resolution of the conflict.

9.4 A search for consensus and agreement, even though this might cause people to feel that fundamental issues of principle have been smoothed away.

10   *Decisions about evaluation in the school or college are made by:*

10.1 Senior members of staff without reference to colleagues.

10.2 Members of staff who have the designated responsibility for making such decisions.

10.3 Members of school or college who have acknowledged expertise in the relevant area.

10.4 A variety of people, in the belief that participation in the decision-making process is desirable for its own sake.

11   *The environment outside the school or college (parents, the community, the LEA, the DES) is seen as:*

11.1 A competitive world in which evaluation must be exploited by the school or college to achieve advantage.

11.2 An orderly world where evaluation is part of an official system of formal accountabilities.

11.3 A complex world which well-managed evaluation activities can help to reshape and improve.

11.4 A world that basically is one of goodwill, in which evaluation is an important means of securing and maintaining co-operation.

DIAGNOSING CULTURES OF EVALUATION: SCORESHEET

1 The evaluation culture in your organisation

Please insert your score for each item from column 1 in the appropriate box. Remember: score 4 for the statements which are closest to your view, down to 1 for those which you feel are least true.

	Power	*Role*	*Task*	*Support*
	1.1	1.2	1.3	1.4
	2.1	2.2	2.3	2.4
	3.1	3.2	3.3	3.4
	4.1	4.2	4.3	4.4
	5.1	5.2	5.3	5.4
	6.1	6.2	6.3	6.4
	7.1	7.2	7.3	7.4
	8.1	8.2	8.3	8.4
	9.1	9.2	9.3	9.4
	10.1	10.2	10.3	10.4
	11.1	11.2	11.3	11.4
Totals				

2 Your preferred culture of evaluation

Please insert your score for each item from column 2 in the appropriate box. Remember: score 4 for the statements which are closest to your view down to 1 for those which you feel are least true.

	Power	*Role*	*Task*	*Support*
	1.1	1.2	1.3	1.4
	2.1	2.2	2.3	2.4
	3.1	3.2	3.3	3.4
	4.1	4.2	4.3	4.4
	5.1	5.2	5.3	5.4
	6.1	6.2	6.3	6.4
	7.1	7.2	7.3	7.4
	8.1	8.2	8.3	8.4
	9.1	9.2	9.3	9.4
	10.1	10.2	10.3	10.4
	11.1	11.2	11.3	11.4
Totals				

In developing the questionnaire, we have applied the four cultures – power, role, task and support – to the issue of evaluation. In the *power culture*, evaluation processes are primarily concerned with control. The senior manager or managers are concerned to ensure that all members of the organisation are behaving in ways which the leaders deem to be 'correct'. Information is likely to be collected informally, especially from individuals whom the senior manager trusts, and evaluated personally by senior staff. This approach is designed to ensure that the leader's vision for the organisation is being interpreted and undertaken appropriately. Competence, in this model, is about being able to undertake tasks in ways that are established by the central authority. Initiative, and risk-taking, are bounded by an understanding of what the leader would see as appropriate.

In the *role culture*, in contrast, evaluation processes are undertaken in ways that fit the notion of administrative necessity. They are likely to be systematised with clear lines of responsibility and well-defined reporting procedures. Such processes may well use a good deal of paper, and increasingly new technology as well, to produce a variety of reports and statistics in standard format. Qualitative data are likely to be distrusted: the requirement here is for order and administrative control. Evaluation responsibilities will be clearly defined in relation to the organisational hierarchy, and competence will be measured in terms of the prompt and orderly submission of returns and 'correct' behaviour in relation to established rules.

In a *task culture*, the emphasis is on using evaluation activities for problem-solving. If a school or college has a problem about meeting the needs of parents and the community it will, in a task culture, set up an *ad hoc* team to evaluate the issue at hand in *ad hoc* ways, perhaps using quite informal methods. Responsibilities for evaluation are likely to be shared and shifting, being based more on expertise than on formal authority. In such a culture, competence is seen in terms of rapid response, the ability to solve problems, and the ability to operate in a team in ways that are not hierarchical.

In a *support culture*, people are encouraged to like and support each other in the belief that, if adults care for one another, this in turn will find expression in caring for pupils or students. Competence in this sort of organisation is defined in terms of the ability to give and receive care and support. In such a school or college, evaluation would be undertaken in counselling mode in a supportive environment. There would be an absence of blaming, and lapses of performance would be treated as a learning experience – *not* ignored but rather used as a lesson for future development. Processes of evaluation would be facilitative and would be person-centred. Interestingly, in discussions of business organisations that are led by women, there is evidence that this sort of culture is emerging as a powerful way of working together.

Of course, these cultures rarely exist in their pure form. For example, a variation, which perhaps has aspects of both the task and support cultures, can be found in some schools and colleges. Here the notions of autonomy and self-development are stressed: it is believed that the organisation *really* exists to fulfil the professional aspirations of individual staff. For example, being an excellent teacher is seen as a personal aspiration and a professional fulfilment and is a gift that one makes to the institution. This is a very individualistic culture in which people can only come together if they choose to do so. Its members will resist 'official' or 'imposed' forms of evaluation which they will take as a professional affront, because competence is seen in terms of individual self-assessment against professional standards. Evaluation is only tolerable in this culture if it is based on peer review freely entered into by consenting professionals. This kind of culture, with its emphasis on professional autonomy, is becoming increasingly rare in educational organisations.

Clearly, those responsible for managing evaluation need to consider the match between the way in which they manage and the characteristics of the organisation in which they are working. If these organisational characteristics are taken as given, how then should evaluation proceed? This question, however, begs a further one. Are some kinds of organisations more conducive to the development of effective evaluation processes than others? What if we do not take the organisation's characteristics as given?

Changing the culture

The answer to this question will be partly pragmatic and partly principled. Considered pragmatically, the way in which evaluation is managed will depend upon its purposes and the legitimate demands of stakeholders. A contingency approach suggests that a variety of methods may be used depending on the circumstances. This should not mean that anything goes, however. Some approaches may be preferred to others because of the values they embody, and some may be explicitly excluded. Our view is that neither power cultures nor an overemphasis on individual autonomy are appropriate for the management of evaluation in education today. Each in its own way fails to recognise the need for evaluation processes to meet the legitimate expectations of stakeholders both inside and outside the organisation. They are both essentially undemocratic. The role, task and support cultures, however, all have something to offer when used appropriately in appropriate circumstances. Each, though, has its strengths and weaknesses. For example, the task culture has considerable strengths in terms of ability to cope flexibly with changing demands and to make good use of organisational expertise. There is a good deal of evidence that many teachers, given the choice, prefer it (Handy and Aitken, 1986). On the other hand, it can lead to problems in relation to the more routine, mundane aspects of work. The strengths and weaknesses of the role culture, in contrast, are the opposite of these. It has a tendency to encourage rigidity and stifle imagination; but it does ensure that roles are clearly demarcated and understood and that the procedures are in place to enable routine activities to be carried out efficiently. The support culture is consonant with much current management literature which stresses the development of shared values: it can perhaps be seen as the 'people' side of the task culture.

A feature of many organisations today – including schools and colleges – is a move towards decentralisation and hence a decline of the power and role cultures and a rise in the task and support cultures. There are a number of reasons for this:

- In a situation where the external environment is increasingly uncertain and rapidly changing, decentralisation enables rapid responses to be made to externally generated demands and encourages initiative.
- When an organisation gets larger – perhaps as a result of merger – decentralisation becomes more appropriate so that the work of the organisation can take place within manageable units.
- Those working in organisations increasingly expect more control over their work. Many professionals, in particular, have a strong preference for decentralisation – a point which may well have been illustrated by a preference for the task or support culture in Exercise 10.1.
- The beliefs of senior managers also seem to be changing, with an increasing preference for 'loose-tight' structures (Peters and Waterman, 1982), where responsibility is widely distributed in the organisation but a strong sense of coherence is maintained through shared 'core values'.

Decisions about the degree of decentralisation in a school or college will have an important impact on the processes of evaluation adopted. Clearly, high levels of decentralisation imply a multiplicity of approaches to evaluation as individuals and teams are granted delegated power to develop their own methods. This point about loose-tight structures, however, emphasises the need to ensure that decentralisation does not degenerate into anarchy and that a strong sense of policy coherence is maintained across the institution as a whole.

The challenge perhaps is to develop a culture of evaluation that draws on the strengths of these three cultures in a balanced way. This might include:

- The establishment of a general culture in which a rich network of professional relationships is developed which are non-threatening and emphasise mutual support and learning – a strength of the support culture.
- Supplementation of this network by clearly defined evaluation tasks carried out by carefully selected teams which draw on a variety of expertise and interests – a strength of the task culture.

- A clear co-ordinating framework which provides systematic monitoring information and ensures that specific evaluation activities are planned and implemented against clear targets that relate to the institution's planning cycle – a strength of the role culture.

The appropriate balance between these levels of activity will depend on the stage of development of the school or college and the situation facing it. Taken together, these may form key elements of a 'learning organisation'.

BECOMING A LEARNING ORGANISATION

Organisations are made up of individuals, yet, as we have seen, individual learning does not automatically result in organisational learning. However, if an organisation is to learn, the total learning which occurs in it must somehow add up to more than the sum of the learning by the individuals involved. In trying to understand this apparent paradox, it is helpful to consider the stage between individual and organisational learning: that of group or team learning. While few may be familiar with learning at the level of a whole organisation, most – perhaps all – have personal experience of groups or teams that worked together to maximise learning. Such experiences often prove extremely powerful. How often have you belonged to such a group, perhaps coming together to carry out a specific task only to find that once this task was completed the group had found the process so helpful that it wished to continue to work together in this way? How much more powerful could such a process be if it were transferable to a whole organisation?

In their book *The Learning Company*, Pedler *et al.* (1991: 1) describe such an organisation as follows:

> The learning company is an organisation that facilitates the learning of all its members and continuously transforms itself.

In this definition, individual and organisational learning are inextricably linked and action in such a company is designed to solve the immediate problem and to learn from that experience. In seeking to explain how these different elements are linked, the authors use the diagram reproduced as Figure 10.2.

In the context of education, the top two circles represent the link between school/college policy or development plan and the way the institution as a whole functions. The bottom two circles represent the individual and the link between what you think and what you do. Therefore the two left-hand circles represent the link between the whole-institution policy and individual ideas and the right two circles represent the link between organisational operations and individual action. In an organisation that is functioning well, there will be a constant but variable energy flow between

Figure 10.2 The learning organisation

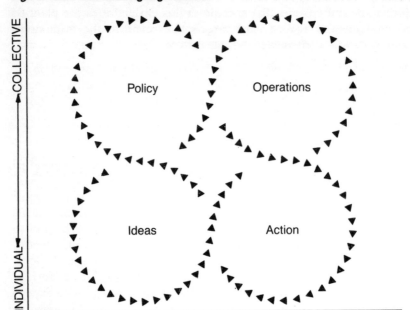

each of these circles. However, you will all know of circumstances in which the energy and information flow is blocked:

- There is little connection between policy and planning and what actually happens at a whole-institution or at an individual level.
- Where individuals behave idiosyncratically within their classroom, out of line with the general approach.
- Where what the majority of staff believe to be the right way forward is ignored by senior management, or vice versa.
- Where there is apparently little connection between what we think and say and what we actually do.

Noting what happens to the conclusions drawn from an evaluation activity will illuminate how well the energy flows in your organisation. Observing where the learning from evaluation stops will reveal the blocks, thus enabling reflection on why this has happened. If this particular block occurs only in relation to a specific piece of evaluation, then the conclusions, and reactions, will be different to those that will be drawn if all implications of evaluation activities are blocked at the same point.

Throughout the cameos, it is possible to find glimpses of organisational learning. One result of the cross-curricular audit in Chapter 3 was a reali-sation that the structure of, and communication within, the college were influencing staff willingness to be involved in cross-curricular planning. In Chapter 4 the efforts to establish cross-cluster evaluation highlighted the absence of, and need for, a common framework and for policy decisions in this area. In Chapter 7 those developing success criteria for careers education and guidance recognised the need to involve other groups, such as parents and governors, in the process. The evaluation in Chapter 8 proved to be particularly rich in learning. The school groups developed close-knit teams and new patterns of consultation. They also used the evaluation process to reinforce and enhance existing open cultures in their organisations. Consciousness of the learning potential also runs throughout the cameo in Chapter 9. In addition, the evaluation process had begun to influence policy-making in this school. This is a key indication of organisational learning: the school had changed and developed, not just the individuals involved in ROA evaluation.

CONCLUSION

The emphasis in this book has been in working collaboratively in teams and groups, involving others as far as possible, linking back into the decision-making processes, and broadening the base that is affected by the evaluation activities. This will not happen if evaluation is intended to cause minimum disruption, to be 'busy work' or a substitute for action. If, however, it is designed to be a process for improving the energy flow (as in Figure 10.2), it can enhance and speed positive change and development.

It is interesting to reflect that the involvement of outsiders in carrying out evaluation, particularly in the context of externally funded projects, has been based on two main factors. First, outsiders with a research background are seen to have the necessary expertise, and, second, they are seen to be neutral observers and therefore able to perceive the central issues more clearly. However, in these two apparent strengths lie equally important weaknesses. First – and insiders need also to recognise this danger – the emphasis on expertise can disempower those who feel themselves to be 'evaluated' and can, therefore, reduce the chance of their identifying with the conclusions of the exercise. In addition, being outside the organisation makes it, in practice, difficult if not impossible to influence the action. Thus partly because of the difficulty in having any real impact on the organisations, as well as partly because of cost, fewer outsiders are now involved in small-scale evaluation. However, impact is a two-way responsibility. If outsiders are to be involved, their work must surely link in to the internal processes of an organisation in a meaningful way. Insiders must be interested in this outside perspective and committed to debating and understanding its implications. Outsiders must also be willing to take part in processes such as those outlined in this book, to be part of the debate and also to be seen to learn.

Well-planned, systematic, critical internal evaluation, where necessary complemented by evaluators from outside the school or college, must be a key to organisational learning. On what basis other than such feedback can development proceed? Such an approach combines several essential elements:

- turning data into information and making such information widely available and not the possession of just a few;
- providing a forum for asking the important questions about what we want and need to know;
- valuing systematic enquiry which can challenge existing comfortable assumptions;
- establishing a habit of shared and open learning;
- requiring a public commitment to action in the light of the insights that have been gained.

Together, these elements add up to a considerable force for coherent, planned but constantly reviewed change and development.

This chapter has outlined the three key dimensions of evaluation: operational and strategic management and the development of a culture of

Figure 10.3 Managing evaluation: three levels of concern

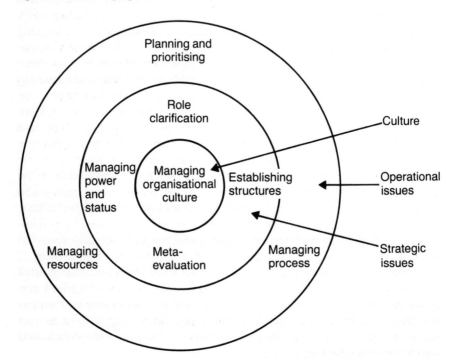

evaluation. It has also demonstrated the potential of evaluation for generating learning at an organisational level, in addition to that of the individual or group. The book as a whole has encouraged you to recognise, value and build on your existing strengths and has offered guidance, advice and examples of possible ways of approaching the issue of managing evaluation in each of the three dimensions.

The overall perspective we have tried to take is shown in Figure 10.3. Whenever the management of evaluation is confined to the outer circle, the impact of the activity is likely to be minimal outside the group most directly concerned. Most is gained by addressing the operational and strategic issues while working to establish a learning climate which places a high value on systematic evaluation at the heart of the organisational culture.

FURTHER READING

The four cultures originally developed by Harrison are elaborated in Handy, *Gods of Management* (1986a) and in Chapter 7 of *Understanding Organisations* (1986b) by the same author. Harrison's more recent development of these ideas, which we use in this chapter, are to be found in his *Organisational Culture and Quality of Service* (1987). An up-to-date and challenging discussion of secondary school cultures is developed by Torrington and Weightman in *The Reality of School Management* (1989a). The authors use a fourfold categorisation of managerial approaches – collegiality, leadership, prescription and anarchy. An instrument for analysing your own secondary school in these terms is to be found in their *Management and Organisation in Secondary Schools: a training handbook* (1989a). Primary school cultures are discussed in *Staff Relationships in the Primary School* (1989) by Nias, Southworth and Yeomans. *Corporate Cultures: the rites and rituals of corporate life* (1988) by Deal and Kennedy is not written for teachers, and its examples are from business and industry, but it contains many relevant ideas. A more difficult – but very challenging – book is Schein's *Organisational Culture and Leadership* (1985).

In *The Learning Company* (1991) by Pedler, Burgoyne and Boydell, the authors use the word 'company' to describe a group of people engaged in joint enterprise. They explore and explain the roots of, and current thinking about, the concept of organisational learning and then offer 101 real-life glimpses of such learning from a wide range of organisations. Garratt also writes about this issue in *The Learning Organisation* (1987) and *Creating a Learning Organisation* (1990) and emphasises what he sees as the central role of chief executives. In the context of education, Reid, Hopkins and Holly identify the 'cult of the individual' as a major factor in limiting the pace of change in schools. In *Towards the Effective School* (1987) they propose a combination of leadership, clear goals, high expectations and school-wide development as the way forward.

Bibliography

Abbott, R., Steadman, S. and Birchenough, M. (1988) *GRIDS School Handbooks* (primary and secondary school versions), 2nd edition, York: Longman for the SCDC.

Adair, J. (1983) *Effective Leadership*, London: Pan.

Adelman, C. (1984) *The Politics and Ethics of Evaluation*, London: St. Martin's Press.

Adelman, C. and Alexander, R (1982) *The Self-Evaluating Institution*, London: Methuen.

Argyris, C. (1991) 'Teaching Smart People How To Learn', *Harvard Business Review*, May/June 1991, pp. 99–109.

Argyris, C. and Schon, D. (1974) *Theory in Practice: increasing professional effectiveness*, San Francisco: Jossey Bass Publishers.

Argyris, C. and Schon, D. (1978) *Organisation Learning: a theory of action perspective*, Reading, MA: Addison Wesley.

Ball, S.J. (1987) *The Micro-Politics of the School*, London: Methuen.

Belbin, R.M. (1981) *Management Teams: why they succeed or fail*, London: Heinemann.

Bryson, J.M. (1988) *Strategic Planning for Public and Nonprofit Organizations*, San Francisco: Jossey-Bass.

Burgess, R.M. (ed.) (1985) *Field Methods in the Study of Education*, Lewes: The Falmer Press.

Caldwell, B.J. and Spinks, J.M. (1988) *The Self-Managing School*, Lewes: The Falmer Press.

Cave, M., Hanney, S. and Kogan, M. (1991) *The Use of Performance Indicators in Higher Education: a critical analysis of developing practice,* 2nd edition, London: Jessica Kingsley Publishing.

Cohen, L. and Manion, L. (1989) *Research Methods in Education*, 3rd edition, London: Routledge.

Darling-Hammond, L., Wise, A.E. and Pease, S.R. (1983) 'Teacher evaluation in the organisational context', *Review of Educational Research*, 53 (3): 285–328.

Davies, B., Ellison, L., Osborne, A. and West-Burnham, J. (1990) *Education Management for the 1990s*, Harlow: Longman.

Deal, T. and Kennedy, A. (1988) *Corporate Cultures: the rites and rituals of corporate life*, Harmondsworth: Penguin.

Department of Education and Science (1987) *Managing Colleges Efficiently*, London: HMSO.

Department of Education and Science (1989) 'Performance Indicators: an aide-memoire from the DES', *Education*, 8 December, pp. 514–15.

Department of Education and Science (1990) *Developing School Management: the way forward – a report by the School Management Task Force*, London: HMSO.

Department of Education and Science (1991) *Development Planning: a practical guide – advice for governors, headteachers and teachers*, London: HMSO.

Department of Employment (1988) *Employment for the 1990s*, London: HMSO.

Department of Employment (1991) *Guidance on TVEI Performance Indicators*, London: HMSO.

Drucker, P. (1974) *Management: tasks, responsibilities, practices*, London: Heinemann.

Easen, P. (1985) *Making School-Centred INSET Work*, Open University in association with Croom Helm.

Easterby-Smith, M. (1986) *Evaluation of Management Education and Development*, Aldershot: Gower.

Easterby-Smith, M., Thorpe, R. and Lowe, A. (1991) *Management Research: an introduction*, Beverly Hills, Ca.: Sage Publications.

Elliott-Kemp J. (1982) *Managing Organisational Change: a practitioner's guide*, Sheffield: PAVIC Publications.

Elliott-Kemp J. and Williams, G.L. (1980) *The DION Handbook: diagnosis of individual and organisational needs for staff development and in-service training*, Sheffield: PAVIC Publications.

Fidler, B. and Bowles, G. (1989) *Effective Local Management of Schools*, Harlow: Longman.

Fisher, R. and Ury, W. (1987) *Getting to Yes*, London: Arrow.

Fitz-Gibbon, C.T. (ed.) (1990) *Performance Indicators*, BERA Dialogues 2, Clevedon, Avon: Multilingual Matters.

Fullan, M. (1991) *The New Meaning of Educational Change*, 2nd edition, London: Cassell.

Further Education Unit (1989) *Towards an Educational Audit*, London: FEU.

Garratt, B. (1987) *The Learning Organisation*, London: Fontana.

Garratt, B. (1990) *Creating a Learning Organisation*, London: Fontana.

Gill, J. and Johnson, P. (1991) *Research Methods for Managers*, London: Paul Chapman.

Gray, J. and Jesson, J. (1990), 'The negotiation and construction of performance indicators: some principles, proposals and problems', *Evaluation and Research in Education*, 4 (2): 93–108.

Handy, C. (1986a) *Gods of Management: the changing work of organisations*, revised edition, London: Souvenir Press.

Handy, C. (1986b) *Understanding Organisations*, 3rd edition, Harmondsworth: Penguin.

Handy, C. and Aitken, R. (1986) *Understanding Schools as Organisations*, Harmondsworth: Penguin.

Hargreaves, D. and Hopkins, D. (1991) *The Empowered School: the management and practice of development planning*, London: Cassell.

Hargreaves, D., Hopkins, D., Leask, M., Connolly, J. and Robinson, P. (1989) *Planning for School Development: advice for governors, headteachers and teachers*, London: Department of Education and Science.

Harlen, W. and Elliott, J. (1982) 'A checklist for planning and reviewing an evaluation' in McCormick, R. (ed.) *Calling Education to Account*, London: Heinemann Educational in association with the Open University Press, pp. 296–304.

Harrison, R. (1987) *Organisation Culture and Quality of Service*, Association for Management Education and Development.

Hastings, C., Bixby, P. and Chaudhry-Lawton, R. (1986) *Superteams*, London: Fontana.

Holt, M. (1981) *Evaluating the Evaluators*, London: Hodder & Stoughton.

Hopkins, D. (1985) *A Teacher's Guide to Classroom Research*, Milton Keynes: Open University Press.

Hopkins, D. (1988) *Doing School Based Review: instruments and guidelines*, Leuven/Amersfoort: ACCO.

Hopkins, D. (1989) *Evaluation for School Development*, Milton Keynes: Open University Press.

Hopkins, D. and Leask, M. (1989) 'Performance indicators and school development', *School Organisation*, 9 (1): 3–20.

House, E. (ed.) (1973) *School Evaluation: the politics and process*, Berkeley, CA: McCutchan Publishing Corporation.

Kemmis, S. (1986) 'Seven principles for programme evaluation in curriculum development and innovation', in House, E. (ed.) (1986) *New Directions in Educational Evaluation*, Lewes: The Falmer Press.

Kemp, R. and Nathan, M. (1989) *Middle Management in Schools: a survival guide*, Oxford: Blackwell.

Kolb, D.A. (1983) *Experiential Learning: experience as the source of learning and development*, Englewood Cliffs, NJ: Prentice-Hall.

Law, B. and Watt, A. (1977) *Schools, Careers and Community*, London: Church Information Office.

Lawler, E.E. and Rhode, J.G. (1976) *Information and Control in Organisations*, Pacific Palisades, CA: Goodyear.

Leigh, A. (1983) *Decisions, Decisions!*, London: Institute of Personnel Management.

Lines, A. and Stoney, S. (1989) *Managing TVEI in Schools: four years on*, Slough: National Foundation for Educational Research.

Lockyer, K.G. (1991) *Critical Path Analysis and Other Project Network Techniques*, 5th edition, London: Pitman.

McCormick, R., Bynner, J., Clift, P., James M. and Morrow Brown, C. (1982) *Calling Education to Account*, London: Heinemann Educational in association with the Open University Press.

McCormick, R. and James, M. (1988) *Curriculum Evaluation in Schools*, 2nd edition, London: Croom Helm.

McMahon, A., Bolam, R., Abbott, R. and Holly, P. (1984) *Guidelines for Review and Internal Development in Schools: secondary school handbook*, Harlow: Longman.

Mercer, R. (1988) *Striving for Effective Change in the Education Service: a guide to the literature*, Sheffield Papers in Education Management, no. 60, Sheffield: Sheffield City Polytechnic.

Morgan, C. (1986) *Images of Organisation*, Beverly Hills, CA: Sage Publications.

Murphy, R. and Torrance, H. (eds) (1987) *Evaluating Education: issues and methods*, New York: Harper & Row.

National Curriculum Council (1989) Circular No. 6, *The National Curriculum and Whole Curriculum Planning: preliminary guidance*, York: NCC.

National Curriculum Council (1990) *The Whole Curriculum (Curriculum Guidance 3)*, York: NCC.

Nias, J., Southworth, G. and Yeomans, R. (1989) *Staff Relationships in the Primary School*, London: Cassell.

Open University (1982) *Curriculum Evaluation and Assessment in Educational Institutions*, Course E364, Blocks 1,2 and 6, Milton Keynes: The Open University Press.

Pedler, M., and Boydell, T. (1985) *Managing Yourself*, London: Fontana.

Pedler, M., Burgoyne, J. and Boydell, T. (1986) *A Manager's Guide to Self Development*, 2nd edition, London: McGraw-Hill Book Company (UK) Limited.

Pedler, M., Burgoyne, J. and Boydell, T. (1991) *The Learning Company*, London: McGraw-Hill Book Company (UK) Limited.

Peters, T.J. and Waterman, R.H. (1982) *In Search of Excellence: lessons from America's best-run companies*, New York: Harper & Row.

Pike, G. and Selby, D. (1988) *Global Teacher, Global Learner*, London: Hodder & Stoughton.

Plant, R. (1987) *Managing Change and Making It Stick*, London: Fontana.

Plunkett, D. (1990) *Secular and Spiritual Values: grounds for hope in education*, London: Routledge.

Reason, P. and Rowan, R. (eds) (1981) *Human Inquiry in Action*, New York: Wiley.

Reid, K., Hopkins, D. and Holly, P. (1987) *Towards the Effective School*, Oxford: Blackwell.

Schein, E. (1985) *Organisational Culture and Leadership*, San Francisco: Jossey Bass.

Scottish Education Department (1990) *Measuring Up: performance indicators in further education*, London: HMSO.

Simkins, T. (1981) *Economics and the Management of Resources in Education*, Sheffield Papers in Education Management no. 17, Sheffield: Sheffield City Polytechnic.

Society of Chief Inspectors and Advisers (1989) *Evaluating the Educational Achievement of Schools and Colleges: the use of indicators*, SCIA Discussion Paper no. 2, Woolley Hall, Wakefield: SCIA.

Southworth, G. (ed.) (1987) *Readings in Primary Management*, Lewes: The Falmer Press.

Sproull, L.S. and Zubrow, D. (1981) 'Performance indicators in school systems: perspectives in organisation theory', *Educational Administration Quarterly*, 17 (3): 61–79.

Torbert, W. (1981) 'Why education research is so uneducational', in Reason, P. and Rowan, R. (eds) (1981) *Human Inquiry in Action*, New York: Wiley.

Torrington, D. and Weightman, J. (1989a) *The Reality of School Management*, Oxford: Blackwell.

Torrington, D. and Weightman, J. (1989b) *Management and Organisation in Secondary Schools: a training handbook*, Oxford: Blackwell.

Training Agency (1990) *TVEI Programme Performance Indicators: guide and supplement for Authorities for Annual Reviews beginning September 1990*, Sheffield: mimeo.

Walker, R. (1985) *Doing Research: a handbook for teachers*, London: Methuen.

Westoby, A. (ed.) (1988) *Culture and Power in Educational Organisations*, Milton Keynes: Open University Press.

Winge, C. (1988) *Understanding Educational Aims*, London: Unwin Hyman.

Index

accountability: aspects of 105; as dimension of evaluation 4–5; involvement in evaluation 107; lines of 104; quantitative approach to evaluation 41
accountability schemes 3–4
action planning chart: of time scheduling 136–7
action research: as qualitative term 41
actions: monitoring of 51–2
activities: scheduling 132–6
adequacy: of information 157
analysis: critical path 136; of data 186–8; of data from questionnaires 174; of documentary evidence 179; of interview data 175; involvement in 190
anonymity: lack of in interviews 176; and photographic evidence 180; in questionnaires 173; see also confidentiality
assessments: external (SWOT Analysis) 57; internal (SWOT Analysis) 57
atmosphere: more superficial than culture 37
attention-directing systems: use of information 50, 159
auditing 14, 62–5; of evaluation activities 48, 49; identifying objectives 62–3; in operational management 213; participants in 63; processes of 63, 65; stage in planning cycle 13; see also monitoring; review
authority (formal): as source of power 194

balance: and auditing 65; between task, group and individual 12; in evaluation 81; overview to show 81; in prioritising process 97; SWOT Analysis and 55, 56; see also bias
behaviour: effect of information on 159–60
benefits: expected from evaluation 128
bias: in data collection 188; in interviews 175; in management roles 11–13; risk of in evaluations 121–2; in sampling 172; see also balance
budgeting: for evaluations 126, 129; see also costs

Calling Education to Account (McCormick et al.) 124
cameo: cross-curricular audit 65–7; evaluating a primary project 184–5; evaluation across a cluster 78–80; evaluation across schools (data collection) 181–3; evaluation to effect changes 203; performance indicators 140–2; planning for participation 102–3
CEG (Careers Education and Guidance): performance indicators for 140–2, 147
change: factors inhibiting or facilitating 200, 201–2
changing practice: as a result of evaluation 193–5
characteristics: of organisational culture 35–6
checklists: for observation data gathering 177
choices: in formal role 25–6; in management 9
classroom observation see observation

(classroom)

clients: defined as beneficiary of organisation 38; as stakeholders 84

clusters: co-ordinating evaluation across 78–80, 231

community education: and response to stakeholders 84

comparability: of success criteria 152, 154

competitors: as stakeholders 84, 85

confidentiality: of documentary evidence 179; and ethical issues in evaluation 122; *see also* anonymity

consensus: about objectives 193–4; *see also* ensemble

constraints: in formal role 25–6

consultation: compared with participation 101–2; involvement in evaluation 107

contributors: reporting to 191

Corporate Cultures: the rites and rituals of corporate life (Deal and Kennedy) 233

costs: analysis of for questionnaire 129, 130; assessing 125, 126; invisible 128

Creating a Learning Organisation (Garratt) 233

criteria *see* success criteria

'critical incident' diaries 178

critical path analysis: in scheduling 136

Critical Path Analysis and Other Project Network Techniques (Lockyer) 138

cross-cluster evaluation: organisational learning in 78–80, 231

cross-curricular audit 65–7; organisational learning in 230–1

cross-curricular themes: as example of need for auditing 62–3, 65–7

culture: cultural assumptions in approach to evaluation 40–1; *see also* evaluation culture; organisational culture

Culture and Power in Educational Organisations (Westoby) 46

curriculum *see* cross-curricular

curriculum audit 62; as pressure on institutions 41

curriculum changes: ethical issues in evaluation of 121

curriculum development: reviewing progress in 69–70

Curriculum Evaluation in Schools (McCormick and James) 16

data: analysis of 186–8; categories of 186; compared with information 49; unmanageable amounts of 77

data collection: documentary evidence 169; interviews 169, 170; key activities 133; management of 180–1, 214; observation 169, 170; qualitative and quantitative methods 182; questionnaires 169, 170; for success criteria 151–2; time required for 129, 131; visual evidence 169

decentralisation: and changing cultures 228

decision-making: contribution of evaluation to, 6, 189

delegation: in evaluation 78

demands: conflicting in role set 33; in formal role 25–6

DES (Department of Education and Science): as stakeholders 85

development: as dimension of evaluation 4–5

development planning: evaluation focusing in 80; and priorities 97

diamond ranking exercise: values and evaluation 42–4

diaries: 'critical incident' 178; for evaluation reports 190

DION (Diagnosing Individual and Organisational Needs) 76

documentary evidence: advantages 178; data collection 169; disadvantages 179; GCSE assignments 180; guidelines 179

Doing Research (Walker) 188

Doing School Based Review (Hopkins) 76

double-loop learning 209, 210

Economics and the Management of Resources in Education (Simkins) 138

Education (Department of Education and Science) 167

Education Reform Act xi

Educational Management for the 1990s (Davies *et al.*) 76

Effective Local Management of Schools (Fidler and Bowles) 76

effectiveness: defined 8

efficiency: defined 8; definition by Joint Efficiency Study 143

employers: as stakeholders 84–5, 89

Empowered School, The (Hargreaves and Hopkins) 16

energy flow: in organisations 229–30, 232

ensemble: achieving group 114–15, 117–18; *see also* consensus

Equal Opportunities: evaluation and data collection 181 182, 183

ethical issues 121–3; in reporting 190

Evaluating Education: issues and methods (Murphy and Torrance) 15

Evaluating the Educational Achievement of Schools and Colleges (Soc of Chief Inspectors and Advisers) 167–8

Evaluating the Evaluators (Holt) 124

evaluation: analysis 18–19; characteristics of 3–8; cultural assumptions in approach to 40–1; definition 2; determining involvement in 108; dimensions of 5, 96, 97; and influencing whole organisation 212; integral to management process 14; meta- 215; perceived purposes of and change 210–11; perception of 11–13; and personal values 41–3, 46; political dimensions in 121–2, 123; problems of 18, 77; purposes of 96, 97, 205, 213; qualitative and quantitative approaches to 41; and research 2–3; reviewing 216; role of manager in 101; stages of 131–2; statements about 45; unstructured 1; and view of teaching 42

evaluation culture: development of 228–9; diagnosis of 217–25; questionnaire to diagnose 220, 221–5

evaluation instruments: (QLT Profile) 151, 153

Evaluation for School Development (Hopkins) 15

examination boards: as stakeholders 85

examination results: attention-directing use of information 50; in information monitoring 53–4; as success criteria 151

expectations: and role 27–32; unclear in role set 33

expenditure *see* costs

expenditure: monitoring of 51

expertise: quality and use of in groups 113, 115; as source of power 194

external support: in evaluation process 106; involvement in evaluation 107

feedback: operational management of 214; procedures for 189, 190–3

feedback meetings: for monitoring and review 48

feelings: identifying basis for 92

Field Methods in the Study of Education (Burgess) 188

flexibility: of questionnaires 173

focus: area of 81; for evaluation 77–8, 80;

examples of 80–1; location of 81; nature of 81; and priorities 91; process of 97; who should be involved 84–5

Force Field Analysis: factors for change 200, 201–2

formal role 24–7

formative evaluation 3

formative (regular) reporting 190–2

funding agencies: reporting to 191; as stakeholders 84

further enquiry: defined 15; as expansion of monitoring process 91, 92

Getting to Yes (Fisher and Ury) 124

Global Teacher: Global Learner (Pike and Selby) 46–7

Gods of Management (Handy) 46, 233

government agencies: as stakeholders 85

governors: as stakeholders 85, 89

GRIDS (Guidelines for Review and Internal Development in Schools) 67, 76; self-evaluation mechanism 4

groups: interviewing in 176; and involvement in evaluations 109; involvement in management process 11–13, 102; problems of 109, 110–11, 112, 113–15; role of 21, 22, 117–18, 119–20; sampling for data collection 171; solutions to problems of 115–21; use of to analyse data 187

Guidance on TVEI Performance Indicators (Department of Employment) 167

hierarchy: in management 10; power and evaluation 226
Human Inquiry in Action (Reason and Rowan) 188

ideological interests 194
Images of Organisation (Morgan) 46
implementation: stage in planning cycle 13
improvement: as purpose of evaluation 205–6
in-depth investigation: as expansion of monitoring process 91, 92, 93
individual: needs of in groups 114, 116–17; role of 21, 22
individualistic culture: and evaluation in organisations 227
individuals: involvement in management process 102; in management activity 11–13; in management of evaluation 80; management of 99–100; need for focussed evaluation 81; perception of information 159–60; responses to information 160; role of in management 9–10; *see also* groups
influence: and involvement in evaluation process 100
information: control of as source of power 194; definition 49; effect on behaviour 159–60; flow of in organisations 230; kinds to be monitored 51–4; management of 159; provided by monitoring and review 48; quality of performance 157; ways of using 49–50; *see also* audits
information management: monitoring in 50–1
input: success indicators of performance areas 146
INSET budget: ethical issues in evaluation of 121
INSET (In-Service Education and Training) sessions: and evaluating a primary project 184–5
INSET session: example of planning for participation 102–3

interests: classification of 196–7; held by teachers 194
interviewing style 175, 176
interviews: advantages 175; data collection 169; disadvantages 175–6; as evaluation instruments 151; guidelines for 176–7; in-depth 173
involvement: in data collection 170; developing strategy for 106–8; in feedback process 189, 190; methods of 102; of outsiders in evaluation 232; *see also* participation

job description: demands, constraint and choices of 25–6
Joint Efficiency Study: success criteria for further education 143–4
judgements: as attribute of evaluation 4

language: terms used in organisational culture 38–9
leadership: involvement in evaluation 107; roles of 101
learning: from evaluation 206, 207–11; helps and hindrances to 209; individual 229; as purpose of evaluation 205, 206; resistance to 206, 207; types of 209–10; *see also* organisational learning
Learning Company, The (Pedler, Burgoyne and Boydell) 233
Learning Organisation, The (Garratt) 233
learning organisations: development of 229–31
local education authorities: as stakeholders 85, 89
Local Enterprise Companies (Scotland): as stakeholders 89
Local Management of Schools: need for 'auditing' 62; response to stakeholders 84

Making School-Centred INSET Work (Easen) 98
management 9–13; definition of 7–8; evaluation integral to 14; formal and informal roles 10; leadership role of 101; operational 213–14; perception of 10–11; strategic 213, 214–15; task and process elements 11
management of evaluation: at

organisational level 80; levels of concern 231, 233; as process 15; Stakeholder Analysis 85; who to involve 99–101
Management and Organisation in Secondary Schools (Torrington and Weightman) 16, 233
Management Research (Easterby-Smith *et al.*) 124, 188
Management Teams: Why They Succeed or Fail (Belbin) 124
Manager's Guide to Self Development, A (Pedler, Burgoyne and Boydell) 16
Managing Change and Making It Stick (Plant) 46, 76
Managing Colleges Efficiently (Department of Education and Science) 167
Managing Organisational Change: a practitioner's guide (Elliot-Kemp) 211
materials: allowing for as resource 126
Measuring Up: performance indicators in Further Education (Scottish HMI) 167
meetings: minutes of *see* minutes of meetings
meta-evaluation: in management strategy 215
micro-political dimensions: Curriculum Development Group example of 203, 205; in management strategy 215; mapping 196–200; in objectives of evaluation 194; of organisations 9; in reporting 193; to resistance to learning 209
Micro-Politics of the School, The (Ball) 211
Middle Management in Secondary Schools: a survival guide (Kemp and Nathan) 16
minutes of meetings: for monitoring information 51 53; as reporting procedure 190
monitoring: and choosing a focus 80; defined 15 48; expansion of process 91; in information management 50–1; *see also* auditing; review
MRE (Monitoring: Review and Evaluation) xii

National Curriculum: need for auditing 62

'Negotiation and construction of performance indicators' (Gray and Jesson) 168
networking: for planning evaluations 131–8
New Meaning of Educational Change, The (Fullan) 211
Nominal Group Technique 91, 94; and priorities 97

objectives: in management 8–9
observation: data collection 169
observation (classroom): advantages 177; disadvantages 177; guidelines 177–8; as qualitative term 41
openness: in choosing success criteria 161–2; necessary to evaluation 6
operational management 213–14
opinion: group access to 113–14, 115–16
opportunistic sampling 171
opportunities 55, 56; SWOT Analysis 55–62
opportunity cost: definition of 126; and management choice 9; in management of resources 126, 127–8
organisational culture 17, 34–9; definition 34; four dominant types of 217–19, 226–7; and learning from evaluation 212–13; in management strategy 215
Organisational Culture and Leadership (Schein) 233
Organisational Culture and Quality of Service (Harrison) 233
organisational learning 229; problems of 212–13, *see also* learning
organisations: development of learning 229–31; loose-tight structures 228; as micro-political 9; role of 21, 22–3; structures in management strategy 215; SWOT Analysis 55–62
orientation to change 194, 196, 197
outcome: monitoring of 53–4; success indicators of performance areas 146
outsiders: involvement in evaluation 232
overviews: of evaluation activity 81, 82–3, 97

parent governors: as stakeholders 85
parental involvement: Force Field

Analysis 200
parents: as stakeholders 84, 85, 89
participants: reasons for choosing
    100–1; reporting to 190–1
participation: compared with
    consultation 101–2; defined 101–2; in
    evaluation 107; planning for 102–3;
    see also involvement
peer review: as qualitative term 41
performance areas: analysis of 155–6
performance indicators: definition 140;
    DES's list of 167;
    input/process/outcome model 146;
    monitoring of outcomes 53; as
    pressure on institutions 41;
    quantitative 139, 140–2; in
    Stakeholder Analysis 163–6; *see also*
    success criteria
'Performance indicators and school
    development' (Hopkins and Leask)
    168
personal development: awareness as
    stage in 12
personal values: and evaluation 41–3, 46
personality: as source of power 195
photographs and drawings: advantages
    179–80; disadvantages 180;
    guidelines 180
physical force: as source of power 195
piloting (trials for data collection
    method) 172–3
plan construction: stage in planning
    cycle 13
planning: and operational management
    213–14
planning cycle (Hargreaves) 13
planning schedule: for monitoring
    information 51
policy-making: link from evaluation 205
political dimension: in evaluation
    121–2, 123; *see also* micro-political
    dimensions
Politics and Ethics of Evaluation, The
    (Adelman) 124
power: in management strategy 215; in
    organisational culture 218, 224, 225;
    sources of 194–5, 196–7
power culture: and evaluation in
    organisations 226, 227
predecessors: in networking 132, 135
pressures: on organisations 41
priorities: and choosing a focus 91;

setting of 97; use of Nominal Group
    Technique to clarify 94
problem-solving: in groups 113–14,
    115–16; information system 50; use
    of information for 159
process: success indicators of
    performance areas 146
process element: in management
    activity 11
product: defined as output of
    organisation 38
Project Trident 180
proving: as purpose of evaluation 205
pupils *see* students
purposive (deliberate) sampling 171

QLT (Quality of Learning and
    Teaching) Profile (Scottish HMI) 144,
    145, 146; evaluation instruments 151,
    153; quality statements 144, 145, 153
quality statements: (QLT Profile) 144,
    145, 153
questionnaires: advantages 173; data
    collection 169; to diagnose
    evaluation cultures 220, 221–5;
    disadvantages 173–4; as evaluation
    instruments 151; guidelines for
    174–5; list of possibilities 172; open
    and closed questions 171, 172–3,
    174; postal 175

random sampling 171
Readings in Primary Management
    (Southworth) 16
Reality of School Management, The
    (Torrington and Weightman) 233
recommendations: presentation of 189
recording: of interviews 176; *see also*
    written records
recording schedules: as evaluation
    instruments 151
Records of Achievement *see* ROA
    (Records of Achievement)
Reflection: audit of evaluation activities
    49; audit of information monitoring
    51; audit (third) 76; dimensions of
    evaluation 5; evaluation reports 6;
    opportunity costs 128; political
    dimensions of evaluations 123; task,
    group and individual 12; when am I
    evaluating? 2
regulators: as stakeholders 85

relationships: and roles 21–4
relevance: of information 157
reliability: of information 157
reporting: formative 190–2; methods of 190; to other interested parties 192; to participants 190–1; verbal 122, 193; *see also* written reports
research: pure 2–3
Research Methods in Education (Cohen and Manion) 188
Research Methods for Managers (Gill and Johnson) 188
resources: control of as source of power 194; identifying 125, 126; management of 214; *see also* budgeting; costs; time
response rate: to questionnaires 174, 175
review: and choosing a focus 80; definition of 15, 48; and managing data collection 181; of specific areas 67; of specific events 71, 72–3; of success criteria 162; time set aside for 80, 81; whole school (SWOT) 102–3; whole-institution 55–6, 62; *see also* auditing; monitoring
review meetings 54–5; as reporting procedure 190
review processes 54–5; areas of difficulty 55; consultation and participation in 103; for problem-solving 50
rewards: control of as source of power 194
ROA (Records of Achievement): evaluation of to effect change 203–4; parents' expectation of 91
role culture: and evaluation in organisations 226; strengths and weaknesses of 228, 229
role management: keys to 33
role performance: effective 34
Role Set Analysis 27–32; role problems in 33–4
role(s): conflicting 24, 33; and expectations 27–32; formal 24–7; in management strategy 215; in organisational culture 218, 224, 225; overload 33; of participants 17, 19; redesign of 33; and relationships 21–4; sensitivity about 17
rules: influence on formal role 24

Rumbold, Mrs Angela: Minister of State for Education 167

sampling methods: of data collection 171–2
SATs (Standard Attainment Targets): and information monitoring 53–4; review meeting for 3
scheduling: of activities 132–6; 'real time' 136; time management 129, 131
School Development Plan: implications for audit 65
School Management Task Force (DES 1990) xi
school reports: feedback of information 49–50
scorecard: use of information 49–50, 159
Secular and Spiritual Values: grounds for hope in education (Plunkett) 46
Self-Evaluating Institution, The (Adelman and Alexander) 16
self-interest 194
Self-Managing School, The (Caldwell and Spinks) 211
sentence completion: for reviews 74–5
single-loop learning 209, 210
Skills 2000 (Department of Employment) 141
skills: generic process 214
sources: acknowledgment of 192
space: allowing for as resource 126
sponsor: leadership role of 101
SSR (staff: student ratio): as success criteria 151
staff: as stakeholders 84, 85, 89
staff development: implications for audit 65
Staff Relationships in the Primary School (Nias, Southworth and Yeomans) 233
Stakeholder Analysis 85, 86–91; and feedback and reporting 190; involvement in evaluation process 100; and success criteria 162, 163–6
stakeholders: and changing cultures 227; classification of 84–5; definition 84, 85; expectations of 87–91; and management strategy 215
standards: for judging success criteria 152
statements: about evaluation 45;

quality (QLT Profile) 144, 145, 153
statistics: in monitoring of information
    53–4
status differences: problems of in
    review process 55; values and 41
strategic management 213, 214–15
*Strategic Planning for Public and
    Nonprofit Organizations* (Bryson) 16
stratified sampling 171
strengths 55, 56; SWOT Analysis 55–62
*Striving for Effective Change in the
    Education Service* (Mercer) 211
student/pupil: as stakeholder 84, 89
student/pupil experience: evaluation
    of information about 95
student/pupil perception: as qualitative
    term 41
student/pupil tracking: method of
    observation 172, 178
success criteria 139–67; for CEG
    programme 140–3, 147;
    data–gathering 151–2; design of
    160–2; development and use of
    154–5, 162; identification of 142–4;
    indicators of 144, 146; limitations of
    167; management of 160–2; and
    organisational learning, 231; as
    pressure on institutions 41;
    qualitative 148, 149; quantitative 148,
    149; setting of 4, 148, 149, 214; in
    Stakeholder Analysis 162, 163–6; *see
    also* performance indicators
summary: of reports 193
summative evaluation 3
summative reporting 190
Superteams (Hastings, Bixby and
    Chaudhry-Lawton) 124
suppliers: as stakeholders 84
support: external 106; in organisational
    culture 218, 224, 225; secretarial
    170–1
support culture: and evaluation in
    organisations 226, 227; strengths and
    weaknesses of 228
supporters: reporting to 191–2
SWOT Analysis 55–62, 102–3
symbolic use of information 49, 159
symbols: importance of in
    organisational culture 38
systematic sampling, 171

task culture: and evaluation in

organisations 226, 227; in
    organisations 218, 224, 225; strengths
    and weaknesses of 227–8
task element: in management activity
    11, 12
tasks: list of 131–2
teachers: and learning processes 206,
    209; orientation of interests 194
*Teacher's Guide to Classroom Research,
    A* (Hopkins) 98, 188
teaching: views of 42
teams 80, 183; management of 99; *see
    also* groups
thinking: time required for 131
threats 55, 56; SWOT Analysis 55–62
time: allowing for as resource 65,
    125–6; for interviews 175;
    management of 170, 214;
    management in data collection 170;
    for questionnaires 174; scheduling
    the evaluation 79, 129, 131, 132
Towards an Educational Audit
    (Further Education Unit (FEU)) 167
Towards the Effective School (Reid,
    Hopkins and Holly) 233
Towards a Skills Revolution
    (Confederation of British Industry) 141
Training and Enterprise Councils: as
    stakeholders 89
triangulation: collecting data in variety
    of ways 157, 181
TVEI (Technical and Vocational
    Educational Initiative) xi; as
    management activity 10; managing
    MRE in xii; response to stakeholders
    84
TVEI-E (Technical and Vocational
    Educational Initiative) Extension:
    auditing 62; cross-curricular auditing
    65–7

Understanding Educational Aims
    (Winge) 46
Understanding Organisations (Handy)
    16, 46, 124, 233
*Understanding Schools as
    Organisations* (Handy and Aitken) 16
*Use of Performance Indicators in
    Higher Education, The* (Cave *et al.*)
    167

validity: of information 157

values: and ethical issues in evaluation 121; influence of on evaluation 4; personal, and evaluation 41–3, 46; in roles 33–4

vested interests 194

visual evidence *see* photographs and drawings

visual evidence: data collection 169

wall conversations: for reviews 72–3

weaknesses 6, 7, 55, 56; SWOT Analysis 55–62

whole-school review (SWOT) 102–3

women: and support culture in organisations 226

work experience: and managing data collection 180

worker: defined as member of organisation 38

written records: of monitoring and review 48; of review meetings 54

written reports: ethical issues in 122; formal (summative) 192–3; importance of 6; for monitoring information 51, 53; tone of 193